THE FIFTH REVELATION

I0081356

Michael Scott

Fisher King Publishing

The Fifth Revelation

Cover image: Painting by Michael Scott

Fisher King Publishing Ltd
The Studio, Arthington Lane
Pool-in-Wharfedale
LS21 1JZ
England

www.fisherkingpublishing.co.uk

Contents

Introduction

Why 'Revelation'?

Hoist by my own petard; of necessity these are a false confection, far too neat. But pegs are needed in making a self-declaration. Big-Knowledge rears its hydra-head. In truth, my eighty-odd years are not at all tidy and not separated into clear phases. Each revelation is spread unevenly over decades, often buried in the unconscious mud and flowering like a lotus now and again. This is the nature of mind; my mind, anyway.

Therefore, the fifth revelation is not actually new, but something I knew for ages. I just ignored it. Until now.

This change, then, its emergence overdue by decades, is the beginning of an essential loss at last. This time I needed to lose anger and fear, the Siamese twins of my servitude. The revelation was that I saw how I didn't need anger the way I thought I did. My last four books reeked with anger and I didn't really see it. The books are true, as far as they go, but the anger is a separate ingredient. It's possible that the anger would be an advantage in effect on a reader, I wouldn't know. Anyway, it's done now. This book should be different. It will record a Houdini attempt to escape. I mean, to escape my own wrath and terror. I mean to drop them on the roadside or in a bin.

If it doesn't work I've had it. But in a way I've had it anyway. I will die soon, that's having it. But before I go, I want to stop being angry and afraid. I expect that's too much to ask of my own nature. But it will be interesting, perhaps.

What were the other revelations? Here they are, the pegs of my story, needed only for reference, as the story is now the anger and fear. But the other revelations are also enmeshed with the anger and fear, so they may need to be displayed here and there. The other books have told their stories already, more or less.

The Other Four Revelations

First. My family were not my friends. Nor of each other as far as I could see. Observing other families I see a similar un-friendship even if love, loyalty, caring, diligence all exist. It must be my idea of friendship that needs examination.

I guess that this is part of the first revelation, as I have strong reactions to the idea and the ideal of friendship, as if I'd been born with the craving for it. Was I? There's a story here. I had two close relationships outside my family when I was sixteen. Both were failures as friendships, which tells me a lot. The other boy was profoundly important to me (interestingly, he was part of an apparently friendly family). For me, it was true love. It faded when we went to our separate universities. Gradually, I realised that the friendship was in my heart more than in his. The girl was an intensely physical partner to me, but I was not her friend nor, I think, was she mine. So that fizzled out too. I needed friendship even more than sexual love, it seems. If so, that is strange, because I was very randy for decades. But when I met my true love, as I soon did, the friendship was immense, as it has remained for sixty years.

Therefore, what is friendship to me? Why were my parents and siblings not my friends? Why did I hang on to them until death us parted? Why did they make me angry, and presumably frightened?

Some definitions that thrill me:

Euripedes: One loyal friend is worth ten thousand relatives
W. Winchell: A real friend is one who walks in when the rest of the
world walks out
H. Keller: Walking with a friend in the dark is better than walking
alone in the light
Mencius (Master Meng): Friendship is one mind in two bodies

In reality, my immediate family were more censorious than enabling, except my mother in my early childhood. Even she became demanding and often intolerant as I grew up. My father evinced dislike and contempt as I rose in the school pyramid to quite giddy heights, for me. As I blossomed into a scholar, my family closed down on me. I didn't know who to blame. So I blamed a mythical being called 'family'. Then, the oddest thing, my father wanted to be my friend. I couldn't quite make it. It was too late, too much damage had been done by those years of tense dislike from him.

I am going on about this because I now see that my fear and rage were being stoked up by the family, while I maintained a stoical, dutiful, sometimes rebellious, demeanour. The anger was deepening and spreading. I was covertly scared of the world and its people, because of familial coldness, while going out into it and jousting for success and recognition.

My mother died when I was thirty-eight and my father died ten years later. I had clung on to them, grimly and painfully, until my middle age. What stupidity. Yet, and here's the rub, I still love them. The almost quenched fire of filial friendliness still burns. Well that's fine. The anger and fear are what I need to drop, and I'll hang on to the love because I know instinctively that I need it. The big need is to accept that there's no blame.

My sister died at the same time as I had a coronary. A strange friendship. I love her too, and without much reservation. She was an admirable woman. And we nearly became real friends at the end.

Second. God is bad nonsense. So much anger in this: I wonder where it comes from. I can't believe that I was a little choir-boy, but I remember it very clearly. And there was a love in me that I still feel. Like the family. But my argument is not with God. It never was. I am an Atheist without animosity to God. I just do not accept that there is a God.

My anger, and fear, have long been directed at the religions and the religious. It is the humans, like the family, who have failed me. How did the choir-boy get to this? The obvious answer is that my other sister died soon after she was born, when I was seven years old. At first I just grieved and wailed. But this God had fucked me up, hadn't he? Well, no, not even that. He'd have to exist to do that. But Christianity had fucked me up, hadn't it? Oh, yes. That sad little grave in a corner of the churchyard preyed upon my child-mind all right. So maybe I went off the choir out of sheer, subterranean fury.

I'd like to think so, but it's too neat; too easy. At about that time I was a wolf-cub in the church pack and, after initial enthusiasm, realised that it was all in league with Sunday School, in fact the teacher of that was also the Akela of the cubs. I felt stitched up. By the people, not the wolves - they're OK. The curate and Akela were buddies, who knows to what extent?

We cubs went camping and he came too. Why? Digging a bit deeper, I confess to being a mystic. I always was. I didn't know it then, of course. Who would have told me? I was already deeply in love with trees, animals, flowers, the nature works. A mixed mass of feelings, hunter plus shaman plus St. Francis; but godly dogma grated.

There was a crunch, an odd one. When I was still young enough to be taken to Harvest Festival service (when my parents were still sufficiently enamoured with each other to go anywhere together) I was in an ecstasy seeing the flowers, fruit and vegetables piled up before the altar. I felt in my real home. Then the vicar brayed at us all about 'God's gifts' to us. I was shocked to my juvenile core. How dare he try to usurp my wonderland!

I admit that I flirted with the Gospel magic even after that internal catastrophe. Christmas still excited me with a strange fervour, and I now recognise that it was Pagan solstice-ecstasy that was whispering in my head. Anyway, my book 'Mystikos' has an account of my attempt to come to terms with mystical encounters. And I have moved on a bit from that now, vide 'Freedom River' 2014.

Third. The human mind is faulty. Yes, this is important for me, because I have only recently understood the basic weakness of my race and it is not pretty. I have said, and will continue to say, that a primary, maybe *the* primary, failure of the human species is its obsession with 'Big- Knowledge'. The hugeness of this revelation has brought everything into perspective and into line. God is in there too. It took me many years to accept the perverse stupidity of the human mind, mine and all the rest. The revelation number three was the sudden awareness that it was only a product of evolution and, like the human backbone, could have serious design faults. I belong to a culture that worships the human mind, that perceives it as godlike, second only to the big god in the sky. My anger at religion was its manifest stupidity, how dare my race be stupid; and the anger with mind theory was how dare it, the mind, be so awful. My fifth revelation, then, is that it is absurd to be angry with the botches of evolution. It is just nature.

The spoilt child in me was enraged because The Big Mother, Nature, had messed up, making us as we are, making us servile, god-worshipping creeps, for instance, or making us mass-killers, for instance. That is foolish. Mother N. has made a lot of other nasties too - look at the dinosaurs, hug a crocodile, kiss a cobra.

Fourth. I've lived a series of errors. This is mainly the Hero Problem. It looks worse every time I look at it.

Yet it is also natural. I am experimental. I am a work in progress. Every man is a prototype. My errors are not errors. Nor are they mistakes. A new word is needed to make this revelation cogent. They were actually discoveries. An experimental man makes discoveries not mistakes. You could say that. The research program, me, was designed to find out how I could be as perfect as possible. I guess.

So I tried a lot of roles, ideas, relationships, places, etc. all in an attempt to get this self as right as I could. I could write up the research notes so as to indicate quite a successful series. Why don't I do that? Why not say the experimental program has been very creative?

Yes, as a mere animal, albeit quite bright, I have done well. Could have done better?

Probably not. Who knows? Who cares?

Chapter One
The Shame of Shane

The Wounded Hero

That's me, and the millions like me. The pretty, small, guardian angel wearing golden buckskin once stole my young heart when I went to see the picture in the Odeon in Silver Street. Alan Ladd was Shane the gun-slinger with the heart of a saint. Unbelievable. Unforgettable.

I am Shane, riding, wounded, maybe fatally, into the distance, having destroyed Jack Wilson aka Palance, the black embodiment of fear and anger. Another fantasy. Can I make it true? No, better, can I make it untrue?

I was twenty-two when 'Shane' was made, and I was already a wounded hero. Who isn't? I had made my first crucial mistakes already. Anger and fear fully established but deeply entrenched. I was thin, depressed, dyspeptic, sexually frustrated, and hating being a research graduate. How could I have got so much wrong by doing my best? I refer you to 'Nirvana Highway', my pseudo- autobiography. That says how it happened. Or 'The Halcyon's Nest', my first novel, in which I am the fictional hero Ossian as well as his pal Ariel. No shortage of self-inflation there.

There is no shortage of self-inflation in any hero.

The fourth revelation shows it. I start by thinking I have made a lot of errors. I say it again on this page: 'How could I have got so much wrong by doing my best'. Hogwash! This is self-inflation, a big, bad, balloon. Why did I, like so many other unwise youths, decide to be a hero?

Well, I didn't actually. I did what seemed to come naturally. I tried to succeed in something that seemed to matter. Not heroic at all, but just normal. Isn't that what all good boys try to do? Yet another budding Shane.

Think instead: why heroes anyway? How did this idea get into our heads and hearts?

There's the theory of Ernest Becker, the 'Denial of Death' man, and his 'immortality project', whereby he sees humans trying to deny death by becoming heroic, as if somehow eternal, part of something big, getting purpose, being significant. This belief just comes from within, says Becker, a 'causa sui', meaning a 'self-caused cause', and I don't know what that means. Well, let's say it's a delusion, and done with it.

For Becker that explains the trouble caused by wonky immortality projects, especially when different ones collide. He cites religion as prone to this wonkiness and blames it for wars, genocide, nationalism, the lot. So much for heroism, then, which is also implicated, says Becker, in depression and schizophrenia when people realise that their immortality project isn't working. Does this theory appeal to me? Is it how my own weakness for heroism reveals itself to introspection? I think it probably does, more or less. It's the causa sui bit that bothers me. Does it feel like a delusion, this wanting to be 'metaphorically' immortal? No, it would be delusion to believe heroism *actually did* give one immortality.

Archetypal Heroism
Let me try another route. Enter Dr. Jung. According to Joe Campbell (in 'The Hero With A Thousand Faces'), following Jung's lead, we are in archetype territory. Here we are, are we? Archetypal heroes? The point is that this isn't *causa sui* but the 'collective unconscious' in origin. According to this we all have heroism in our psychic

bloodstream, or in our human heritage, whichever. Do I believe this? As I have explained elsewhere, ('Freedom River') I don't think much of Jung's archetype belief-system. Does it make sense? If only in regard to the hero? A lot of issues congregate.

I once read all four of Campbell's master works: overarching title, 'Masks of God', and a total of 2,000 pages of mythology, 'Primitive', 'Oriental', 'Occidental' and 'Creative'. It is hard to comment. The problem is not being quite sure of the source- material, despite lengthy footnotes. I suppose I wasn't entirely sure of Campbell's intentions. Coming to the material as a rational sceptic, as I saw myself, I think that I assumed that I was reading the books of a like-minded person. But it is now obvious to me that I was misleading myself. Despite his being sure, I assumed, that all myth was bunkum, and that it was his job to expose the extremity of the nonsense, I remember being worried by the lack of Occamite parsimony in his conclusions. In other words, I failed to realise the probability that Campbell thought that myths were profoundly interesting and valuable. In my innocent arrogance, I thought he was clearing all that rubbish so that people today could have a clean start in the business of coping with real existence. Since then, which was forty years ago, I have softened my position on mysticism, in the sense that I do not now trust the veracity of scientific man anymore than I can credit the religious confections. I have strong mystical experiences and do not pretend to 'understand' them. But I have also reconsidered Carl Jung's expositions on everything and become suspicious of doctrines such as the 'collective unconscious' and the 'archetypes'. For a while, I sought refuge in these concepts as non-religious spirituality. I now see that as special pleading on my part. I needed to come clean with myself. This meant facing up to the primary archetype, the so-called self. I have come to the point where I just don't believe in the self at all. I accept the basic animal self, of course. We all have that, evidently. It is the hypertrophied and solipsistic human self that I now find risible and unnecessary - and also extremely toxic. So when I try, not for the first time, to read 'The Hero With A Thousand

Faces', I am gripped by disgust. I have limped through 200 pages of it and much as I admire Campbell's diligence (and fortitude) I recoil in horror at the vast panorama of absurd beliefs that have corroded human thinking for several thousand years.

Campbell does seem to admire, even extol, heroism. And, it seems, the wilder the better. His own theorising, sometimes hidden in subtexts, suggests that the hero is the most perfect and most laudable aspect of human behaviour. This is because he sees the hero (male or female) as a person who willingly courts danger, even disaster, in order to face his own demons and then bring back spoils of war to his fellow humans.

It is not at all clear that the awareness of the hero is well-established, particularly the issue of monstrous personal self-importance. In fact, Campbell, and Jung for that matter, seem to be bloated with self-importance, in the sense that they seem unable to laugh at their own absurdity.

Plan 'A'

A friend and I have spent many hours examining self-importance, and have fought creatively to challenge it in ourselves and in one another. We have been besieged by heroism. It is all around us and permeates our own being. It is a bloody nuisance. But it is very powerful. Campbell's thousand-faced creature is very near the defining embodiment of the human species. This creature is near enough to being a god to satisfy each of our cravings for recognition, success, valour, and even immortality. All the millions of myths point in the same direction. Therefore, Campbell, and every other hero-fan, takes the gargantuan human appetite for heroism as the proof of its reality and value. I have the temerity to deny this. This friend and I found ourselves using the shorthand term, 'Plan A', to describe and identify the madness that grips us (most people, that is) from soon after birth, and it is worthy defining Plan A before I go any further with this story.

When I was a baby I must have been regarded as a possession by my parents. I say this because when I became aware of my being, say around five years of age, I was inculcated with a mass of absolute mandates. To be fair, I may have inculcated myself. But my parents behaved as though they owned me. I was, in effect, their slave. Nothing in my experience caused me to doubt the perfect rightness of this situation. On the whole, I tried to be a dutiful and willing slave. I was looked after, so why question the arrangement?

The time came when my slavery became irksome. But I usually redoubled my efforts to be a good slave of my owner-parents. Yet a basic conflict was fashioned by the circumstances. I was unfree all the way to my centre and bursting with the need to be my own person. As a result, my version of Plan A was conceived. Or if not conceived, at least unconsciously engendered. There was the outside 'me' who accepted an increasingly complex state of slavery, as the society as a whole also took shares in my ownership, and I tried to fulfil the obligations of that bondage. Then there was the inner 'me', who retreated from the outside obligation into an isolated cave in which I grew and prospered unbeknown to anyone except the special friend of the time - and I remember being pretty cagey with him, too. The idea of success, was important, very important indeed, yet it was unclear whether it was an internal or external phenomenon. This muddled state persisted for decades as I grew older, it still being a matter of confusion quite where success might or should happen, hidden within or flaunted without.

I can see how the madness of heroism burgeons in this existential compost. Add to this the heady brew of superstition and the myths are inevitable. Campbell cites case after case, ad infinitum, to show how humankind have resolved the Plan A inner conflict by introducing spirits and gods into the equation. There are, of course, father gods and mother gods, the chief slave owners, and there are the miraculous heroes who win against the evil gods using the help of the nice gods. Incest is rife, as slave-owner-parent seduces or rapes slave-child, metaphorically or literally. Everything is measurable in thousands or millions as the aggrandisement of self-importance spirals out of control. Ghastly initiation rites are perpetrated, in which the slave is dismembered or the slave-parent is exterminated.

Plan A has to ride on this bucking bronco, somehow, falling off frequently. Hence depression, suicide, schizophrenia. Hence war, massacre, desolation. The mythologist and his scribe have had rich pickings.

But why doesn't it stop? We are still stuck in myths. Inner or outer fantasies. How and when will they be extirpated and reason made the ruling wisdom? Never, probably. But that doesn't mean that the odd maverick like my friend and I cannot make a personal conversion to sanity.

Hero Vaccination
Everyone loves a hero: the essence of Plan A. This is a convenient state of affairs because there is no Plan B. Or so my friend insists and I have provisionally agreed. Let's test that assumption, given that Plan A is crazy: a fool's hell/paradise. If we abandon Plan A, what is left? Well, it might be nothing if we were actually able to get rid of the primary dichotomy involved. But would it really be nothing? Would we not return to the Void from which we first removed ourselves into a life of ambiguity and external slavery? The big question may be, does a hero retrieve a position in the Void? This needs deconstruction to make any sense.

The clue really is in the nature of heroism itself, which is a hugely exaggerated state of arousal of the human mentality. Campbell's massive excursion is of great importance, as is Jung's ploughing of the same jungle territory, but it is an importance that consists of a colossal warning. Our so-called Plan A is the everyday enactment of the grand absurdity of our race. It is as if we are permanently in the rutting mode of the red deer or the feeding frenzy of the great reptiles and carnivorous mammals. We are feeding upon ourselves, making an insane banquet of our anger and our fear. And because we have such a lavish intelligence we behave as though we can think ourselves through the ordeal of existence. What else can we do? It seems that this pathetic Plan A is all we have and our great tragedy is that the Plan does not work.

So, we are bound to suffer unless we actually have a Plan B.

Campbell's gigantic myth-fest celebrates a disaster. We are a failure in action. I mean the whole human species is a disaster, so far. The mythology of humankind merely delineates our tragedy. We are truly magnificent fools. We are truly terrible creatures. We are truly wonderful generators of beauty and love. And the universal Plan A is an endless nightmare. The nightmare is heroic. We, as a race, are living a disease. It is a disease of half-awareness. We know something but it is inadequate in nature and content. We either go on living with the disease, as if inevitable, or we change our Plan. That is the issue.

How could we vaccinate our species from the disease we call heroism? (And, incidentally, from the many 'isms' which are ancillary to the main sickness.)

Shane, again

Another look at this Western epic, and I feel that it is a pathetic comedy now the enormity of Campbell's vision has hit me. The noble gun-slinger is preposterous in his total inadequacy to comprehend the true nature of being. Then, at the opposite pole, there is the pure Buddhist, for whom the myths and fantasies are endless. The story of the Buddha's enlightenment in the 'The Hero With A Thousand Faces' is horrifying in it grandiosity and sick in its copious detail. It is unlikely that a Buddhist would have done any better than Shane in confronting and defeating evil, the reality being so intractable compared with the doctrine.

The Three Poisons, Greed, Hate, and Delusion, are merely an oriental formula for the state of Shane's world. I am not persuaded that, for all their effort over millennia, that the various Buddhist sects have actually achieved some credible form of Plan A. They sound good but are they really good?

My twin horrors, anger and fear, emerge undiminished through the smoke of centuries. They are the twin negative energy-packs of the racial Plan A. Have they ever been absolved into a Plan B?

The Jesus Plan

As with the Buddha, the character and nature of the man or myth, Jesus, seems to be inclining towards a benign and effective Plan B. Again, as with the Buddha, it is impossible to disentangle the reality from the flimflam. They are both buried in a swamp of swindle. Yet an idea does shine through. What a pity it has been so horribly mangled.

Imagine Jesus-Buddha, or Buddha-Jesus, without the gaudy and meretricious flimflam of the religions, being in the situation of Gun-slinger Shane. How would, or could, they have done better than merely killing a nasty human being?

It is the same for me and everyone I know. How could we have done better with some Jesus-Buddha brilliance in us? How could we be improved by some Socratic shrewdness or some Epicurean generosity? There is a trace of something different in the wasteland of Plan A, isn't there? Or is it just another futile gesture in the ingrained idiocy of our species?

In one sense, Buddha-Jesus was bursting with self-importance, part of their problem of the Plan A Hiding-to-Nothing. But their message was the opposite of self-importance. Somehow, this seems to me to define our task. As my own self-importance shreds, and my self-important fear and anger diminish, I am increasingly noticing how this feature dominates all human activity. A few examples may show what I mean.

There is a bright youngish professor who appears frequently on TV screens, and his latest foray is titled, 'The Human Universe'. Whose universe? Ours? Or does he merely mean the universe through our eyes? Could be Plan A obscurity. Or Plan A confusion. In the program he repeatedly says that as we humans are probably the only intelligent animals in the whole universe, we are extremely precious. Translated, that says humanity is the most important species because it is very intelligent. How could this statement possibly be justified? Is it not absolute nonsense? Unique we probably are, but so is the English badger and the American Bald Eagle. Does that make them extremely precious, too? And the Ebola virus? And the malaria parasite?

This Cox goes on to explain how the human species must find a new source of energy to keep itself going, fusion energy being his favourite. Yet he at least understands that the human race will become extinct sooner or later. And that the planet will disappear, too. But it's 'no surrender at the Alamo' for Brian. We keep going for as long as possible because we owe it to our preciousness.

Then there's the huge store of millions of seeds in a secret vault, for when we lose everything on earth but ourselves. Wonderful, you'd think. But it appears that the seeds are of agricultural crops. He, Cox, seems unaware that agriculture is implicated in our demise, and has been the main factor in our mad over-population. (Kew, at least, is storing a vast collection of seeds of *wild* plants.)

In another dimension, there's the sad self-adoration of the knight, Parzival, in the mediaeval prose-poem by W. Von Eschenbach. This lame-brain warrior, Parzival, reaches the end of his quest in spiritual maturity, according to the text. But there's no indication whatever that this has happened. At most, he has been domesticated. Where are the signs of transcendence? Nowhere? As in every hero, transcendence is absent in the final achievement. There is, at best, mere fame. And that is all that self-importance seems to crave.

If Jesus-Buddha did transcend, rather than just enter a fairy-tale realm of eternity fabricated by over-excited clerics, it could have been the defining moment of human becoming. But it didn't happen, because Plan A was still the received wisdom of that age as it still is.

The Knowledge Factory

Brian Cox also keeps on about **Knowledge,** asserting that it will solve most of our problems. I think it more likely that Knowledge has caused most of our problems. I mean heroic knowledge, of course, the knowledge manufactured by religion, science and old wives. Heroic knowledge, the Plan A knowledge, has been my main mind-diet too and much good it has done me, in my dreams. In Joseph Campbell's master works, the 'Knowledge' is the enormous mountain of myth. It does, however, contain a clue that might lead us to Plan B. Amongst the gods and demons and saints and daredevils, and their grandiosity and their sheer messiness, there's a different theme. In this, the heroic act is in facing one's own human nature. No gods, no bardos and resurrections, no dismemberment by cosmic forces, but a humbler process whereby each of us can become aware of the terrible qualities in our deeper nature. The 'dirty backside' of the so-called self, is the true reality of our baser state of being. The 'bucketing' in these waters reveals horrifying details of what we are actually like. It is absurd to see the journey into this territory as heroic, but that is how we invent glory for ourselves where no glory can possibly exist.

The true story of 'Shane' would be less about his killing of an evil man in a saloon, and more about the discovery of the villain in himself. Generally speaking, this is not something any of us like to do. We would prefer to see the evil we commit as atypical, an aberrant event for which we may seek absolution. It is not comfortable to think this behaviour is endemic in our nature. There is, therefore, a weird irony about the idea of heroism: the enemy is usually within and the approach required is humility rather than bravado.

In my anger and fear, I am quite villainous. I behave badly. Excuses proliferate. *But I feel under duress. It's not my fault, I am doing my best, I am having a hard time.* No, this is a cosmetic view: the reality is that it's the real me.

The Real World

The same is true of us. All of us. The human race is villainous. It may also be 'precious' to some minds, though only human ones, I guess. However you do the numbers, the bottom line on humanity is failure, failure to be a meritorious species if anyone is judging. It is impossible not to be bamboozled by what is beautiful and wonderful in the human. It is a mirror, after all: one man, like me, looking at other humans, can only see himself, they are all I am.

I have been ill with a viral attack for several days, and was occasionally delirious. Not entirely a bad thing, however horrible to endure, because it forced me to a crisis. I needed to make a personal renunciation of the villainy within and without. My anger, your anger, my fear, your fear, are the base from which our behaviour stems. Call it 'energy', if you want a neutral word, providing that you remember that energy is power to do something. Remember how often our energy is used to do villainous things.

What villainous things do I mean? Ruining the earth, for a start. This is just a point of view, not an absolute truth. But I am at heart a sentimental naturalist and I think and/or feel that all living things have inherent validity. Therefore, when I see vast tracts of the surface of this dear old planet being flayed alive, and entirely for human need or greed or waste, I feel very sad/angry. It could be argued that a top-predator is bound to behave like this. Yet *this* top-predator makes it known that it has moral standards. I find it hard to reconcile morality-claims with the annual murder of some 150 billion fellow mammals and other sentient creatures to feed the human population as it grows uncontrollably. This is either malignity or psychopathology, probably both.

Then there is the subject of this chapter, heroism, which is held up to be the human jewel in the crown. It involves a vast miscellany of symbolic behaviour, as the work of Campbell shows. I am intrigued by the fact that he loses himself in hyperbolic joy at the scale and content of myth, yet chills out occasionally into a very rational comment as follows:

Wherever the poetry of myth is interpreted as biography, history, or science, it is killed. The living images become only remote facts of a different time or sky. Furthermore, it is never difficult to demonstrate that as science or history mythology is absurd. When a civilisation begins to reinterpret its mythology in this way, the life goes out of it, temples become museums, and the link between the two perspectives is dissolved. Such a blight has certainly descended on the Bible and on a great part of the Christian cult. ' (p. 249, 'The Hero With A Thousand Faces'.)

I am bedevilled either way, in that I loathe the myths themselves, as insane misrepresentations of natural existence. Therefore, whether in their original form, as in rampaging, blood-letting, Christian proselytising, or in their less obvious form, almost civilised codes of conduct (however misconceived, as they typically are in Catholicism).

So, back to my viral crisis. It was extraordinarily hard to bear, apart from the damage to my body, because my mind seemed taken over by another system from the one I usually operate. I seemed to be some kind of living computer programmed to do endless tasks of comprehension based on inexplicable data. I didn't sleep for three nights. On the 'third day', ironically, I sat in our small conservatory and tried to haul myself back to my sort of normality. I was in a type of meditation, I suppose, though not intentionally, because I was merely trying to hold on to some degree of well-being.

What then happened was three violent series of mental attacks upon the human world. I was the attacker, using the full range of ancient and modern armaments. I remember nuking Mecca, the Vatican and Buckingham Palace. I was driven by a colossal rage. I destroyed the whole of human civilisation and most of the human race. It took a while. And when I had finished, I felt a serenity beyond anything I have previously experienced. I was clean, at last, and free at last, as well.

What I had destroyed were the very symbols that Campbell describes, but including governments, institutions, schools and universities, and the places where Knowledge is manufactured and processed for consumption. I have live over eighty years in a global mad-house. Which is what humanity has made of the earth, a pretty barbaric and violent place before we got at it. My internal explosions are laughable in the sense that they are empty noises, but they matter to me because they show me the almost infinite rage and terror I feel at my core. And that is something I have been trying to tame for all this time. What a hope.

Well, what, if anything, was the point of my internal explosion? It was not going to make any difference to the poor planet. There has been altogether too much of megalomaniacs believing they could reconstruct everything. But, without inner convulsion, how could any of us be shaken out of the disastrous Plan A and lead to a personal view of Plan B. Clearly, in my case, I think we have to start with a clean sheet. Everything must go, as the saying goes. Well, maybe that process has happened in me, so I have to stay with that.

Self-Knowledge

The essence of the subject is that the only form of knowledge that leads to transcendence is the inconveniently termed Self-knowledge - inconvenient because it seems to confirm the value and importance of our worst parasite of them all, *self*. This needs explanation. To use self as a convenient pronoun-substitute, like 'one', or 'I', a mere grammatical label, is obviously innocent enough. Metaphors are like this, too, mere labels. But what happens when the label takes on an identity, and becomes real? I have self, I have anger and I have fear, but I am not a thing which *is* self, anger, or fear. This mistake makes all knowledge corrupted.

It is this error that makes the first breach in the great continuity between man and the rest of nature. We may be no more egoic than any other animal, yet calling out the word that specifies our egotism means that we aggrandise our beingness beyond coherent sense. My Burmese cat is immensely egoic, but he cannot say so in intellectual language (it would be a nightmare if he could!). The human mind is blessed, if that's the right word, with unusual intelligence. It is an instrument capable of exerting great power, more or less effectively. But what the human mind cannot yet achieve is a kind of sense of proportion. There have been various stabs at it over the centuries, but generally we are crazy with self-concern. I mean self-concern in the aggrandised sense, i.e. that all human creatures seem more less full of self-importance, regardless of age, culture, education, or anything else.

I don't know whether it is inherently immoral to be self-important, but must surely be practically immoral, in that it prevents each of us from actually connecting with another human in uninflected terms. Maybe we can with animals. Maybe not. We probably patronise any animal but the human and we try every device available to cope with the incompetence we suffer in human interchange.

Chapter Two
The First Fence

From the Depths

I might have known, knowing what I know. Fancy trying to override the forces of the unknown unconscious. I would master my fear and my anger, would I? The fifth revelation, my foot! So I have been shown who's master, I think. The unconscious isn't dumb. It runs everything, don't I know? Well, sort of. It's a stand-off, probably.

It also reminds me of the Charles Wales controversy, and the indignation of 'Republic':

'The royals are free to say what they like to our elected politicians, to lobby for their own interests or on behalf of Middle Eastern dictators - all in secret. That has to stop. The voters have the right to know what power and influence they're wielding and in what way. So we need the Freedom of Information laws changed. We also know from revelations last week that Charles expects to be an activist and outspoken king - yet demands secrecy when it suits him This is a real threat to our democracy that has to be challenged.'

Hear! Hear! Of course. And my unconscious mind seems to be writing 'black spider' letters to me using invisible ink. But irritating megalomaniacs, royal or otherwise, can (theoretically) be silenced, as was the first King Charles, let's remember. But each of us has a 'black spider' within us which is not so easily disempowered. Like

Parzival and Feirefiz, we are each fighting ourselves. I am in the Depths of Unknowability, not able to distinguish between myself and my alter ego.

'Republic', on the face of it, should be pushing on an open door. All they want is the abolition of the monarchy in Britain. That would seem a very modest ambition. A parliamentary democracy and a monarch are chalk and cheese. So why is the level of support for the monarchy so high - why, indeed, is there any support at all? I can hardly complain of the disloyalty of my own non-conscious mind towards my goals, when some sixty per cent of my countrymen endorse the madness of a democracy with a king. Does this madness come from the same place, I wonder? Is there a sort of Jungian collective lunacy that runs both our inner lives and our collective endeavour?

I confess to the suspicion that the human mind is, in fact, deranged fundamentally. I mean genetically and biologically incapable of performing optimally. As I have written elsewhere, evolution has produced a chimaera and nature is taking a while to exterminate it. In my own case, I am struggling with this heritage. As the saying goes, '*Those whom the gods would destroy, they first make mad*' (Euripides, allegedly).

My fifth revelation was that I should unburden myself of fear and anger. I knew, obviously, that I would be asking for trouble in trying to change habits of a lifetime (and probably of humanity's lifetime). But the unconscious doesn't seem to fight rationally. There is no rational reason why it should, as it was the conscious mind that dreamed up this particular mind-set. Like the laws of gods or physics, the conscious mind assumed it was genuine and superordinate, not realising that this was just one more fantasy. There seems to be a Yin/Yang dynamic between unconscious and conscious minds that cannot be resolved and that is dangerous when glossed over. Worst of all is the conflict that breaks out when one or other tries to be king. It is unrealistic to behead either mind-king and we are stuck with both, apparently till death us do part.

Where Is Sanity, If Anywhere?

Psychiatrists make a living out of sorting the sheep and goats of the farm in our minds. But who decides what is the optimal condition? I had assumed that I, the superordinate me, the possessor of the mind in this case, was justified in making the decision to drop fear and anger from my existential baggage. That's the way kings and queens used to operate, even deciding the religion and taxation of the people in their so-called kingdoms. It is absurd, surely? It was absurd of me to decide that 'I' would cast aside fear and anger. Wasn't it?

Revelation Number Five seems to be guiding itself in a new direction. For example, it seems that I have no actual human rights in this matter. There is no apparent universal law on 'my' side. The current trend in my psyche is that fear and anger have every right to dominate my life. That this rule is enshrined in a dark and inaccessible place is certainly implied, by my logic, anyway. What on earth do psychiatrists suppose that they can or should do about this rule? Or clerics or lawyers, or anyone else who has a need to control the existence of others.

There is, implicitly, a new variation on the Theory of Mind in this situation, i.e. every situation. The basic form of the theory is:

Theory of Mind (often abbreviated ToM) is the ability to attribute mental states - beliefs, intents, desires, pretending, knowledge, etc. - to oneself and others and to understand that others have beliefs, desires, and intentions that are different from one's own.

The key phrase for Revelation Number Five is 'oneself and others', in that the 'one self' is also, effectively, 'others'. Just as I, or you, consist of billions of individualistic biological selves and others, as cells and micro-organisms, so I, or you, presumably, also have a number of psychological or existential selves, including those hiding in the unconscious mind. Each of us is an unruly, or not-to-be-ruled, community of mental associates. We don't know this because we are encultured to believe in an autonomous individuality of the 'whole' person. I am surprised by my own waywardness when I fail to behave to 'the required standard', a criterion obtained from who knows where or why, except that it is in 'the list of things to be done'.

Appropriating Evolution

The heroic mode of humankind, and its god-fixation, is seemingly the result of our assumption that the entire phenomenon of life is all about us. This connects to the equally weird conviction that evolution has been a progressive, even semi-divine, process that has reached its objective in the production of the human species. We have stolen a reality, we have commandeered a world that doesn't belong to us any more than to any other living form. Does any human, apart from me, think that this is what has happened?

Moreover, am I alone in the conviction that our conscious mind has usurped the rest of our thinking apparatus? Does it seem the case that our minds are controlling devices that put everything else in the shade or treats other perceptive impulses as subordinate to the big-mind-over-everything? What about mind-work such as intuition, inspiration, gnosis, transcendence, and similar adjuncts to the conscious think-machine? Do we see them as secondary, primary, paramount, or hallucinatory? How could we decide between them? Is there any consensus whatsoever between any or of all the mind-states?

A visiting alien might well ask of human earthlings, 'Who do you think you are and what do you think you are doing with that bit of grey matter you flaunt as if it is sacred?' And do we think, as we behave, that our thinking is the crème de la crème of the universe? Do you believe that your mind is the acme of evolution, the very point of life itself?

Well, of course it is, as far as our limited vision can tell us. We are absolutely solipsistic. We have no idea what the universe is actually like, however we prod it, because we have only one of billions of mind-sets and consciousness-states. We are unique and we are not able to see absolute reality, if it exists at all.

Dance of the Bees

Just for example, the scientific, i.e. the conscious mind in rational mode, has judged the dance of the bees as mere instinct. These little animals have dance routines that indicate the direction of food for gathering, and the distance to be flown to the food-source. It is 'built-in' knowledge, so to speak. The bee doesn't work out the process. It is automatic. Whereas human navigation is a conscious process. We think it all out. This is the conventional wisdom of bee navigation versus human navigation.

Do I believe it, I wonder. Starting with the language, I am disturbed by the cosiness of the science. Of course I accept that an animal that only lives three weeks and has to change occupation from carer to forager in that brief career, must get a lot of guidance from automatic programs. Besides, its brain is very, very, small indeed. But we, with our massive minds, have no idea how the bee does it. The next thing that bothers me is the assumption about our own navigational power. Regardless of maps and sat-navs, don't we have some sort of sense of direction? Not very good, perhaps, in urban man. And we can all get lost in a forest. Or a desert. Or on a motorway. But how did Stone-Age man do it? How, for that matter, do cats and dogs do it?

Thirdly, and most puzzling of all, how can the sensory apparatus of a bee or a human be regarded as an evolutionary *achievement?* Is it not merely a *phenomenon?* Would we congratulate a supernova on its explosive performance? In other words, by what divine right does the human judge phenomena as good, bad, developmental, progressive, or destructive? What are our criteria and where are they located?

The Gender Enigma

A recent dream led me to recognise how faulty was my own judgement on the phenomenon of gender. I should say at once that the judgement is neither simple nor obvious. It has never been a straightforward matter in my life. Thinking about it after the dream, my gender attitude seems as in-built as a bee's navigation. But can that be true? How did I acquire an attitude to women different from my attitude to men? Has my gender-attitude evolved over millennia or did it happen in five minutes when I was ten years old? Does anyone know the answer?

In any case, I am intrigued and a little disturbed to discover that I have two categories of gender attitude, not just one as I had previously assumed. Once past the most inflammatory episodes of adolescence and early stag-behaviour, I became a modern man of tolerance and liberalism towards female humans. In my conscious mind, I was an exemplary aspirant towards fairness, tenderness and sharing. I wanted women to take greater control of the great engines of life, whether actual machinery or the control of governments and institutions. I would hector people about the way women were side-lined, overlooked, exploited and subjected to male cruelty.

That I was still a predatory male in basic nature, I knew, but I tried to restrain my inclinations, with a great amount of frustration. Nevertheless, I was doing the right thing by my cultivated moral scruples. What I didn't know, because I refused to know, was that I was a chauvinist pig manqué. I would have a quarrel with women and be convinced that it was a fair fight because I was treating her just as I would treat a man. At the least, it is now clear to me that my other attitude to the female was ambivalent. I claimed to prefer women to men in every way, I declared that women should rule the world because they were better people than men, yet I now realise that I harboured a secret dislike for them.

This is important because women are so important, genuinely crucial to existence, and in a gender workshop a decade or two ago, I did experience, as a temporary woman, the superior qualities that females possess. Yet the importance of this discovery is a more general one, i.e. that I cannot assume I have achieved full awareness in any context because my mind operates, as do my emotions, at several quite different levels. Thus, in the matter of heroism and of my inconvenient fear and anger, I am a mass of contradictions and evasions. As are we all, I imagine. At best, I am a partially evolved muddle. Not only that, but while I claim a degree of completeness, even wholeness, our old enemy entropy is busy undoing my carefully constructed edifice of maturity and wisdom.

Evolutionary Addictions

Correcting the illusion we all share, it must be said that evolution is not at all the process we crack it up to be. For a start, it is an absurdly anthropocentric idea, as already discussed. For me, it displays no characteristics of a production process whereby new models are produced to satisfy (or create) new needs of consumers. At best, evolution is like a river, flowing from one place to another without rhyme or reason. I like evolution as a biological process because it is so eccentric. And, so far as I can see, utterly purposeless. It can't help doing what it does but it is all accidental.

I can see it another way, using my perversely varied mentality. I could, for example, say that energy moves naturally towards manifestation as form. Or that consciousness is the inevitable yet still glorious product of energy interacting with matter. In a mad moment, I might even assert that it is as if there is a great genius out there somewhere who is thinking himself into us. If I go completely loco I could agree that the maker of the universe is lonely and humankind is the ideal plaything to keep his Lordship happy.

Whatever the mechanism, evolution makes addicts for itself to play with - mindlessly, of course. The universe is a giant toyshop in which habits are made and games are played. Evolution is the brainless toymaker. Humankind would be a very amusing toy for a brainy addict - and some humans enjoy the surrogate role of critic or romantic as if observing human nature from a safe distance. Meanwhile, the rest of us, me for instance, suffer our evolved addictions and even try to make sense of them. For human kind the most prevalent addiction must be this latter habit. We want to make sense of it all. Indeed, this addiction to discovering information is the key feature of the hero, the person, often male, who digs down into the abyss and comes up with answers for the rest of us. In the process, the hero takes on the twin ogres of fear and anger, his own or anyone else's that comes into play. He seems a simple fellow, this hero. Does he not realise he is merely a sacrifice by the majority to keep themselves in spiritual or physical comfort? Fame is for idiots, you might say.

Evolution is a Dracula that feeds on knowledge. Its teeth are the genetic spirals and the blood it drinks is the flow of life over the surface of the earth or in the waters of the earth. The phenotype, the forms it creates from its appetites, is the concreted sculpture this mad artist creates. Progress is the last thing Dracula the Evolutionist is aiming for. He just wants blood. While poor, mad, human beings remain addicted to the delusion of their own special preciousness.

What is Human Intention?

Forgetting the nonsensical ideas about evolutionary progress, what actually is it that mankind, the Frankenstein pseudo-genius, actually wants to achieve? What does the mad hero want to make of, or for, himself? Much as I dislike myths (because they finish up being taken literally) there is one that seems to me to express all the muddle and error implicit in actual evolution as opposed to the romanticised view of it as a march of progress.

Ceridwen's Cauldron

In this famous Celtic tale of divine skulduggery the goddess, a bad-tempered, foolish, Narcissist, has a very ugly son whom she wishes to make very wise as compensation. She sets up a cauldron of magic contents and cooks it for a year. As in evolution, the chances are slim for any improvement because, as with genetic mutation, only a tiny bit of the brew will be magical and the rest is poisonous (most mutations are harmful). The boy, Gwion, stirs the pot and three drops spill out onto his finger, which he sucks to relieve the pain. These are the only portion of the brew that can make a miracle. Ceridwen is enraged and chases the boy, intent on killing him. He evades her by repeated physical transformation. (The process of growing up is inherently unpredictable.) She eventually catches him and eats him. (Fortuna can destroy as well as transform). He is born (again) and she can't bear to kill him because he is so beautiful, so she throws him away into the sea (or river, etc). But he survives this journey (into the unconscious!) and becomes the great poet Taliesin.

Whose Purpose?

The Celts valued poetry, it seems, so you could say this tale is about the achievement of poetic creation. Yet poetry is a dubious 'achievement' in that it endlessly analyses existence, often critically. More than this, the myth shows how chance operates, disguised as magic. The story is cataclysmic, however you look at it. Ceridwen the goddess is frustrated. Gwion 'dies' twice, once inside Ceridwen and once in the water, but emerges from both hazards in one piece and transformed as a bonus. A cataclysm becomes a miracle.

Somewhere in this myth, as in the unromantic version of evolution, chaos contains the seed of new life, different life, perhaps change for the sake of change. But does it indicate change *towards* some goal? While a pure scientist ought, by professional standards, do his genetics in the spirit of utter objectivity, he is only human, with the emotions that militate against the pure spirit. He cannot resist seeing the 'invention' by nature of the opposable thumb and forefinger as a fundamental *improvement* in primate anatomy. Even if this is only buried in his subconscious mind, the geneticist is affected by the concept of progress.

The fear that the universe has no purpose is closely allied to the fear of death in each of us. If I were not angry for any other reason, there would still be the fury over the pointlessness of my existence, the rage that goes with the fear that all my effort has been futile as I am about to disappear for ever. I am a hero if I try to establish a truth that confounds nihilism. I become angry and afraid as I discover no such truth.

Pure Luck

After two millennia we may still have failed to get a clearer picture of existence than the old idea of the goddess Fortuna. She is actually nonsensical, because she is a goddess who controls nothing. What is the point in being a goddess if your divine realm is pervaded by mere chance? But, more pertinently, what if the universe is actually a chance process? You can draw up *laws* of physics as much as you like, but do you really think there are lawmakers? My own experience of my unconscious, such as it is, derived from dreams, accidents, illness and so on, suggests that I am all too aware of the reality of chance. If so, that must be a common reality for my species, as I don't think I am all that unique.

Oversimplifying the mind, it is as if my unconscious is actually all-knowing while my conscious mind makes laws of its own. By 'all-knowing' I mean without guile or logic. I mean, seeing life as it is, both hateful and lovely, and being free from perfection-neurosis. In my conscious mind, busily controlling my existence, I am addicted to perfection, if only the *idea* of perfection. So I would embrace the emotional treasure of progress as a feature of the world and the universe. But it is not so simple. Making life more bizarre and complex, there seems to be a submerged state of mind that deals with hope, desire, fairness, love, beauty, etc. as if they were real possibilities. In other words, my all-knowing and innocent unconscious has another side to it, the opposite side, which entertains a warm and positive view of existence. To complete this gavotte in the skull, my conscious mind also apprehends imperfection and sometimes sees it as interesting, or beautiful, though usually comic or tragic.

Living in the Real

This is impossible in practice, if only because we cannot possibly know what is real. The minimal analysis above shows the bewildering complexity of awareness, conscious and unconscious (I assume there is unconscious awareness, though it is another confusion). But it must be possible to live differently from how we have been doing it so far. For the last few tens of thousands of years, we have followed a set pattern of awareness which attempts to override or outmanoeuvre the complexity of existence. During my brief, long, life I have gradually shed this pattern as its absurdity has increasingly revealed itself. Which is why I am reaching into the darkness and trying to shed light as well as the delusions. But what is my purpose, actually? It may sound odd, but I think I have a strong yen for integration. Thus it is that I wanted to ditch fear and anger. I got that wrong to the extent that these emotions are alive and endemic in my mind at all levels, and to ditch them would be to ditch my mind, which I don't regard as desirable just yet.

Integration still beckons, however. Just as the good Buddhist pursues mindfulness, I am pursuing the state of integration. I am aware that this is similar to the old word, truth, which was used when human thinkers idealised the possibility of there being such a thing. Nowadays there is a phrase, 'holding it all together', which, if a bit desperate-sounding, is not a bad translation of my goal.

Chapter Three
Therefore Integration?

Mystic Marriage

We have been here before, again and again. It is one of the nuggets in the Perennial Wisdom. But in the past the object of integration has tended to be resolution, unification, or individuation (a la Carl Jung). I do not desire unification. I accept my multiplicity as real, if that is the right word.

It is, I suggest, the mystic marriage idea that causes, or symbolises, the existential muddle that besets us all. This is the great myth of 'wholeness', which can be an extremely ambivalent ambition. The problem is illustrated by Jung's attempt to distinguish between (selfish) individualism and (unselfish) individuation, a clever distinction that evades the danger of the self as a context.

I think it is a false distinction, mere word-play. The real difference is between integrated wholeness in and of the living world and its meagre opposite, egoic individuality. Of course Jung and his predecessors, going back to Aristotle, were right to question the narrowness of individuality which is not connected or inclusive of others. But Jung was also pursuing the conjoining of spirit and matter and of conscious and unconscious awareness: his definition of individuation was the bringing together into a unity the various elements of the mind and spirit. It is this that seems to me to be sheer arrogance, as if the various parts of the psyche could or should be cajoled or bullied into being unified in some way. Perhaps they wouldn't want to be, who knows?

Above all, the Jungian obsession is with the self, as something unquestioningly the core of meaningful existence. I am profoundly at odds with this idea. But my use of the term 'integration' puts me in suspect territory, because integration could mean exclusive regard for one's own state of being. I don't mean that. I mean integration with all being, the opposite of excessive self-focus.

I also mean acceptance of my inherent fragmentation; acceptance of the muddled, endless, foibles and whims and enthusiasms that swirl around within all parts of me and others. I think we need to surrender more to the unknown, to accept the absolute mystery, and come off this complacent assumption that we can ever gain comprehensive knowledge of anything.

The very idea of the mystic marriage chills me to the bone. It is very Christian, which is bad enough, but it is also patronising and creepily heroic too, as if the function of holy femininity were primarily to back up heroic maleness, including bodily sacrifice. Jung was from a Christian background and his work is contaminated by Christian belief-systems even if he claims to be free from them. His coniunctio mysterium is a myth of enormous complexity, including alchemical references, but it is overwhelmingly concerned with the combining of opposite parts to make a new, complete, whole. My experience of humanistic psychology also had this emphasis on transformation by blending or joining different elements of the psyche. The gurus I met were all obsessed with bringing together the disparate into a resolved unity. From physical sexuality at one extreme to reclusive meditation at the other, Western therapy has landed securely on the field of unity. In this safe meadow, the seekers after wisdom celebrate diversity and worship unity without any apparent embarrassment over the fact that they are completely different phenomena.

The Paradigm Shift

I have to revisit the idea of integration. My sense of the Void and the Great Continuity is strong and inexplicable. I cannot accept the idea of the archetypes or the gods because my sense of the ground of being, the mysterious nothing that is everything, is far greater than these personifications. I think I am driven into the fifth revelation by the realisation that fear and anger are somehow superficial or maybe derivative rather than vastly important.

If my sense is right, we, members of the human species, are failing to wake up and see a real truth. That real truth is probably that we know nothing and will never learn very much, because we are neither equipped nor designed to transcend the trivial. On the other hand, we can certainly appreciate that there is an enormous mystery, even if it is neither our business nor our destiny to comprehend it. We have been trying to understand the mystery for fifty thousand years or more, and we are still trapped in triviality and ignorance. Nothing shows this better than the repeated claims of astrophysicists that we are about to break through a fundamental knowledge barrier. Over and over again. How long does this game of hide-and-seek have to go on before one honest physicist (or archbishop) admits he is totally stumped and without any answers whatever?

So we could, theoretically, give up being archetypes, especially myths like the heroes or the wise men. This would be a paradigm shift of potentially massive proportions. As a base, we'd have to accept and agree that our accumulated knowledge and our recorded history are worth nothing. But our willingness to accept our ignorance, and a set of new responsibilities, would more than make up for any feeling of loss. That would be the beginning of a wonderful awakening. It would, ironically, be a gigantic, racial, act of heroism. It would be bravery without arrogance. Could we conceivably do such a thing? It would be a global act of integration, in that it would be a process of discarding all human foolishness while taking on a completely new scale of perception. We would be integrating our best qualities into our collective being and simultaneously discarding all the lies and beliefs that have piled up over the millennia.

Anyway, if my race won't do it, I will do it for myself alone. I will shift my own paradigm.

How? First I have to de-construct my value-system. Forget the species, Homo sapiens sapiens, this is all for me. I won't copyright or patent it. But anyone can join me if they like. This is my odyssey but it doesn't have to be solitary.

I am not a hero, so there will be no send-off. I will just slip out into the night and follow the moon over the hill. Metaphorically, as I am too old for an actual physical journey. Maybe I will have to dream it, or let it dream me. Which is an interesting idea. What kind of dream would it be? Rather like the ones I am already having, perhaps. I could do worse that letting the dreams speak for themselves. And do an Ockham analysis? Watch out for the next dream, then.

Dream 1. A condensed wildlife panorama waking me up with the thought: *In biology, everything is connected and nothing is determined.* This does summarise the position I have reached, now I think about it. The trend in science is to discover the cause behind the event, whereas my suspicion is that cause is a mistaken viewpoint. An oversimplification at the least, because the inherent chaos of the world systems make it impossible to extract anything as one-dimensional as cause. Think of the swallow migrating to Africa and back to Shropshire and try to produce a clear determining factor. The reality is too beautiful and terrible for simple causation.

Dream 2. As it happened, a thought sequence with illustrated backdrop (i.e. panic-stricken withdrawal from alienated family/false friends and frantic attempt to find my beloved woman who, when I found her, could not be 'mine'): *I am alone. There is no complete connection with another. I crave a complete connection. I am terrified to be alone.*

I am nearly connected. That makes it worse. Nearly is worse than nothing. Because I am actually alone. Where is my other? There is no other who can be my complete connection.

How can I face this truth? It is time to face it. This is my fear and anger: to be alone.

I wonder if this fits with the crazy 'mystic marriage' idea. One way to outwit aloneness could be to invent a 'conjoint self', or a marriage with a god, or to aggrandise the self into wonderful icon. The truth is quite successfully obscured in a cloud of vaingloriousness. Prayers and hymns and battle- cries and even sobs in the dark may serve to create a sense of another's presence in one's existence. Then there is the hero-business, outfacing terror and using rage to explore hidden realms so as to come up with the treasure and receive plaudits.

Not content with all those options, I also secured a fine partnership with an actual woman and have lived with her for sixty years. We are both failing in health and vigour, now. Our dependence on each other as ultimate rescuers from isolation looks increasingly fragile. Aloneness grins evilly at each of us from the wings of the stage. It is going to get us: no escape.

I remember once writing about aloneness with great confidence. Now I can't find that text. How did I do it? More interesting, why did I do it? Did I find something valuable in aloneness alongside the existential terror. I can't believe it. Perhaps I didn't publish it because I didn't believe it.

Now, however, is probably the time to address this monstrous fear. Not that I expect to defeat it - that is what ill-fated heroic behaviour is about - all I want to do is to see it without too much denial. This means moving into aloneness and experiencing it with absolute intimacy, a parody of the mystic marriage in which the myth is seen for what it is, a servile evasion of reality.

I ask the obvious question, at last: **why is it so terrifying to be unconnected to another, any other?**

Dream 3. The artist's nightmare. I have been personally and privately driven by the need to create visual imagery for over fifty years. But in this dream I am holding an exhibition and the fifty or so visitors all ignore my work. Do I concede that I am a failure? Or is the failure in the minds and attitudes of others. To what extent, I wonder, sitting alone in a corner of that exhibition room, is art a private occupation and to what extent is it a public action? I drink some rancid wine and resolve to leave the exhibition almost as an act of imaginative suicide.

Dream 4. Maybe that's the wrong question, as the next two dreams suggest a *tribal* factor (and it should be asked why recluses, hermits, and eremites actually choose to be alone). So Dream 4: I am a member of a musical ensemble, a choir or operatic group, and I find it both exciting and intimidating.

Singing has, in waking life, been important to me and I did a lot of lieder work in my sixties and seventies (too late to be really good). Now, though my voice is still functioning, it is a diminished force. In the dream I am aware of that and also that my companions are much more professional. The dream ends with my agonising over what to sing to show them what I can do. I feel a fraud and a failure.

I take it that this is an exclusion dream, or one showing a fear of being rejected or just not belonging. This is not so much a terror of aloneness as a grieving over being unacceptable or beyond the pale. The same feeling, differently nuanced characterises the next dream:

Dream 5. I am a grey-suited man meeting a group of grey-suited men. My credentials are an issue. Why am I with them? I am in a different business. They try half-heartedly to engage with me, but there is an atmosphere of distrust, even of pantomimic absurdity. The body-language, the smirks, the edgy questions, all signal to me that I shouldn't be there. As with the music group, I rather want to belong but I recognise that I am not one of them and leave.

These two dreams remind me of several experiences I have had in which I have tried to influence organisations or groups of people to change their modus operandi. It has usually been focused on a strategic objective. My advice was often rejected, or accepted with bad grace, perhaps because fundamental change is not usually welcome to people. Or maybe I was just not very good as a consultant strategist. Anyway, I have always felt the rejection personally, however hard I tried to remain neutral. I remember that I was also at odds with my family when I embarked on a university career because they apparently rejected the changes in me. It is, therefore, a life-theme of mine that I am unsuitable, odd, alien, and unacceptable. At the same time I am extremely intolerant of what I perceive as stupidity in others.

This means that my need for a loving relationship, which is strong and undeniable, tends to conflict with my dislike of a range of negative behaviours in others. I do, therefore, often feel rejected or excluded. I have usually taken this as normal existence, however painful it may feel.

I now wonder if it really is 'normal existence' and it occurs to me that I may be emotionally prone to reject others when they displease me. Therefore, I am depriving myself of loving possibilities because of my arrogance. In reality, therefore, I am perhaps producing the isolation that frightens me so much. When I think this, though, I experience indignation over the immorality of bending the truth so as to keep friends close to me. The isolation is, in that case, my own creation and I should live with it as the price of my own conceit. Quite heroic, in a way.

Having confessed all that, I have to point out that friends do put up with me to an extraordinary extent and that I am grateful that they do. I need them, probably more than they know.

After Five Dreams
Interim, how is the paradigm? Well, I think, in the sense that the turbulence and inner chaos of my psyche fits well with the idea that the human mind in general is much more of an imperfect mess than we generally accept. My self-image is really rather preposterous. I see myself as a rational, sceptical, perfectionistic and honest man. I am constantly discountenanced by aberrant tendencies, as I see

them, but put them aside as irrelevant to the main theme of myself. Like my mystical experiences, the behaviours that don't fit the main theory are side-lined, denied, or kept in a sealed box. The stresses involved in this continuous adjustment can hardly be imagined. Without alcohol, drugs or therapy, I have to work hard to maintain an approximation of so-called sanity. There must be a better way of managing my life than this. Freudian and Jungian therapeutic devices are still unacceptable to me, because they are drawn from the very belief-systems that cause the trouble in the first place. I will dream on, for now. My subterranean resources are being very productive.

Dream 6: Night Reverie. I am, in so-called real life, a participant in a play-reading group, which is reviewing its practice. Lying in bed at 5 a.m., I started to think about the plays we had read in the past two years. It was pleasantly retrospective and I thought I'd write a list for the group so that we could all see where we had travelled.

Here's the list:

The Doctors Dilemma	*Shaw*
An Inspector Calls	*Priestly*
Major Barbara	*Shaw*
The Birthday Party	*Pinter*
Tempest	*Shakespeare*
Macbeth	
Measure for Measure	
Othello	
Twelfth Night	
Death of a Salesman	*Miller*
Night of the Iguana	*Williams*
Hot Tin Roof	
Admirable Crichton	*Barrie*
Winslow Boy	*Rattigan*
The Deep Blue Sea	

The Browning Version	
The Importance of Being Earnest	*Wilde*
Antigone	*Anouilh*
Two/three plays	*Ayckbourn*
Under Milk Wood	*Thomas*
Abigail's Party	*Leigh*
Noises off	*Frayn*
Six Characters in Search of and Author	*Pirandello*
Look Back in Anger	*Osborne*
Hedda Gabler	*Ibsen*
Three Sisters	*Chekhov*
The Hostage	*Behan*
Roots	*Wesker*
The Prime of Miss Jean Brodie	*Jay Presson Allen*

It proved useful for the strategic discussion. But what struck me was the fact that my colleagues could hardly believe I had remembered so well. It hadn't occurred to me. But now I see that something quite odd had happened. From no record but my memory I had retrieved a great deal of data. These plays obviously meant a lot to my sub-conscious, as I had not given them a thought at the conscious level until that early morning reverie.

What does it mean to me in the general context of my odyssey? Clearly, plays and acting matter to me. Even though I cannot remember the parts I read, in most cases (I do remember disliking being Prospero, Macbeth and Othello, but this is interesting too. What does that mean, if anything?). Are these play-readings an opportunity to explore who and what I am? It feels like it. More than that, it is also a way of accepting my limitations and qualities, as if the truth is being offered to me adventitiously: I see myself in the fictional other. I dislike the qualities, for example, in the three characters I mention above. I find the various forms of egoism and stupidity in Prospero, Macbeth and Othello very nauseating. In a way the plays fail for me because there is not a clear and transcendent enough exposure of the flaws of these offensive men. Maybe I should re-evaluate the plays and admire the objective dismantling of the principal characters by the sharp sword of Shakespeare. Maybe I will. In the other plays, an immense range of feelings is triggered in me. Again, maybe I have been insufficiently aware of the power of the plays. But sometimes I have been affronted by what seems the lack of awareness or awakeness of the playwright.

There is no guarantee that a Shakespeare or a Chekhov are actually very aware beings. Thinking of Dylan Thomas or even Pinter, I can't quite eclipse the notion of how flawed they were as human beings. And this is an important message to myself. We are all flawed, and all muddled, and each of our egoic selves is weighed down with foolishness and vainglory.

This could mean that the theatre, or at least the written works of playwrights, gives me and others a rich data-base for exploring our own lack of integrated awareness and, more important, offers a way of maturing to a higher state of being with consummate humility. It also, incidentally, puts the authors of the plays in an altered category, in that they offer themselves naked to their fellow humans in the substance of the plays, a kind of self-sacrifice, even an act of heroism? What an irony that is, for me. Maybe I really have to backtrack on heroism too, depending upon the specific agenda of the hero concerned. I could hardly object to a heroic playwright fearlessly exposing his own absurdly heroic poses.

Dream 7. My wife/partner and I visited a house to discuss new business prospects with someone. She met us and was gracious but vague, telling us her friend was a wonderful cook and we would have a beautiful lunch. She disappeared. Then her husband, also gracious but vague who chatted and drifted away. Lastly we were confronted with a disagreeable misanthrope who sent us packing because there was nothing worthwhile to discuss. We left, driving down a sunny, pretty road, wondering if we had been misled or merely fortunate to escape. We didn't think it particularly odd as potential business situations often evaporated after initial enthusiasm. It was usually hard to make any progress in new ventures, as we well understood. Cocktail-party meetings also tended to lead nowhere too.

What does this mean to me now?

Essence

My friend and I discussed the Plan A/B again and it was like swimming in cold blancmange. We almost understood each other but my perception was that our minds were refusing to engage fully with each other. I don't wish to be witchy about this, but I do feel that forces behind recognition are at work here. They are probably just unconscious processes, but I do feel balked in my effort to reach this personal paradigm I have targeted. It may be that it is this aim that is at fault. Here again, my conscious mind is giving instructions to the rest of my mind and the result could be rebellion.

As I set the objective as de-constructing 'my' value-system, some 80% of my mind may have not signed up to the venture. Perhaps my total value system, muddled as it may be, suits my whole mind perfectly. And, in that case, the conscious 20% is being an arrogant upstart.

My dreams have gone on but they have shut down on conscious recall. It is as if they are hiding or sulking or teaching me a lesson, fanciful though that may seem.

Anyway, 'Essence': my friend thinks that his confusion or disappointment or desperation for a Plan B, or whatever he thinks is his problem, could be solved by the activity of this 'Essence'. He doesn't know quite what it is, but it seems to me that it could be the whole mind trying to express itself.

Now, my term 'whole mind' is interesting, I realise, because it has two meanings, i.e. 'whole' as in 'total' and 'whole' as in 'integrated' (euphemistically called 'healed'). I think that the wholeness that I am trying to negotiate is both of those meanings and I suspect that when I think, 'de-construct my value-system', I am prejudging and overwhelming from an intellectual standpoint. My 'whole' mind may dislike this intensely and I couldn't blame it if it did. It would have been more accurate and helpful if I (as conscious mind) had said I wanted to listen to the whole orchestra rather than just the conductor's lectures. The word 'conductor' is also significant, coming to consciousness to mean, perhaps, the one who thinks he is in charge. Which he may be, some of the time, for some of the music, but surely not for everything in the music (what about the composer, for example? Or the soloists? Or the 'leader'? Or the 'first' violin, French horn, bassoon, etc. What about the audience?) Does a different way present itself? And can I have my dreams back, please?

Carer-Breakdown
'I can't do this any more,' I say, with absolute finality. 'I am leaving and never coming back.' This to my wife within a few weeks of our diamond wedding-anniversary, a declaration of love with thorns. Her disablement is the ostensible reason, and her reluctance to do the required exercises. But what do I think I am doing? Is this insanity, or what? She has seen me fling all the cards in the air before, and stays steady through it. What part of my whole, composite, mind is doing this? It is a dream enacted in nearly real life, after lunch, in our kitchen. I tell her I will take my pension with me, and everything else will be hers: enough to buy a live-in carer and keep her in luxury for years. Where am I going? I haven't the faintest idea; well yes, the faintest, like a tough rope over the branch of a tree and me kicking at the other end of it.

It is true that I have had enough of the carer-worrier role. For four years I have been at or near my extreme stress-limit. But in the internal turmoil of my mixed-mind I know this is just a farce, even as I appear adamant in my despair.

The gales blow themselves out eventually. I am back to normal, if that is what it is. But the storm has shown me how mixed I am, shown me the different forces acting inside my psyche, as if I didn't know anyway.

I admit to her that this stress is life-long, life-endemic indeed. I have never been happy and it's too late to start now. Whereas I have always been happy, and it's too late to be unhappy now. She says I have a lot left to do in my life. She won't admit to the same for herself. She is merely holding on. My job is to forge ahead. Oh, really? That is the main problem. I, or some part of me, has always been forging. Now, that part of me, or nearby parts, want to lie down in peaceful pastures. For a while, at least. I could take a month's holiday. Alone. What hell that would be. Even worse with a friend other than the one that I am leaving.

I ponder the absurdity of trying to integrate all this absurdity. I will, of course, dig in, carry on, and make the best of it. But how to make the best of it, that's the interesting rub. I get a brief flash of insight. I see that this chaos is the stuff of the mind itself. It is temporarily going ape on the parade- ground. But it will line up neatly again any moment now. Has it seen enough to understand its own panic? Can it see that what was scattering the pigeons is mere hysteria? How can that madness be encapsulated in the whole without poisoning everything?

This waking dream, a day-mare, just shows the scope for raising my game to a gentler realm. She, wisely, says it is an opportunity. Well said, that woman. So there is a vague image of wholeness   in all this confusion. Maybe it is my friend's so-called essence. Maybe not. It feels more like a mental organism not quite winning in the survival-of-the-fittest competition.

Does a mind have to win that race? Why not walk in last? Oh yes, if smiling.

Another Friend
Feeling guilty, bruised and stymied by my own mind, I confessed the turmoil to a friend who was once a psychiatric nurse. He said I was 'depressed'. That is apparently a technical term. He expanded on it by saying my writing was too detached, it didn't weep on the page. It would be more effective if I didn't keep an intellectual distance between my feeling and my words. I think he thinks that I live too

much in my head and do not love my body enough. Possibly true, but I write to achieve comprehension rather than catharsis. It appears that he has similar problems, however, and that meditation has gradually turned round his state of being. I had stopped meditating some years ago and I think that was a mistake: something practical to take up again.

I find the conversation deeply helpful as it works upon me. One reason for it is that I am afraid of my own anger and unpredictability, and it also leaves me ashamed. This 'confession', because of his empathy, has allowed me to relax and, moreover, accept my own nature.

Coincidentally, a poem I wrote for the Group has been very well received, described, to my delight, as 'beautiful'. The content of the poem is, I feel, relevant to this chapter, because it does contain more fellow-feeling than I usually express and should certainly express more.

The Registration

His head, white-haired, leonine, wild-etched, stretched
Towards her, eyes searching, challenging, blue-black.
He was waiting in his darkness, listening for the message
To escape, to safety, anywhere but here, tight-lipped-angry.
She held out in the bleakness, tensed for the strike, fists
Hidden beneath apron, tired of meeting madness, old age,
The ferocity of broken being, the mediation, giving, loving
With no love to give, facing the alien as if a friend, smiling.
'Your name is Gwion?' she began, 'Surname, I suppose?
The white lion roared. 'Fool! I am Gwion Bach ap Gwreang'.
The registration form shook in her hand, the wrangle wept,
The joke died, replaced, he was eventually 'Lloyd George'.
She let it go, a pseudonym for a pseudo man, a vagrant,
Victim of the Welfare, the problem of acceptable disposal.
'Date of Birth?' she said. He smiled. 'Plinlimmon, top of.'
He explained. His mother was impregnated on the mountain

By a blind shepherd who remained anonymous. Try again.

'I must know when, not where.' His brow contracted. Thought.
He said it would have been weeks after starting on Plinlimmon.
Yes. She could follow that. The year, Lloyd? How old are you?
'Thirty thousand, about.' She looks quizzical. 'Days, my dear.'
She calculates. Years? He nods at eighty two. Clarity. At last.
Nearly there. The year agreed. 'At least we need a month.'
'What's that?' 'Lloyd, I want to know the month of your birth'.
'I am a druid. I don't do months.' 'But everyone does months;
Don't be silly, Lloyd.' They are nearly friendly now. Pleasant.
'Put down Imbolc, then. That will do, I'm sure.' 'When is that?'
'Imbolc is Imbolc. That's it. My mam fell pregnant in summer,
See. So I was born in winter, obviously.' 'Which winter month,
Then? You must know that.' 'February?' 'Or January, say?'
He tries: 'Yes, put down both of those. It wasn't Christmas.
I am not a Yule log. Nor have I purported to save the world.'
She gazes at the registration form. It is unusual. Unique.
It would not be impossible to like this person, they each think.

Wherefore Revelation Five

Alive and well, I begin to realise. An ambition may have been thwarted by reality, in that anger and fear are formidable psychic ingredients, not easily put down. Like familial heavyweights, maybe they have to be lived with not ostracised. The guru may tell us to 'leap beyond fear' but it is done in a single, spectacular, bound. My phrase, the hackneyed, 'Well, we shall just have to make the best of it we can,' is completely apt. Perhaps it would have been a better way to start this book. More than that, perhaps it would have been a better way to face up to life, instead of the Plan A nonsense of being heroic.

In fact, thinking of my parents, when I was heading for university and social success, they had already been 'making the best of a bad job', for years. I have the photograph of them on their wedding day and they look so young, happy, and rather beautiful. It didn't last long. Poverty and work and worry soon ruled their roost. I couldn't get away quick enough, even if I did weep with home-sickness in my first week at university. I still cannot fully understand how a contemporary of mine, also Michael, could actually choose to be a farm-worker. It worried me then, in the 1940's, as it still does. What did I think I was doing and what did he think he was doing? I have no answer to either question.

Chapter Four
Imbolc Approaches

The Chase

I am no Gwion Bach but I sometimes feel Ceridwen's hot breath on the back of my neck. I have been running for decades. Away from where and towards what? My fifth revelation was apparently the fact that my epic heroism, driven by fear and anger, drove me to excesses of self-tasking which have been ultimately pointless. This is a self-dramatisation that cannot stand up in court. Nor can the self-imposed sentence that I will simply give up being afraid and angry. The best I can try for is a state of being in which I feel ordinary. Or do I mean normal? Or blessedly unimportant?

Yes, it seems so. But what does that mean in practice? What will the cold spring be like when I reach the festival of Imbolc in a few weeks time? I am sure that fear and anger will be there, ever- present attendants upon my various life-processes. The question is, can I respond to the emotions in a better way? That does seem possible, After all, my life-long habit has been to pretend that they don't exist or that they don't apply to me. Therefore they have always taken me by surprise and been all the more powerful forces in the ambush. Also, my failure to own these forces - who else do they belong to but me? - intensifies their effect, as if they have no right to be there. In this sense, if in no other, my second friend is right to say that I am too much in my head - it is true, as well, that I am extremely fond of thinking and rather wary of feelings.

Teaching Dream

At last, another dream allows itself to be remembered. In it, I am leading a group of ten or twenty people in some subject or other, perhaps gender politics or socio-sexual malfunction; I don't know, it might have been something else entirely. The group are sitting in rows and instead of standing at the front like a proper lecturer I am in the middle of one of the rows.

Significant, this, because it may mean that I am halfway toward resolving a profound question but doing it in the wrong way. The question is, how can any of us presume to teach anyone anything. I love to teach, as my writing all these books indicates, but I am deeply suspicious of the teaching impulse. And the practice, too, since it is so often an abuse in one way or another. As in healing, so- called, how can I be so arrogant as to think I know what another person needs? The 'professional' teacher/healer will stress the 'training', which confers special skill on the practitioner. Yes, but who does the 'training'? Where or what is the ultimate authority for the truth being proselytised? It doesn't actually exist, yet to run our civilisation this phantom certainty is absolute. Apart from rebellion, of course, which is just another form of teaching.

In the dream I am teaching from the middle of the class, as if making it truly democratic - which it cannot be. I am the authority in the room and I shouldn't try to pretend I'm not there. It is the worst solution, because everyone knows I am counterfeit. Standing at the front I would at least be a clearly identified target for anyone who cares to challenge me.

Several people become antagonistic. My worst nightmare as a teacher comes into the room: they say that this is a pointless charade, or words to that effect. I ask why they are here if they don't want to know what is being explored? There's no answer to this, but the insurrection grows. There is anger everywhere. Why are they angry?

I am mortified and frightened. I am not sure where the fear and anger are coming from. Is it just me? Or is it all in them?

Two women are leading the rebellion, but they are not very angry. They could even be friendly. I realise that they are trying to help me. They try to explain the cause of the problem. They are inarticulate, but I just perceive that it isn't the subject that's bothering the 'class'. I also realise that it isn't particularly an aversion to me, specifically. It is, for no particular reason, an outbreak of anger (and fear?) that has suddenly irrupted as if there was a vacuum into which these elements have suddenly entered. As if the fear and anger had been waiting in the wings, looking for a way into the gathering.

My mind or body changes gear. I stop being a victim, a role which I realise had been waiting for me - also in the wings, presumably. I took action, as if the dream itself changed gear. I said to the people in the room, 'Would you please put the chairs in a circle, facing inwards?' I wasn't sure they'd do it, but now I didn't care: my fear and anger had evaporated. This was their show, not mine. I could get out of there any time I liked. And I would, if necessary.

I waited. The men were the most truculent, but they nevertheless helped the women move the chairs and then moved their own as well. My idea was to invite anyone to talk about the subject, in any way they chose. Or any subject, actually. Just a get-together, I thought, a way of being in relation to each other and ourselves. At this point in the dream, my wife woke me and asked for help. The ideal end to the dream.

As it happens, and it certainly happened, a third friend, female, had brought a DVD of 'Bagger Vance' for me to see. She was certain it would 'work' for me. 'But I loathe golf,' I protested. 'The golf is unimportant,' she asserted, 'It's the spiritual truth that matters'. Well, the actor Will Smith certainly did a fine turn as Krishna, playing a spiritual caddy, reprising his ancient mythic goal as the adviser to Arjuna, who had refused to fight. It is a film that, like the Arjuna myth, praises heroic warriorship. In that sense the film is counter-intuitive to me now, in that heroism seems an invalid way of being unless it is also transcendent, beyond the dross of power and glory. But as played by Smith, and directed by Robert Redford, the heroism was of the same kind as in the practice of Zen archery. That is heroism I can admire and attempt to emulate. The focus is on one's essential 'true gift' and the abjuring of all grandiosity. I love the principle of that. The practice is the most difficult thing a human being can attempt.

Synergy of the Messages

After all these decades of pursuing an evasive truth, like the Zen stories of the catching and domesticating the bull of spiritual pride, I have at least finished up in the Void which replaces the false glory of holy knowing. I was certainly trying too hard. And my pride was too great for any wisdom to find a place in me. But I was desperate to fulfil Plan A and become a whole person. In the mutinous context of the dream and the self-discovery in the film, the emotional charge in real wholeness came clearer to me.

Where does that leave fear and anger? Certainly they are still in residence. But there seems to have been an expansion in the role and meaning of these important emotions. It is, I think, and as Adyashanti seems to think too, a matter of how love enters the scene. Whatever that word is meant to mean, in the soft power of love there is a re-framing of fear and anger. Maybe love can even make allies of fear and anger, allies in the sense of power-animals, supporters in the psyche. My power- animals have been a big, black cat and a wild boar. These are hardly gentle beasts. Yet, when in a helpful or witnessing role, their power is wonderful. It may be mystical imagination, but how does that matter if the wholeness of being, and the awakeness of the spirit, are enhanced by them?

Friend number 2 needed me to recognise my strong tendency to depression, including my intellectual pessimism. When I was convinced that they were the absolute truth, i.e. that they accurately mirrored nature, I was undoubtedly depressed - and have been for years and years. But there is no absolute truth. Not as far as I can see, anyway. So why put everything in the shadow of darkness and misery? It is a choice, is it not? And I can reserve my main rage and fear for the endless acts of cruelty enacted by my species. That, at least, is positive. And it is almost certainly real.

The Botanist

Was botany my one true gift? Particularly as it included a desire and skill in illustration? Like the other Michael, I could have followed my singular star. He wanted to work on the land. I wanted to find and nurture plants. No much difference between us after all. We might have become adversaries, if I had become a zealous opponent of all-consuming agribusiness. Or maybe not. I worked for farmers' interests for twenty years, as it happened, and very much disliked it. But I did the work diligently. It was just a mistaken venture. I'd have done better to follow the way of the naturalist, if only I'd had the discernment to find it. It would have been a hard road to travel, I know, assuming I would have avoided commercial exploitation. It hardly bears thinking about, come to think of it. But it seems even more repulsive to imagine being a professor of botany in one of the universities. Far too political for me, I'm sure.

So I have made a garden and painted trees and landscapes. This is a sure-fire combination for bankruptcy. So I have done a salaried job as well, Krishna save me. Apart from the monthly pay and the pension, this life-time of labour was really pointless. Not that it was unpleasant or excessively stressful - though it could be very hard at the time of take-over bids or market- collapse. But for someone with a tendency to pessimism or depression it was a voyage of empty despair. Could I have done this foolish thing as a deliberate act of self-degradation? Or did I think I would be a world-ruler? Surely not either of these. The truth is much duller. It was just that I didn't think hard enough about the existential reality. I suspect that my mind was a romantic ragbag of nonsense. I was much more stupid than I could possibly have recognised. And I was undoubtedly very badly educated indeed. None of my teachers seem now to have had the slightest clue about life. They just did a subject, like the foolish version of me in the angry classroom dream above.

My subject was botany, or so I imagined. That seems crazy to me now. It cannot possibly be true. What was I trying to do? Botany was a depraved, or more correctly an elevated, version of the priesthood vocation, perhaps. It was a form of secular worship of the divine. I walked in the actual Garden of Eden, as I experienced the hills and vales of south Gloucestershire. What a mad youth I was. I am reluctant to admit it, but I do suspect a pagan fervour at work. I was intensely curious and potentially avid sexually. I knew nothing of paganism and had renounced any contact with Christianity. Yet something was driving me that was quite irresistible. A 'good' student', a strong athlete, a handsome youth, all those 'gifts' preposterously overbalanced me. The three university years were frantic and exciting. I was a wild creature with a civilised veneer, I think, and needed strong guidance that never materialised. If anything, I think I was exploited rather than helped, but anyone could say that of themselves.

The Real Me
If it actually existed, what could have been my true nature. And what is it still?

I am pleased to feel embarrassed by the degree of self-importance that has entered this chapter, if not before, but, unexpectedly, the book is going in that direction regardless of my initial and futile goal of stamping out undesirable emotions. I have already written one autobiography, more than enough you'd think. But here I am, indulging in another. I don't apologise. It is necessary.

That previous effort, inadequately hidden behind a fictional author, Nathan Wise, was a naively straightforward account of my first 56 years followed by 130 pages of psycho-babble and guru-lore. Then, at the end of the book, I invented another figment called The Paraclete, a composite being, who transcendent in one way or another. It was 1999 and I had come to certain conclusions. Fifteen years later I don't seem to have got much further. This is a sobering thought. Here was the final 'Paraclete report' in that autobiography, referring to the effect of a dream:

Nathan awoke and realised that the dream referred to his own lack of faith throughout his life. This lack of faith at his core, and the fear associated with it, was an error. Certainly the world was a very unsafe place, but he had blamed himself for that unsafety. He had worked himself into the ground trying to make the world safer by becoming more faith-worthy in himself.

Recognising that his self-disbelief was a mistake made it possible to slough off the anger he felt about the world, as it was not his fault that it was dangerous. Indeed, as I had been trying to show him for seventy years, the world and he were much of a muchness. Given this self-belief instead of disbelief, he could realise that he was actually quite good as well as quite unimportant.

I wish all my work came to such a fortunate culmination. Nathan's last few years can now be happy as well as highly aware. Figment that I am, I can feel a sense of achievement about Nathan. And, figment that he is, he can feel a sense of achievement about me.

Note 'fear' in line 2 and 'anger' in line 5. I am still where I was fifteen years ago. I hadn't realised that. He was already aware of the failure of Plan A. What have I been doing during these fifteen years? I suppose I could argue that the case I perceived at the beginning has been analysed and expanded in some ten further books. I have spread the word (to deaf ears?). But have I moved personally? Am I up against the intractable me? It looks rather karmic, I must admit.

I mean karmic in the sense of things coming back in a circular motion. Have I done all this before, have I been all this before, and if so, when? It is very counter-intuitive, but there it is. I don't do reincarnation, so I don't see it as a past life. But I am beginning to see how I just keep on repeating things in this one life. Habits as you might say, habits I have failed to recognise. It begins to seem that the real me is just a series of habits like evolution is just a series of accidents. There is a delicious sense of freedom in this absurd process: it happens despite everything so why worry and why plan, I just won't notice just how deja vu is my existence.

The Big Bully

Another dream: I knew this man, before cancer killed him. He was big. Over six foot high. Maybe twenty stone. Formidable beer-belly. I was always daunted by him. He lived a few doors away. He was a judge. And a big drinker. He made me feel small and inadequate - or I allowed myself to be intimidated by him. And so it was in the dream. He was standing to the side of me and half- addressing other people (as he would in court) but his words were directed at me. I was being humiliated, quite successfully, but the charges were lacking in detail. Basically, I was just no bloody good.

I woke up feeling quite scared and remembering the few occasions that I had met him. I remembered that when he was drunk he was overbearingly affable and extremely controlling. He had seemed to dislike me but his wife said he was nervous of me because of my 'personal development work'. I gathered from her that he was afraid of 'that sort of thing' and didn't want her to be mixed up in it. In mature retrospect, if such a process is really possible, it seems that he and I spooked each other. But we both practised Plan A till we were blue in the face so that even a shred of male bonding was out of the question. I should, of course, have been more skilful, and so should he. There are lessons here of some importance.

I am also contemplating another big bully in my life, a female cousin whose career had been in teaching English to sixth form and above. She had attacked me in my 'psychological work' and also in my attempts to write novels. There was nothing I could do right in those areas, (She acquired my paintings voraciously enough, yet that didn't appease me at all, such was my pride and conceit.) By the time she had done her worst, I hated her. The hatred alarmed me, but there it was, as big and grotesque as she was.

Then I thought of lesser bullying, on the surface at least. At university I had 'converted' from flowering plants to fungi because the resident mycologist, snappy little fellow though he was, far exceeded the ability of all the other staff in the botany department. So when I got a good degree, he was the obvious (and wrong) choice to be my research supervisor. There was a very pleasant young taxonomist, who might have got me researching with him, yet I didn't rate him enough to ask him to take me on. So I started my research career in the worst possible way. I wanted to work on symbiosis, a big deal for the fungi. But the little-big man decreed that I should spend three of my precious young years uncovering the dirty secrets of a pathogen of onions. I was appalled, and unhappy, but hadn't the courage or confidence to say no.

I have to look at my own tendency to dominate others, too, often to the point of mental bullying. It's standard Plan A procedure, after all. No excuse for it, but it's what the culture demands despite liberal pretensions. It now seems to me that I have always fought in a crowded saloon, like a stubbornly English Shane, but without much true heroism. My passion for nature's beauty has kept me going, plus the love of, or with, a few precious people. But the main action seems always to have been this endless tussle of egoic will against egoic will. I can't think of a profession in which it does not hold sway. Even friendship tends to succumb to the bullying tendency.

Observer Error
This is common enough throughout our race: we pronounce truths on partial or negligible evidence and call it intuition or wisdom or inspiration or some other fraudulent process. By ordinary observer error I failed to see my own culpability again and again, while feeling fragile or betrayed by others.

I learned how to be an effective bully in my childhood and teens, it is easily picked up and added to a ready-made disposition to win against others. There were some strong friendships and a lot of weak ones, but the main event, frankly, was to get my own way. Erroneous observation was my passport, and sometimes I was a bully and sometimes I was bullied, often being unsure of which way it was going. Like liability, it is hard for the involved observer to know who should take the blame in any particular situation.

In the three examples of my feeling bullied, by the big judge, the egregious cousin, and the mycological martinet, my life was changed by the experience. The first two undermined my faith in myself and my apparent gifts, serious but not fatal, and then third ruined a promising career in biological science. My family had already done some groundwork in the bullying process. All my university holidays were spent doing manual labour to prop up the fragile family finances. I was never thanked for this obligatory favour. My father ignored me for most of a decade, making me feel unloved and valueless. My mother expected me to be her personal guardian angel. My brother and sister seemed oblivious of my existence.

In all these interactions, it is impossible for me, the error-prone observer, to know who caused what. I may feel done down, but that is not necessarily true when everything is considered. Every one of the many persons who bullied or neglected me were struggling with their own demons. In the real world, whatever that may be, we should focus on the undisputed bullying deliberately and cold- bloodedly perpetrated on the weak, innocent, and vulnerable. There is plenty of that around, everywhere, and it doesn't get enough attention. Why have I not devoted more of my life's energy on that opportunity to do really good work? My only excuse is my stupidity. At least, I think that's the cause, unless I am deliberately misanthropic.

Solstice
December 21; not long to Imbolc now. By the middle of January I should write a poem on the subject of doors and windows. At first, the subject fails to stir me. Then a thought floats up from the substratum: there are far more doors than windows in the human mind. What on earth does that mean? I remember a ritualistic

exercise from ten years ago. At first, there was a windowless room without an apparent door. A crowd of people were talking loudly at one another. Our first task was to find the door. Nobody seemed to care about a door. But I saw a possibility of a door and tried to open it. No handle. I pushed. No movement. Then I thought hard about it being open, willing it to let me through. Then there was just a large hole, like a cave. As my eyes adjusted I could see the lineaments of a passage-way.

I walked into the passage. I was alone. It was a long walk, but the tunnel eventually met a circular barrier, apparently made of opaque plastic, though quite rigid to the touch. I knew, by some hidden psychic instinct, that on the other side of the barrier there was the Void. In recent years I had been increasingly interested in, and affected by, the Void. But this was the first time that I had ever felt capable of entering it. I hesitated, rather afraid, but profoundly interested.

Always before I had been just an observer. The idea of the Void was that it was fundamentally ambivalent, more so than anything else in existence. To enter it was taboo because I was a bit of something and the Void was hostile to things. It was a fertile nothingness out of which nothing and everything issued. I might cease to exist if I entered it. The possibility of psychic death hovered. Yet I had to do it. This was a reality-border, as if a division between completely different realities. For years I had sought the real reality, as if it were a thing to be discovered. So, here it was, I had to drop my guard and step through the barrier.

I did so. A simple step. I walked through the absolute barrier between non-Void and Void. Now I was in the Void. What was the reality of it? Was there anything that a mere human could recognise? I don't know. What I saw in front of me and, come to think of it, all around me, was a milky way. I mean that I saw billions of points of light apparently unbounded by any limits whatsoever.

I had previously experienced strong mystical and scientific doubts regarding the reality we all seem to think we occupy. The conundrums of quantum mechanics fed my soul like manna. Of course this was reality, and totally unknowable at that. This was my beloved Great Continuity. And so on. But the vision after passing through the 'plastic' barrier was transcendent of anything so humdrum as mere knowledge, or even of the tiresome concepts of reality. This was absolute existence, comparable in some ways the notion of absolute zero. And it certainly wasn't that hackneyed image, The Milky Way. I was not looking at the edge of the universe.

If it is possible, I would like to feel the meaning of quantum physics. I am a non-starter in maths and physics as academic subjects. Yet I feel this powerful urge to share the experience of being a Voidal entity, as if I am clear about the fact, even without living the substance of it. It could be the text of my doors and windows poem. The idea is eccentric enough to pass muster. Doors and windows could pass muster as the 'furniture of quantum living'. It is a poem daring me to write it.

Pushing out the boat of irrationality, whereby I might hope to sail into super-rational territory, the pot-pourri of metaphors and mind-stretching and quanta must be well-stirred like Ceridwen's cauldron. Maybe there will be a few drops of magic substance to change the state of being that chains us in a tight and strangling embrace. Imagine it.

The blackness around the 'stars' seemed to be a different Void, a continuum of doors. The points of light were the widows, as metaphorical as the doors. How different are the mind and the universe? It can be imagined that the Void, as experienced through mind, has meaning, however baffling. But the universe seems quite meaningless, and the stars are merely burning globes in almost infinite distance. The physicists and astronomers peer into the space beyond us and try to make sense of it, at least to the extent that the human mind can be made to seem as if it, itself, is meaningful. The stark possibility is that neither the 'little' Void, the one in our heads, nor the 'big' Void, the one pervading the whole universe, have any meaning whatsoever. If that were the case, what does thinking 'mean', and what does feeling 'mean'?

Thus we create the metaphors, the symbols whereby we conjure up meaning where it may not exist. The doors and windows in the human mind would be devices for creating the illusions of significance. There must be something on both sides of a door. Windows reveal another world beyond the one we look out from. But then there is the reality we can neither understand nor derive comfort from: the quantum field, in which doors can be windows and windows can be doors, where waves and particles are interchangeable. We invent gods and then struggle to make sense of them as they also embody ambivalence, we cannot rely upon the gamble that divinity stands for anything.

I have argued that there is true freedom in this all-pervading lack of meaning. I think it is true. But I know that it is hard to live without meaning. The furniture of my mind keeps me occupied if not satisfied. I like my doors and windows, even if they reveal neither something nor nothing beyond my imagined world. And in that case, is imagination somehow inherently both true and false?

The poem waits to be composed. It is actually written above, without rhyme, reason, or metre. But it is too sober for a poem. The truth is wilder and more absurd that prose can render. That does not guarantee that the poetic confection will tell the story any better. Here goes. A poem for Imbolc, the herald of Spring, when the earth goes crazy.

Quantum Openings

Confusion stalks the halls of physics, where thoughts
Think they might be both/either waves and/or particles,
And little Quantum David slays the Einsteinian Goliath.
Two universes, then, at least, if not many more, makes
Mockery of sober science, trying to have and eat cake
Of fruity logic. Their house is out of order, in their heads
A truth tries to speak, is muffled by professorial rectitude,
And there's no-one else to speak it, no maverick voice.

Physics? Just one more religion! Would be the rebel's cry,
Another mansion in the house of cloudy aristocrats, gods'
Home-base of inventions, where desires are made manifest.
Everything is in the human head, the skull-universe of man.

Choose another animal: there's another cosmos. Millions,
Yes, millions of different worlds, ours is one, just the one.
Look into your head, O human, and see how your quantum
Fantasy operates. It seems so various. As well it might, being
Imagination in action. In your skull-residence, little universe,
There are many openings and closures, as you'd expect from
Quanta, if you would only surrender to their conceptions, not
Cement yourself in fixed fictions, those existential roundabouts.
How you use your personal cosmos is up to you, but choice is
A quantum predilection: so how do you live there in your head?
The skull-house has many openings, little galaxies of suns, not
Determined by decree, no certainty, unknown, shanty-mind.

Think doors and windows, making walls ridiculous, think open.
Why do you have so many doors and so few windows? Mind
Abhors a vacuum (nature doesn't care) and fills it with assertion,
But the wildness of reality breaks through pretence, doors open,
New doors are made, windows flash and pierce: your skull-home
Is rebuilt each moment, it is a mental quantum field, meanings
Slide, slip, disappear; unnecessary trivia for the disposal men.
The monster lurks outside, tricking your mind beyond your walls.
Let him in, face him down, his sickness is in his authority, priest,
Or pedant of experiment, smell the odour of sanctity, the fatal
Smell of hubris, they think they make the world by their magic,
They forget the world makes them, particles or waves, or both.

Does that give my picture of the 'truth'?
True enough, I think; but they, Einstein, Bohr, and Heisenberg, the
oldies, and Brian Cox, Jim Al-Khalili, and Hawking, the 'newies',

are wrong in a more subtle yet more important way, as we all are, because of the nature of mind itself.

It's not unlike my minor error (I mean microscopic because of my unimportance, the error is cosmic) in thinking I could ditch my fear and anger. This 'fifth revelation' has already eclipsed itself by deeper realisation. Fear and anger are encoded in my mind and its emotions. Likewise, the wonderful, brilliant physicists (I am not being sarcastic) have rightness encoded in theirs. Science is driven by the need to be right, even though the goal is claimed to be the elimination of wrongness. Rather like my fifth revelation, the scientist is determined to cast out error.

Like my (and their) impulse to extirpate fear and anger, the need to destroy wrongness is a burning desire. Karl Popper put it more forcibly, he said that the point of science was to assume error and then work to prove the error, until the work proved rightness. This is really nonsense. Popper was making an impossible claim, turning a metaphor into a fact. Yes, science should assume a theory is just a theory, but would a person really spend his life trying to disprove his theory if he didn't have at least a sneaking conviction that it was probably correct? Scientists are not saints, even if they behave as if they are.

I want to dig deeper. The whole human thought process, at least in the West, but probably throughout our species, seems to be round the wrong way. It's not unlike the chicken and egg version of cause and effect. As it happens, the chasm between Einsteinian physics and quantum mechanics is just one symptom of the overall malady. The overriding problem is something like saying, 'Well, if it's not this, it must be that, otherwise the problem is insoluble'. I suppose the problem might be the very idea that there are such things as problems and solutions.

What if evolution, as a process, has been stuck in the groove of 'success', as a biochemical response to the earth's environment? This question seems asinine, doesn't it, because we have all been taught that evolution is about the survival of the fittest. That is success surely? In approximate terms, we have also been taught that energy systems tend toward disorder, i.e. entropy, unless some other process holds them back in a state of order. Or it may be expressed as entropy being constant in a 'closed system'. As an evolving species, or an individual organism in its biological operation, are not closed systems, they are entropy-changing in nature. One solution to this possible conundrum is to say that a living organism, and the evolutionary process, causes increased entropy i.e. disorder in its outside world in exchange for increased order within its own process. Seven billion human animals must therefore be inherently bound to make colossal increases in the entropy of the world. The disorder we humans create seems to bear that out.

These are simplistic arguments, yet they begin to illustrate what I mean about the human mind's presumption regarding the nature of nature and especially of its own nature. The concept of success is as slippery as an eel. The mind is not necessarily a very useful instrument of understanding, nor is it at all clear what it is trying to do in its daily life. Just how wedded is it to the slippery idea of success, or of progress; and if it is thus devoted, can it ever do anything but fail?

The Quantum-Void

What shape is it, this mind of ours? Typically success-oriented, I decided to oust anger and success from my behavioural range. I called this a revelation. But I hadn't considered that a revelation could extend in time and/or space. It is now clear that my fifth revelation is a process not an event. But my need for success is so ingrained, and perhaps unconscious, that I thought that was it, I had apparently succeeded in making or acquiring a truth.

My Plan-A friend was desperate for a truth upon which to rest his head. My thankful grasping of the Fifth Revelation was paralleled by his discovering 'Essence'. My solution was illusory, though not useless. But we were both reaching out for a success, a rightness, with which we could be happy, whole or fulfilled. It is as if we are driven by the need to be 'right' in some fundamental way.

The idea the nature is fundamentally a quantum phenomenon is both satisfying and problematic (appropriately enough) because it doesn't seem to fit the classical model in which predictability rules. Humankind needs predictability, just as it needs rightness and wholeness, so the quantum version of reality is a poisoned chalice.

Ever-determined to find rightness somehow, there is immense and expensive work being done to make sense of quantum mechanics. Hence the TV programmes by Jim Al-Khalili. Everywhere on earth, people are trying to be right or find rightness (except the enormous number who are starving, homeless, or dispossessed or violated by other people); politics, religion, philosophy, science, law, education, medicine, militarism, and even terrorism, are all devices aimed at getting rightness, i.e. being successful. The existential Void is full of striving. Yet it is still a Void.

The picture changes if it is accepted that the Void is actually the human mind. It is the human mind, in that case, that is the existential phenomenon, that is, as it were, everything we experience. Our collective error is that we think it is real, an actuality outside ourselves albeit inclusive of ourselves. Our human mind is, on this assumption, a quantum phenomenon. Its behaviour is unpredictable, in can be two things at once, it can happen across space and time, it can be a particle or a wave. Of course it can, it is mind, that is what mind does.

Being the mind of all humans, the Void is any shape or thing we like to imagine it. The empty phrase 'It's all in the mind' is the absolute truth that rules our existence however we deny it. It can be a spectrum, a sphere, a vast plain, a tiny point, a black hole, a universe, a chimeric creature, a god, destiny, the great continuity, the mystery, the ground of being and, for my friend, essence.

While scientists delve and spin to find the hidden reality, and non-mystical clerics claim to know it as a god-given fact, there are many human beings who take a third position on the truth that must be discovered. These are the people who take a mystical or transpersonal stance on the unknown. They are a strange bunch in many ways. Many of them are famous for their power and charisma. They are the spiritual rather than religious authorities. They are often extremely vocal authorities. In some ways they outplay both the scientific and the religious truth-makers. A lot of them are very erudite psychologists or teachers. I personally find them much more attractive and often convincing than the scientific/logical or religious/faithful majority of our species. I do not consider them to be right, or successful, because they are generally trapped in the certainty of a hidden reality. They are also consumed by the fires of rightness and progress. But I still like them. Why?

Essence People

Who am I talking about here? I could name a dozen people, some contemporary, others long dead, such as: **Adyashanti, Krishnamurti, Ram Dass, David Bohm, Ken Wilber, Alan Watts, Annie Besant, George Gurdjieff, Gautama Buddha, Epicurus, Eckhart Tolle, and A-Hameed Ali.**

How heterogeneous can you get? Well, that's the point. These people do cover an immense range, and there are massive differences between them. But for my purpose they are virtually identical. And there are hundreds of others, perhaps thousands. Still not enough for our suffering world, but how much worse would we be without them?

I like these people because they are examples of humanity at its most aware and involved with the idea of humanness, and even their pottiness, where it exists, is somehow liberating to my own psyche. I suppose they appeal to me because they are a fracture line across the self-obsessed, dogmatic, armoured-plating of conventional wisdom and traditional certainty. This is not a one- hundred per cent distinction, everything being mixed and muddled in matters of the mind. Similarly, there are essence-people I have excluded because of their particular fixations, people such as Rudolf Steiner, Carl Jung, and Deepak Chopra.

My Plan-A friend has a strong regard for the twelfth person in my list, A-Hameed Ali, who writes under the pseudonym of A.H.Almaas. In deference to my friend I bought Almaas's book, 'Essence'. I am reading it at the present time.

Almaas both confirms my regard for essence-people and repels me by his immense presumption. This is the trouble with the wonderful human mind, it knows no limits to its own magnificence. I keep remembering that the human mind is just another invention of scatty evolution and that it's really no big deal. Yet I have to live with one inside my own head. It demand attention. It is always bloody thinking. It doesn't even let up when I am asleep, but rattles on with dreams. (In this early morning's dream I attacked and threw out two men from my house, and I nearly killed them in my rage at their criminal intent.) So I ought to be more tolerant of Ali from Kuwait.

I could excuse myself because of my distaste for the Sufi overtones in the book. But I won't. Having started it, I must keep going and maybe learn something about my own mind as I collide with that of Mr. Almaas. I will explore this in the next chapter.

Chapter Five
Deepest Reality?

Symbol or Actual

As I do have sympathy with the idea of 'essence' as the original or fundamental nature of a human being (or any other creature) I approached the book with cautious optimism. Halfway through, I still cling to the expectation that I will derive some benefit from it. But the optimism has been severely tested.

I accept that the nature of my own mind-set is antipathetic to esoteric theory claiming to be fact. Mr. Almaas is an esoteric theorist claiming to offer actual facts. In this way, he veers towards the steamy swamp of religion and I reel away in disgust. Much of the text proselytises Sufi lore, with friendly nods to the Rig Veda, Sri Aurobindo, Idries Shah, Bhagwan Shree Rajneesh, and Chogyam Trungpa, as well as a wide range of psychologists and healers. Most of this company have little appeal for me, partly because of my own disenchantment with the glorification of the self and the endless worship of the power of the human mind, psyche, soul or consciousness.

Yet, apart from these tendencies of mine, I have been fortunate in my mystical and imaginative life and I do like the idea of a ground of being or a great continuity of existence. So, in some ways, I am just as bad as the motley bunch who shelter under the umbrella of spiritual esotericism. The main difference, I suspect, is that I also cherish Ockham's (Occam's) razor.

This means that when a symbolic or metaphorical concept is printed as a solid entity, I get very restive. As I have written elsewhere, Jung's archetypes are very problematical for me. It's rather like my being able to accept the message of a Jesus or any other guru, but balk at the whole divinity caper.

Therefore, as a substitute for the disastrous Plan-A that dominates the consciousness of most people on earth today, that is, the universal obsession with 'success', spiritual esotericism doesn't work, being just another brand of the success contagion aggravated by delusion. I can't see how my Plan-A friend will cope with it. But that's really another issue.

My issue, here, is how I resolve my feelings about the 'Diamond Approach' peddled by Mr. Almaas. For now, I am in psychic shock. This book disorientates me seriously from page 54 onwards, by the insistence that essence is actually a substance. At first, I couldn't take in this monstrous suggestion. I read on, hoping I had misunderstood. Maybe he meant the fact that a human person is made of trillions of living, sentient units, both cells of the human kind and those of the vast number of 'alien' residents. Maybe he saw in this immense variety a deep pattern I had missed. This would be exciting. But no. He specifically excludes 'the various substances and fluids' in the body.

Here are Almaas's exact words on p. 54, para. 5:

'Essence, when experienced directly, is seen to be some kind of substance, like water or gold, but it is not a physical substance like physical water or gold. This is a very difficult point to make. Essence is experienced as a substance, a material. It has characteristics such as density, viscosity, texture, taste and so on, but at the same time it is not a physical substance. It belongs to a different realm of existence.'

Precisely the same words are quoted in another of his books

'Essence with the Elixir of Enlightenment', p.56, so he obviously means what he says. How can this be anything but insane fiction? If not, it is earth-shattering in its significance, as it seems, in effect, to put some actual physical 'godness' into the human body.

Mind you, the language he uses about essence is very uneven and discursive. At times, the idea of essence as substance seems to give way to other concepts, and elements such as soul, presence, subtle energy, seem to take centre-stage. Maybe I am just too un-Sufi to follow these ramifications. And I am certainly alive to the basic idea of essence being the most important factor in my existence if I use the term in my way, i.e. *as the core of my being.*

Losing It

Moving on from the conundrum of substantiality, there is the question of loss of essence. I am familiar with this concept. Indeed it drives the system known as The Enneagram, in which the human personality forms as a replacement and a distortion of the human 'true', fundamental, and indeed, basic, essence. The author almost overstates this. In his narrative, the human baby starts full of essence and it drains away in him as he grows up, particularly in terms of the love relationship with the mother. Although I have made much use of this concept in my later life, I still found myself protesting at the apocalyptic horror of the process of loss in Almaas's text.

It is extraordinary how the book fails to explain how and why the essence-loss occurs. It's all the fault of the egoic push of the usurping personality, sure, but why does that occur. Is it bad parenting, bad culture and bad teaching? Almaas doesn't say, as far as I can tell.

This is intriguing. Does he really believe that his Sufi culture, for example, actually destroys essence? Or any other culture? Why do we humans sacrifice our essence for the sake of the meretricious personality. I suggest that it is a Plan-A process; that we destroy essence because we believe in success, or heroic achievement, or just power. What is Almaas's explanation? It seems to be that the growing baby gradually realises there is less love in its life, that a hole opens up in the love-matrix. Holes lead on to bigger holes. And personality is made to fill the holes. That is much the same as the Enneagram story. But I wonder if it is true.

Evidently, the picture here is one of supposed victim-hood. The most precious quality in infantile existence is seen as being cast aside, leaving the child, and hence the adult, scarred for life. Are mothers really so inept? Is the environment actually so hostile to the expression of love? Or is it a basic flaw in human nature, a spontaneous burgeoning of resentment or anger that becomes the breeding-ground for a set of personality traits which are intended to protect the self as it swells in importance? Is it possible that infants, and youngsters generally, are pre-set bombs planted in us with inevitably explosive results? Which is the chicken and which the egg?

As he proceeds to the 'retrieval' process, in his case the 'Diamond Approach', Almaas concentrates on the way the infant tries to 'merge', or hold on to merging, with its mother:

Merging Love and Dual Unity

'Whenever there is any loss of the symbiotic union, the dual unity with mother, the child experiences the loss of merging essence. To repeat, this is because, for him, the merging love aspect of Essence is he and his mother together.'

(Essence with the Elixir of Enlightenment, p. 93)

I could well understand this symbiotic state, especially applying to the first few months of a baby's existence after birth - it is, after all, a continuation of the uterine state partially interrupted by the birth event. One way of seeing this is that human infants are all premature, having heads that have evolved to massive proportions thereby making ordinary mammalian birth inherently dysfunctional. One of the human defects is, therefore, this state of serious inadequacy in the first year or two of extra-uterine life.

Coming to terms with the environment is the primary task facing the human after nearly a year in the uterus and another two out of it. What surprises me is the naivety of the view that what happens next is a disaster. I am well aware of the evils attributed to the personality/ ego which emerges from the 'coma' of babyhood, as I have studied them in detail when working with the Enneagram, but I am now far from convinced that the conventional wisdom is correct. I certainly concur with the idea that the human personality is full of error and even disease, but what now strikes me as dubious is the assumption that the environment is to blame, especially the baby's main early environment, its mother. Whatever we may think of essence, or any other vital equipment of the human psyche, there is too little thought given to the mechanism by which the personality becomes such a problem. And, consequentially, there must be doubt concerning traditional methods used to solve the personality problems.

The Cause

As many others do, Almaas blames 'external forces' for the loss of essence and the assumed damage to the merging state. Both religion and psychology tend to see it as a kind of 'fall' from grace or equanimity. The assumption, not altogether consistent, is that the new-born human is pure and that the purity is stained by contact with the world. Let's try a different model.

The unicellular human has the full genotype within it, from which it develops into a phenotype, the multicellular organism that emerges from its mother's uterus after nine months of rapid growth and development. It has an inner mandate to survive despite being more or less disabled by its still incomplete development. Some animals are luckier in their heritage, being able to walk almost immediately after birth. We just happen to be the unluckiest animal on earth (except, perhaps, the kangaroo or the giant panda) in terms of new-born activity.

On the other hand, we have a remarkable brain, which may or may not be the source of our mind, and indeed our essence, or soul (it is entirely conjectural what these are and where they come from).

It is this brain/mind that must now tackle the world and live in it, usually with the dedicated help and attention of another, or several other, mature human individuals. Does this really seem such a bad deal? Falling in love with our devoted minder is an inevitable hazard, but couldn't we do a better job of that with some gratitude rather than griping because the care wasn't quite perfect for us?

Perhaps not; our needs are unlimited and nothing could possibly compensate us for having to make it on our own in some way and at some stage. So we scheme and plan and dissemble, we shout, fight, throw things, sulk, get depressed, we smile, simper, laugh, caress and hug. It's called personality. It's how we get hold of the world and shape it to our relative satisfaction.

This personality we have contrived is not necessarily the perfect answer to the existential state. We blame it on others. Sometimes that's fair, sometimes not. Who can judge the precise balance between our culpability and that of others? One thing is certain, the personality is a composite phenomenon. It is a collective creation, with our individual input being primary.

The Cure

There's no doubt in my mind that the individual human personality is truly pretty awful. In this, Almaas does a favour to us all by ramming home the point. The personality does need fixing. It just doesn't work. I happen to think it is the result of a faulty 'design', an evolutionary fiasco, whereas he seems to think it is a spoilt perfection, in a toxic environment. I have my idea of a rescue system, and he has another. It is very arrogant of both of us to think we can solve this problem, whichever it is. But why not? It's just our personalities/essences doing their worst/best. Let's compare.

First, I refer to another Almaas book, 'Facets of Unity: The Enneagram of Holy Ideas', and quote two key phrases:

The Perspective of the Holy Ideas

As we have noted, the present work expands on the understanding of

the Holy Ideas as it has unfolded in the context of the development of the Diamond Approach. At the same time, the perspective of the Holy Ideas actually provides a context for understanding some of the underlying basis for the method of inner work that constitutes the Diamond Approach. The Diamond Approach developed in a context that included the understanding of the Enneagram as a map of reality and a sacred psychology.
Facets of Unity, p. 10

The Perspective of Unity
As will become clear in the course of this volume, the method of the Diamond Approach is based from the outset on the perspective of unity, as revealed by the Holy Ideas. At the same time, the student is not expected at the beginning to understand or appreciate this view; on the contrary, students begin by working with the actual, limited egoic identifications they find themselves in. Truthfulness about, and openness to, the limitations of the deluded ego state are central to the method. Thus, for example, a central attitude encouraged in the student's exploration into her character is the attitude of allowing, that is, attempting to take a non-judgemental, non-controlling position with respect to whatever arises in her inner experience.
Facets of Unity, p. 12

The cover of this book displays the Enneagram circle, slightly distorted to accommodate the Diamond design, which is elaborated by nine starred points. Therefore, the Diamond Approach is to a degree merely a well-known and widely practised system with the added spin of the essence-concept. Also, near the end of the 'Essence' book, there is a section on the importance of developing full awareness in the process of re-framing or restructuring the personality.

At this point, the sense of deja vu becomes unavoidable for me. In one way or another I have been practising these methods for decades and affirm their relevance and importance. I was puzzled by the term 'Diamond Approach' and baffled by the idea of a substantive and physical 'essence', but now I can see how they are really just embellishments of a system in widespread use. If I have any problem with Almaas's methods, I can now understand that he is really using a well-tried method of working (he calls it the Work) and bolstering it with a (dubious) notion of Essence as material, and inserting a multiplicity of references to the Sufi religion. Otherwise, it's a typical embodiment of transpersonal psychology with some added ingredients and garnishes.

Missing Factors

I am glad that 'awareness' is added as a crucial feature of 'The Work'. I have written extensively on this subject, though I prefer Adyashanti's word, 'awakeness'. It seems clear to me that the personality is a strategic device undermined by the tendency to be asleep, i.e. to act automatically rather than consciously. At one point, Almass seems to be saying that we must destroy the unconscious so as to become fully aware (p. 126 of 'Essence'). That must be poetic licence. I can't favour the destruction of eighty per cent of the mind. However, there must be quite an excavation job done in the deeper regions of the mind so that fullness of being can be achieved.

What I miss in Almaas is any idea of the causal nature of the mind itself. I think he seriously underestimates the responsibility of the human mind for its outrageous behaviour. I suppose that I am also saying that our so-called essence is not so good either. I think there is fundamental 'badness' in the human, in the sense that we are inherently the same as our fellow animals.

This is a preposterous value-judgement, of course. There can only be 'badness' as defined by human opinion. We don't know whether other creatures have sets of values, any more than we know if there is a supernatural court of judgement, i.e. a god-tribunal. The point here is that Almaas's 'essence' is, in effect, a god within each human, i.e. a perfection within an imperfection. A common religious belief, to be sure, but, like the absurdity of 'original sin', it fails to understand the basic biology of man and other animals.

This brings me to another deficiency in Almaas's thinking. Although he refers fulsomely to psychological work of various kinds, he seems to ignore the more fundamental sciences. I mean 'fundamental' in the sense that they deal with nature as a whole rather than merely the function of the human psyche. Science is certainly overblown and unreliable, so it deserves wariness of approach, but can any serious thinker ignore, say, quantum mechanics or Darwinian evolution? In exploring the human personality, does it make any sense to disregard the more or less known facts of genetics and the workings of logic-systems and mind-theory?

There is another deficiency for me, that is the fascination of the entire living world. I admit that this could just be my idiosyncrasy, but trees, for example, are of immense significance to me. They are a different order of existence, which is interesting in itself, but they confer such extraordinary benefits on humankind. Then there are the wonderful flowers that grace our lives. Medicines and essential oils make human life more tolerable. Walking through fields, or woods, or by rivers, has powerful mind-healing effect. And, overall, the grand sweep of nature, both beautiful and terrible, puts our petty selves in proportion.

Next, I think of the arts. As a painter, my life is greatly enriched by just the act of painting, while poetry is the most powerful form of words for me. Music has overwhelming effects upon the mind and emotions. No doubt these are used in the Diamond Approach, yet I wonder if the full importance of artistic imagination is reflected in The Work.

Extraneous Factors

Religion is superfluous for me, so how could I appreciate the Sufi content of Almaas's work? Similarly, I find offensive the repeated use of the word 'holy' in listing the supposed essences in his Enneagram book. I can certainly recognise that religion is a huge factor in the human psyche, but has Almaas or his religiously inclined associates considered the probability that religion is a toxic element in the dysfunctional human personality? I do regard religion as a massive error in human behaviour. Why? Because it converts sheer fantasy into mendacious fact. Thus, Almaas and his ilk automatically assume that they can utilise religious dogma in explaining their work and purpose. This is insanity as far as I am concerned.

As my book 'Mystikos' demonstrates, I am all too familiar with mystical, or 'spiritual' experiences. More than most religious believers, I, an Atheist, have always had a rich mystical life. As the events or emotions I experience are unproven by impartial evidence, I take them as part of my overall human experience. I have no difficulty in attributing them to my particular personality, just as I accept other features of it. On the whole, I love my mystical experiences and dislike my personality. I do not, however, pretend that I am in overall control of my life, nor that I am any kind of model citizen. I rather dislike gurus, too, because they seem to me particularly asleep in respect of their own personalities. There is true irony in the proselytiser of awakeness who is actually quite asleep in his own self-assessment.

Finally, the most difficult area of superfluity, for me, is the evident need of (we) gurus to teach others how to live. I am nowhere near resolving this contradiction. Almaas, and I, and thousands of our fellow humans, are in daily breach of our own commandments. We have elected ourselves to be the teachers of our contemporaries and of future generations. We might abjure fame as Narcissistic, but we seek fame 'for the sake of the work'. And what is 'the work'? It is the stuff we want the rest of the world to hoist upon their shoulders, or inject into their brain, to make them more like the paragons we think they should be.

If challenged, our defence is typically that we want humankind to be happier, or better-behaved, or (even) more successful, so we feel obliged to teach them how to do it. If we see ourselves as healers, the excuse transforms into wanting people to achieve wholeness of body, mind or spirit. Here again, we think we know what is needed and are determined to get others to follow the 'Path'. In other words, all this do-gooding is really just another version of the infamous Plan-A. It isn't a breakthrough into a better way of being, because it is just another form of the already-established way of being.

The ultimate irony, for Almaas or for me, is that the more aware/awake we become, the more we risk sinking into a different and deeper asleep-ness. How would we wake up from that?

Chapter Six
The Awareness Paradox

Errant Thoughts

In a slightly stupefied (though teetotal) postprandial state yesterday, these words came into my mind:

Is it possible that, although I am aware of being aware, might I also be unaware of being unaware? And that while I can be awake to being awake, could I be asleep to being asleep?

There seems to be more thought needed, or more experience, of the unaware/unawake states. Shouldn't I look particularly at the likelihood that by coming aware/awake in one part of my consciousness/being, I might incidentally (or even consequentially) be more unaware/asleep in another part.

After all, classical physics seems to work in that way, e.g. every action having an equal and opposite reaction (Newton's Third Law of Motion) while in the Quantum Field everything is topsy-turvy.

At least, this seems to fit with the bipolarity of my passing moods, the swing from contentment to despair without apparent reason (except my inherent tendency, often counter-phobic, to be afraid, and my chronic dissatisfaction with my own state of being). I will blame myself when I see myself as unaware/unawake, and even if I have advanced in awareness versus unawareness, there is a counter-argument from within myself.

My apparently automatic need to succeed is easily rapped and denounced in my 'intermediate' mind where I am neither quite aware nor quite asleep.

I have been writing about Almaas and thinking about Adyashanti, gurus who are devoted to the virtues of awakeness. More specifically, I wonder about their actual awakeness in the light of my above ruminations. It is impertinent, even monstrously arrogant, of me to question the mind-state of the mighty, I know, but they are only human. At least I think and hope so.

Adyashanti is a man of huge charisma and appeal. I have not met him, but I have listened to him speaking and read his words. I think he is a marvellous man. I love what he says. He can teach me any time. But there's a 'but'. I slightly suspect that he might enjoy being famous and influential, however absurd that may seem considering the substance of his message. If that is true, does it mean he is at least a bit asleep?

As for Almaas, even more so. If I accept even the most basic version of his belief in Essence, then it is my Essence that is reeling away from his. How can it be that I don't like him, even dislike him, and don't trust him, when all I have to go on is a couple of his books and a handful photographs of him? Am I being asleep, unaware, unawake, in this personal animosity? Or have I picked up some subtle clues without being aware of it? I do not trust my judgement in this. The man is practically a Sufi saint, full of love and the desire to help humankind be happy. What's to dislike?

I understand why I have come to dislike heroism, and also why I dislike heroes while admiring their courage and selflessness. I have not, however, considered that this attitude is asleepness on my part. It almost certainly must be.

Goldeneye

I am being pernickety; sitting aghast on New Year's Eve, stupidly watching a 'James Bond' film, I realised that Adyashanti and Almaas are saints in this dreadful culture of ours. Today, I could even see myself as a little bit of a saint compared with the revolting men depicted in the film. Simplistic heroes and villains, admittedly, but what they reveal about the asleep personality is a hell on earth. As if I needed further confirmation, I also sat through some of 'Dark Knight' (because I wanted to see the legendary performance of the drug-slain Heath Ledger as The Joker). It was even more vile in some ways than 'Goldeneye', partly because Ledger achieved a portrayal of evil rarely equalled even in this blighted world. I looked up online opinion and was further shocked to see how viewers thought it a wonderful film.

Nevertheless, I opened the Almaas book I mentioned in the previous chapter (ie 'Facets of Unity, The Enneagram of Holy Ideas') with foreboding, because the 'Essence' book had been a trial to read. I think this other book will be too. And I wonder how it is that the foul violence of the two films is as much a function of the human mind as the mushy semi-religion of the Almaas books. In one sense, the horrible films and the glutinous books have a similar lack of awakeness, because there is no sign in either of what I would identify as the sense of proportion that surely distinguishes the human character at its most transcendent.

When I worked with the ideas of Transpersonal Psychology, I was aware of a state of being beyond the self-absorbed fervour of either evil or good beliefs. In that sense, I think the so-called Essence is self-bound and suspect, whereas the transcendent aspiration can take the psyche out of this sink of self-importance. When starting to read 'Facets of Unity', I was immediately gripped by revulsion at the word 'holy', because while it may imply the highest discernment it can also mean the pit of bathos. The nine 'holy ideas' are described by Almaas as constituting 'a map of the view of reality as a unity'. Apart from the sleight-of-mind trick of making nine elements equal a unity, do these 'holy idea' really make sense, I asked myself. In other words, do I believe them?

The Holy Ideas
1   Perfection.
2   Will.   (Freedom.)
3   Harmony.   (Law. Hope.)
4   Origin.
5   Omniscience.   (Transparency.)
6   Strength.   (Faith.)
7   Wisdom.   (Work. Plan.)
8   Truth.
9   Love.

Well, for a start, I don't really comprehend them. I know what the words mean in the dictionary sense, but they don't seem to relate to each other, especially as components of unity, or oneness, as I take it they are supposed to be. The immediate impact is worsened by some of them having additional words. I have inserted these in brackets. All sixteen words are preceded by 'Holy'.

On the face of it, far from 'believing' anything about these words, I experience them as a complete muddle.

I was diagnosed as a 'Perfectionist' some years ago, after a few years of accepting I was a 'Counter-phobic Six', which was based on the experts finding that I was a 'fear-type'. I now find that Almaas labels number six with the words 'strength' and 'faith'. Therefore, my holy ideas have been a pretty mixed bunch. I confess that I still don't really understand where or how I fit into the Enneagram system and, frankly, I think I am past caring.

However, it occurs to me that I could at least explore Almaas's picture a bit by assuming I could be either number One or number Six and seeing where this takes me, bearing in mind that the principle of unity makes it necessary to know all nine holy ideas with great familiarity, or so it is claimed.

The Fear-Type

I will start with 'fear', as I was taught to characterise this Enneagram type. In those days, the fear- types were either a phobic six or a counter-phobic six, i.e. you were generally scared of life and in a general panic, or you toughed it out and behaved like a demented hero. Or you could do both, alternately. I understood that easily enough and could see how it fitted my personality. The 'fixation' (of the personality-mind) of a Six was cowardice, and the 'passion' (of the personality- heart was fear or doubt). Of the several names given to this personality type, 'Questioner' was typical, although 'Devil's Advocate' and 'Trooper' were also used.

In that system, the 'holy' elements in the Six were faith (holy idea) and courage (holy virtue), similar to Almaas's holy ideas for the Six. The explanation of the term, 'holy faith', for the Six-type, is given as, *'the experiential realisation that Being is the inner reality and inner truth of every human being'*. Almaas defines 'holy strength' as, *'the perception that the inner nature of the human being is Essence,'* and, *'as a result of this perception, the transformation that occurs in the soul is Holy Faith.'* It would be a typical reaction on my part to dismiss all this as circular cant, because there is no evidence for the description except the description itself. In other words, it is a delusion.

However, since the whole point of the book is to show how all the holy ideas work together, there is in the Six description some references to other types. For example, Almaas says that the Five-type view of man (at the holy idea level) is that his soul is inseparable from the rest of existence, and that the Seven-type views the soul's development as inseparable from the unfolding of the whole of existence. In sum, the 'unfoldment' of the soul is part of the 'unfoldment' of the whole universe.

Gobbledygook this may appear to be, and it may even be gobbledygook, but to my astonishment something clicked in my mind when read this (on page 232). I felt that I had no need to do any more critical examination of the text and that the book had done something vital for me. Then I had one of my damned dreams and the click became louder and clearer.

[Mother Dream: helped by an unidentified second person I am putting on a dark blue dress belonging to my mother. My purpose is to repair or recondition it for her to wear. I am having difficulty getting into it but it is important that I do this for her.]

Of my many mystical or spiritual experiences, dreams or actual, I think this is the most vivid in terms of feeling something I might name as my soul. I sense that 'soul' and 'mother' are very close friends. I am also aware that a powerful bond between my mother and me loosened as I grew up, to the extent of effective alienation. I blamed her, of course, but that was unfair of me. We just grew apart, to my considerable disadvantage and distress, I may say.

Also, I do have a fervent inclination to see all life as connected, something I see as The Great Continuity. This is a god-substitute, I suspect, as I have to worship something. The combination of Great Continuity and Void is my version of divinity, I imagine. It could be actually no less gobbledygook than Almaas's convictions.

Also, further, I can get past the nonsense and feel the sense. The Diamond Approach to the Enneagram is no worse than any other story of what we are. I will read on.

The Soul of a One

I have been a Perfectionist for a long time, ever since I gave up being a Six. Type-One was attributed the 'fixation' of resentment and the 'passion' of Anger'. As well as 'Perfectionist' this type is called 'Reformer' and 'Teacher'. The holy idea was perfection and the holy virtue was serenity.

I fought against my Perfectionist label for a long time. I disliked most of the features of the type, for a start. Helen Palmer, a prominent Enneagram teacher in those days, gave a list of type-One 'preoccupations' which included:

Puritanically demanding internal standards with self-criticising stream of thought.

Compulsive need to do right thing and be correct.

Belief in own superiority and comparing self with others.

Fear of making mistakes.

Do-gooder with displacement of disappointment-anger onto outside targets.

Double self, worried self and playful self.

Attention focus on error in others, superb critic
As if these were not bad enough, I also felt consumed with disgust at the badness in the world and was really furious with the idea that everything was really perfect. This was totally absurd to me. Yet I couldn't ultimately disagree that I had those frightful personality traits, and I eventually came to understand the 'perfection' being emphasised by, for example, Sandra Maitri ('The Spiritual Dimension of the Enneagram'). Her words, on the second page of her chapter on type-One, made me choke with rage:

'We see that all that exists has a fundamental rightness to it and that everything that occurs is correct and perfect.'

I am so affected by the violence in nature that I don't even want to perceive perfection in everything. Yet I can see what Almaas calls the egoic mind in action. I understand why he thinks this. But there is an error, as well. He, and his mentor, Ichazo, assume that there is a process in reality which has purpose and rightness. This 'one goal' concept is an extreme position of divine intent. On this basis, evolution or the laws of motion are somehow endowed with supremely magical power. If perfection merely means 'this is the way it is, accept it', I could just endorse it, but if it means 'this is divinely created and purposeful', then I could not. (Not that it matters all that much either way, in practical terms.)

What it does mean, for me, is that although I would certainly judge the world as imperfect, I have to live with an idea of perfection - I mean I can't help being like that. I suppose that it's perfection second-class, i.e., this is the way I am, I have to accept me.

Anyway, I have still to absorb the whole story in Almaas's Chapter 14, which begins with Ichazo's dictum: *'The awareness that Reality is a process, moving with direction and purpose. Within this movement each moment is connected by the process with the one goal, and thus is perfect.'*

To elucidate this dogma, I needed to know something of Ichazo and from various sources I gleaned an approximate view of the last few decades of Enneagram work as follows:

It seems that Oscar Ichazo was the initiator of the Enneagram system as used today. He had accumulated a large body of ideas before others such as Claudio Aranjo and Sandra Maitri joined up with him in the mid-twentieth century. Ichazo's teachings are intended to help people 'transcend their identification with, and the suffering caused by, their own mechanistic thought and behaviour patterns'. Naranjo brought psychological insights into the picture and Sandra Maitri seems to have added a spiritual dimension. Helen Palmer added teaching-skills to the mix.

Ichazo's theories about the fixations are founded on the premise that 'all life seeks to continue and perpetuate itself and that the human psyche must follow universal laws of   reality'. He understands the fixations as aberrations from 'an essential state of unity'. The primary difference between modern psychology and his theories is that he has proposed a model of the components of the human psyche, but modern psychology has preferred to focus on observed behaviour instead of an essential model from which aberrations develop.

According to Ichazo, a person's 'fixation derives from childhood subjective experience (self-perception) of psychological trauma when expectations are not met in each of the instincts'. Young children are self-centered and thus experience disappointment in their expectations 'because of one of three fundamental attitudes: attracted, unattracted, disinterested.' From such experiences, 'mechanistic thought and behaviour patterns arise as an attempted defence against recurrence of the trauma.' By understanding the fixations, and practising, self-observation, it is believed that a person can reduce or even transcend suffering and the fixations' hold on the mind.

As a perfectionist-reformer I am fatally attracted to the idea of undoing the damage apparently suffered by every individual person in the first years of their lives and the consequent deformation of their being into the mechanistic personality. On the other hand, I am a natural sceptic. As a result I am seriously challenged by the Enneagram dogmas. And how do I build my newest impressions of the Enneagram type-One into the changing picture of my Fifth Revelation? Most of all, in what way can I come to terms with my soul, if I have one and if it is making itself known to me?

Holy Perfection, Unholy Rage

Almaas starts the Perfection chapter by linking three holy ideas, Perfection, Truth, and Love (ie numbers 1, 8, and 9) and declares that all three are 'true at the same time'. (At the personality-level, these three are said to be the 'anger-types' of the Enneagram, and that they have different ways of managing their anger i.e. denial, suppression, and enjoyment in 1, 2, and 3, respectively.)

There is no explanation for the claim that the three ideas are all true at the same time, except, presumably to emphasise the unity of the whole schema of the nine. But I suppose that perfection, truth and love do have a theme linking them, and they certainly appeal to me; in fact I feel a particular connection with the ideas of love and truth, which may add up to my sense of a soul.

My mild agreement is soon swept away by astounding claims, however, which I can summarise as: the assumption in the book is that the author (and his associates) are able to see without judgement, whereas in my view the content in this chapter is entirely judgemental and subjective. The determined stance of not having an opinion and not minding, as it were, is itself dogmatic and shows delusional thinking while claiming to eradicate delusional thinking.

On page after page I am baffled by the endless reiteration that is, basically, that seeing the world as perfect is being objective while making judgements about the world is delusional. I am not denying that the world is perfect, but I do think the language of the book fails to take this dogma to its full conclusion. It may be a fault in the language itself. For example, if I say, 'What is, is simply what is, and in that sense is perfectly itself', then I am describing a 'perfection' that I can totally accept as universally correct. I am not making any judgement, but merely accepting that the universe is as it is. Now, of course, that is a tautological statement. Yet it does apply a steadying force against rampant distortion of the very obvious truth.

Almaas's 'perfection' is not of this kind. Paradoxically, it is actually he that is making relative judgements about perfection, it is he that fails the truth test. How? Because he has a standpoint which he believes, or assumes, to be correct, and is castigating different standpoints. If he were consistent, he would have to see that all standpoints are perfect because they exist. This means that even if it is delusional of someone to say they are Jesus Christ, that delusion is as perfect as anything else. How, otherwise, could the universe be said to be perfect in the 'value' sense.

There are attempts to hide this truth, such as: *'This sense of the intrinsic rightness of the reality that is inside and outside everyone is a feeling, a recognition, an action, of intelligence. It involves no conceptualising about perfection. Holy Perfection reflects the intactness, the completeness, and the glory, of what is'* (p. 143). This is one huge value judgement. And it is contradictory; words like 'rightness' and 'glory' conflict with 'no conceptualising'. This is seriously muddled thinking.

Or it is careless drafting. For example, Almaas uses the word 'feeling' and 'intelligence' as if they were describing the same process. That is a bad mistake. But worse, he would deny emotions, or feelings, when it suits him. Say I am scared or grief-stricken, as I often am, why is that feeling a delusion whereas feeling that the world is perfect is not a delusion. Why is one sort of feeling accepted and another rejected?

For that matter, why are delusions not accepted as elements of total perfection? If the Holocaust is perfect why is madness imperfect? Almaas is trying to have his cake and eat it. Either everything is perfect or it isn't. Worst off all is the arrogance which claims its own veracity. Ichazo and Almaas and the others were surely right to expose the horror of the manufactured personality, but the implied (or even explicit) claim that they have transcended that unfortunate state is just too breathtaking to be given serious consideration.

Consider this: if I were to say, 'having considered the history of humankind, I realise that I see how mistaken all people have been, and still are, not to realise with absolute conviction that this is a perfect world. Unlike me, they are all imperfect in their error,' would you not suspect I might have becoming overtaken by unacknowledged egotism? Yes, the Enneagram personality analysis is very good therapy, used wisely, but every teacher of it needs to beware their own egotism.

My Perfect Soul
In amongst the flagrant misuse of language and logic, Almaas, Ichazo, Maitri and the rest have compiled a massive gift for the human race. If only they had found a better way of presenting it. Like any of we flawed creatures, the Enneagram Workers have been carried away by their own emotions while castigating the rest of us for ours. They are not unique. The Romish Church, as Stephen Fry called the Catholics the other day, speak love and perpetrate its opposite. Politicians fervently lie. But the Enneagram has strengths that we all need, leaving aside the religious doctrines. The core of the Enneagram process for me is that it is a framework of pursuing increased awareness and awakens of our being. All too often, the process bogs down in doctrine or false logic, but it's probably as good as we can get in this imperfect world. I bless my soul.

Chapter Seven
Imago 2

From our website, Scotts Gallery:
Imago, a novel

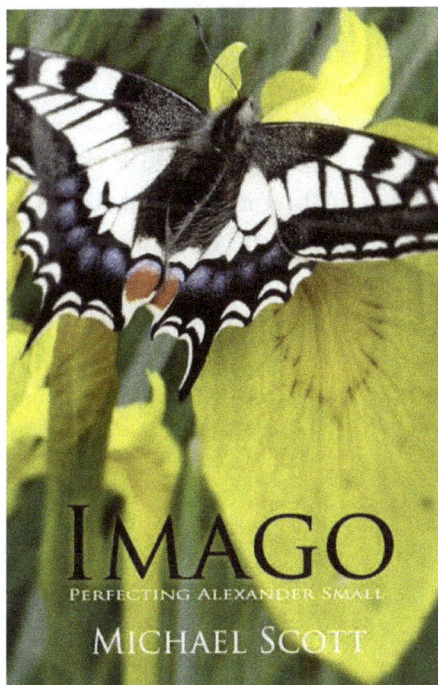

There are two meanings of 'imago'. Biologically it is the final stage of insect metamorphosis, e.g. the butterfly; while psychologically it is the perfect human inner self, the ideal image. In this book, the main character, Alexander, is trying to find his own imago, as if it still exists somewhere, while circumstances push him through a development towards maturity.

A review, by Elizabeth Crabtree, puts it this way:

'Michael Scott's "Imago" is a serious and very funny novel about how male psychology may interfere with personal relationships and spiritual development. Alexander T.H.E. Small, Doctor of Ethology, retires from his academic post at the age of sixty-five. He sets out with his devoted, long- suffering, enraged wife, Elinor, to recapture his childhood. What he finds, with the help of Elinor's immaculate intuition, and expert machinations, is a new home where he can make a new life with new friends. This is a profound book with all the greater impact for being a comedy.'

It's not hard to see the autobiographical import of this 1999 book. I was still in my sixties (just) when I wrote it, and though I was not intentionally depicting myself, there are significant personal elements - how could there not be?

To an unknown degree, the imago is similar to the idea of the essence. I think I prefer it, given the idealistic and often ambivalent way the second word is used by Almaas and Co. There is a precision and objectivity about the word, imago, and no-one pretends (I hope) that it is a substance within the body rather than a potentiality in the psyche.

I wonder, now, if Alexander's depression was really a matter of neglected, suppressed, or damaged essence or imago. The suggestion in my 'Imago' (the book) that loss of childhood was Alexander's feeling is perhaps truer than I realised when I wrote it. As early as page three, Alexander is having a quarrel with his newly acquired therapist, Dr. Friend, a PhD in history, a Professor Emeritus, author of a book on the other, the 'Great', Alexander, and, therefore, as far as the 'patient' Alexander was concerned, a fraudulent therapist:

'Do you realise that you are obsessed with your childhood?'
The question was so interesting that Alexander forgot he was talking to a deranged imposter.
'Obsessed'!? With his childhood? In what sense could one be said to be obsessed with something which had determined one's whole life? Wouldn't it be madness not to be obsessed with that precious, misused, wasted, of all that was and was to become?

Near the end of 'Imago', (p. 366) Alexander had made some important friends, one of whom was Jamie, a ten-year old having trouble with his father, Jack. By this time Dr. Friend had also become a very close friend. The three of them are sitting on a grassy hillock, grappling with the existential problems explored in psychological alchemy, the endless journey through nigredo, albedo, rubedo, and the exquisite aurora. Childhood has rapid movement through the four colours, with gold being preponderant while it is allowed to be. Jamie was losing his 'Golden Secret' too fast under the heavy influence of his father:

A boy-child like Jamie, and maybe the one Alexander had been, ranged easily across the spectrum, taking black, white, red, and gold as they came. He could move back and fore, or round and round. He had yet to learn how to compartmentalise, how to keep off certain areas, and he was resisting the learning. Alexander could only glimpse the fleeting reality. He was not ready to go head-first himself into the sea of gold. Yet it seemed that this child was being dragged away from it. How could he resist it? How could Jack push Jamie away from it? Jamie possessed, for the time being, the wisdom that Alexander still had to regain. Was this the connection between them, here on this small hill?

So many ways of seeing the Golden Secret: soul, essence, void, aurora, awakeness, holy idea, nagual... imago, and yet so many ways of losing the inner being which make our lives shine with beauty and love. In this chapter, I want to revisit imago, the image of completion in an insect's existence, and perhaps perfection in a human existence. When I wrote 'Imago' I was unaware of something that is particularly relevant to my current existence. I now realise, belatedly and helpfully, that 'imago' comes to us in its religious garb as 'Imago Dei', a Latin tag meaning 'Image of God'. Hence, it is 'perfection', allegedly, as God by definition is regarded by believers as perfect. So, a human is potentially perfect because we are made in the image of the perfect god.

Never mind the contradiction between Original Sin and 'inherited perfection', laughable as it is, because what really bothers me is the implication that my only chance of realising my own imago is to acknowledge its derivation from a mythical deity. I am finished before I start. This must be why Almaas and Co. stress the 'holy' element in their Enneagram concept. It comes from God, in some mysterious way, presumably.

It is necessary for me to disengage 'imago' from godness and, indeed, to free from deic ownership all other allusions to the essence or soul, etc. Even if God did exist, I would have to point out the serious imperfections both in God's make-up and in God's 'creations'. I don't need to do that, unless someone insists upon the existence of some deity or other, because the idea of a perfect imago is enough of a delusion to deal with as it is.

I am suggesting that we need to use the word 'perfection' with extreme caution and discernment, otherwise we may just make fools of ourselves. I want to protect the word 'imago' from contamination by supernatural or superstitious implications. Imago, in my terms, is the ideal wholeness of the person rather than some celestial fantasy. At the end of the novel, my character Alexander had made great advances in his state of being, but was still very confused about his role on this planet. As well he might be.

An important theme of the first 'Imago', is Alexander's relationship with Elinor, who develops during the book from doormat to acerbic critic, much to Alexander's discomfort and benefit. And it is the idea, even the imago of marriage that, Alexander attempts to define in the last words of the book:

To be a Manichean (he means one who experiences a world of moral dualism) *is to know beyond any shadow of doubt that everything in the garden is not lovely, never was, never will be. It means knowing the black and the white in absolutely everything. Therefore, marriage is fine so long as it fuses the good and the evil into a higher form, the mystic transfiguration, from which a cornucopia of glory flows. It is the grail-stone of the mystic marriage. I think that is probably what I think, since you ask, as I think you did* ... *(p 391).*

Clearly, the idea of a perfect world contrasts mightily with the idea of a morally dual world. But leaving aside the old fantasy of two gods, one bad and one good, it seems to me that however continuous the great continuum may be, it contains as much bad stuff as good. Nature is just that, a mixture of hell and heaven, of beauty and vileness. How can anyone, even the high-minded Almaas or Ichazo, gaze upon the actual world and pronounce it absolutely perfect, except by using the word 'perfect' in a most bizarre way.

Therefore, how to live in it, practically and existentially? I am still working at it, fifteen years after inventing Alexander Small. How, in fact, can I conceive Imago 2? This is my cosmic leap, or at least my wobbly step across the Rubicon rivulet.

The Tyranny of Words
I like 'imago', as a word and as an idea, but it symbolises something more sinister than completeness or quasi-perfection. It shows how words take on a life of their own, and are so protean as to confuse anyone who uses them. Until I came across Imago Dei, I was happy to have a word that apparently described wholeness or completeness. Now the word is devalued for me by being tied to a delusion, as I

see it. It seems that all these words for the 'ground of being', Void, Essence, Soul, whatever, are really quite untrustworthy because of their shiftiness of meaning.

As I have written elsewhere, it may just be that the human brain is poorly designed for thinking. I am serious about this. Astrophysicists are still arguing about the universe, as if they could possibly know its real nature, and we all argue about life as if we could possibly comprehend that. As in the matter of words, there is a dangerous assumption that actual knowledge is feasible. We forget that we are merely organic algorithms with no designer to explain us. So we explain ourselves using the algorithmic data fortuitously implanted by the evolutionary process, meaningless but apparently purposive.

At the time of writing, there is a terrible frenzy in France because some satirical cartoonists have been murdered by some Islamic terrorists. The reason given is that the prophet Muhammad has been insulted by the words and drawings of the satirists. France and other countries are making great play of the absolute necessity of 'free speech'. Words and death are here conjoined, as has happened over and over again in the perilous journey of humankind. There is insanity in it all. Where does my beloved 'imago' figure, in this nightmare of semantic hatred?

Words were allegedly invented for the purpose of communication. That's the anthropologists' excuse, I guess. Or were they intended as weapons as well as tools? They certainly function in both capacities. Words and the imago do not seem to be seriously related at all. Imago is an idea or an ideal even a metaphor or a poetic trope. It is not a 'thing'. Nor for that matter can soul or essence or Void be things. They are ideas or idealisations.

Whereas 'freedom of speech', or Muhammad, seem to be 'things' in the sense that they carry behavioural indicators. But people commonly make the same of 'imago' and the other ideational words. Indeed, it is a common error to make words into things, especially making them act as tools or weapons.

So, not only is the human mind error-prone in its thinking-capacity, it is also incompetent in its ability to do communication. The result is mayhem and murder, hardly the work of a useful evolutionary process. Unless mayhem and murder are, in ways not evident to me, satisfactory outcomes of the accidental adaptive procedure known as survival of the fittest.

Therefore, what do I think of imago, as an idea or an ideal, given these considerations? My answer is that it is the best, if not the only, useful tool in our mental box. Thus, Imago 2 is a positive reappraisal rather than a burial ceremony. Nevertheless a death and a burial is necessary: I must destroy the outrageous misuse of the word, or its equivalents (soul, Void, essence, awakeness, etc), as things, factual objects to be used as missiles or sacred relics. The imago is most emphatically not an object of worship and certainly not the substance of an icon.

The Free Imago

It goes where it will - it is an idea, so it can roam as free as a quantum particle/wave. I do not have to push it, nor, indeed should I try to push it. It will die if it is made into a thing. We are at the edge of rational thought in this area. How could, similarly, soul be not a thing. If it is an idea, or a substance-less ideal, it cannot exist as a thing, ever, or anywhere. When I die the idea may remain, the soul cannot die because it does not live, it is an idea. Like the much-debated universe, it was neither created nor had it always existed, it is merely an idea in the human mind. When clever professors measure the universe they are only scanning their own brains. Brains do exist, in that lumps of multicellular porridge can be spilt from the human skull, though it is not known if they are also minds. But a brain in a specimen jar is not active in mindful terms. The mind has moved on. The mind is probably just an idea, like the imago, and probably the universe. As we think it exists. So it is that words can be seen to have dubious meaning.

My many so-called mystical experiences are, I now suggest,

manifestations of my nascent imago. Or of my essence, to be fair to it. Or of Almaas's 'holy ideas', to be fair to them (although I erase 'holy' to avoid mental dyspepsia). I am suggesting that my imago has been showing its influence repeatedly in my life, usually when I least expected a moment of wholeness. Often, too, it was forced into disguise because I misinterpreted its nature. I was living a mistake.

The Great Error

It has been revelational to use the imago idea to approach the Enneagram problems. But even more enlightening is the sudden perception that my thinking (and that of others generally) has been the wrong way round. I had just not taken Existential awareness to its greater status, i.e. the realisation that it actually is 'all in the mind'.

I will try to explain how back-to-front has been my mindset throughout my life. Although I abandoned theistic models at a very early age, I still continued to accept that my reference-point was external. Even up to very recently, in discussions about, for example, consciousness, there was still a question mark over the origin, the source, of my or everyone else's consciousness. I had the ingrained thought-habit that focused on 'inspiration' as at least partly an incoming phenomenon. Therefore, I regarded my 'mystical experiences' as somehow fostered by the external world in some way.

Hence the phraseology: mystical encounters in nature. God may have disappeared from my address-book but was still operational at the subliminal level. This is the reason why thinking about soul or essence or the Void involves a mental and emotional impulse to look upwards or sideways to see how the influence arrives in my centre of being.

All the time, however, there was a protest movement active somewhere in my psyche. While I quite clearly refuted any idea of divine intervention in my existence, I was muted and muddled about where my awareness originated. The mystical flavour of the 'collective unconscious' was strong upon my psychic tongue. I looked to the world of nature as a source of spiritual comfort or struggle.

Even the notion of a five-point carousel of terror never quite settled inside my mind without seeming to have an existence of its own. Yet I balked at the stream of consciousness as an incoming flow. I just never managed to turn off that tap.

There are excuses. I do listen to other people. There is incoming information. I did experiments when I was a scientist and drew inferences from the results. I trust my multiple senses, up to a point. I trust my rational process, up to a point. So there actually is an incoming stream of data. So the thought-habit would automatically assume a source for the other kind of experience, the so- called spiritual or mystical or transcendental flow. It never occurred to me that it was entirely from within myself. Even now, writing the words, I shudder slightly at the arrogance of such a notion.

Imago Dei Exposed

I shudder far more at this:

Then God said, 'Let us make man in our image, after our likeness. And let them have dominion over the fish of the sea and over the birds of the heavens and over the livestock and over all the earth and over every creeping thing that creeps on the earth.' So God created man in his own image, in the image of God he created him; male and female he created them. (Genesis 1:26-27)

This is the central error of religious imagination. Here is the human mind deifying itself. And thus it has remained deified. I cannot claim to be surprised by the sleight of mind. It is a natural bit of solipsism, a specific form of it, in which everything belongs to the divine self, the human divine self, the self that is identical with God's self.

In fact, this double-self is of course a mirage. We each know that we are not actually God. But we have it on the authority of the Holy Bible, written by God, that we are exactly like God. This is pretty secret, because it would not do to noise it abroad. So we praise God, our specific God, and derive massive authority from our deep, secret, identity with God.

The profound falsehood should be exposed. We have reversed the horse and the cart. The created form starts with the human imago not with the projection called 'God'. It is genuine and true that each human being has an imago, an image of completion or wholeness. We get confused and convert it into a self or an ego or some such toxic by-product. We call it 'ambition'. We call it 'hope'. We call it essence. We even, in rapture, call it 'the source' or 'the ground of being' or, in my own case, 'the great continuity'. In a good mood we may call imago by its romantic name, love, or truth, or beauty. In a bad mood it becomes depression, despair, or failure, i.e. imago frustrated.

The big lie, however, is that we conflate all these elements of the human psyche and call the whole thing by a very different sort of name: we call the imago by the name of 'God'. Then, to endorse and expand the untruth we have made, we call it the imago of god.

Why would we get rid of it from our deeper being? It can't be that we are ashamed of it. It is, after all, the best part of us, as an idea or potentiality. I can only assume it is the pathological condition that afflicted and afflicts millions of us, the Lawrence of Arabia Syndrome. Or maybe poor old Shane. Or Alexander the Great. Put simply, it is megalomania. To misrepresent one's own essence as a deity is the ultimate sick aggrandisement. Fame at last. As they say.

The Actual Imago 2

This thrives, however. I am revivified by realising that I belong entirely to me, and than all my vainglory and fairy-tales are just my own inventions. I am free for significance beyond my own minute being. Nobody is watching me (except, perhaps, security services). And a few friends, now and then. Imago Dei is dead, long live Imago Me/I. If it exists. Even as an idea, only an idea or an ideal, how can I trust its reality when I so distrust the concept of perfection?

How is imago distinguished from that impossible tyrant? At

first thought, I saw no reason why an idea should not be perfect, so long as it is only an idea not a thing. Then doubt crept in. How would I know that an idea was perfect? Could I be sure that it was beyond the possibility of improvement? Almaas and Ichazo would say, 'Certainly it is perfect, as everything is perfect. Only egotism asserts otherwise. You are not free to judge perfection.' And on they go. But not with me. The only way I could fall into line with them would be to say, 'There is no such thing as perfection, so forget the whole problem.'

I could leave it at that. But in the apparently real world, perfection is an apparently real thing. We are bombarded with perfections. At its worst, perfection presents itself as absolute extremism, as in a terrorist whose fundamental certainty assures a place in paradise for committing murder. At its best it claims prizes and plaudits for outperforming all competition. That's how it works in the apparently real world. But in an actually real perfect world it wouldn't work at all. Such a perfection would have to be dropped into the Void and disappear or reappear as an acceptable process of change.

Perfection is a cul-de-sac. And not only is it a dead-end but it is a dead concept too. Human existence must deal with all kinds of imperfection, that is our natural situation. Imago, on the other hand, is an idea of moving towards some form of completion of a process. The butterfly may have imperfections, a variation in colour, or a parasite, or less than six legs, but it is still a butterfly. It is as complete as it can be. Now if that is your definition of perfection, so be it. This kind of perfection therefore exists only in the context of a random distribution, a Gaussian curve of variation. That is perfectly all right. But it is emphatically not perfection.

If all else fails to convince the perfectionist, it may help to emphasise the facts of genetics. The genotype is much more of an imago-process than any kind of perfection. For example, mutations occur which may invalidate the reproductive process. Imperfection is built into the very fabric of our generative capacity. Our foetal development may abort spontaneously. We get ill. We die. It is correct to say that all such happenings are normal for the imago but can anyone seriously pretend they are perfect?

At this point, I have either demonstrated the absurdity of perfectionism, or I have failed to make my case. It is time, I guess, to let the matter rest and move on. Can I just rest in the certainty that there is at least an imago in there somewhere? In me, I mean; as my inner model?

Imago Intentions?

Does the imago ideate purposive change? Or does it grow like a happy weed? Not that Convolvulus lacks a purpose. I doubt that it ideates, however. But I am not sure my imago ideates either. Where, if not in my imago (soul, essence, awareness) does my purposive change originate? Is it an emotion? Is it will? Is it volition? Is it motivation. How useless these words are. They give no explanation, they tell us nothing.

Monkeys and cats and dolphins, all agreeable and intelligent animals like some humans, must presumably have will, volition, motivation? And if insects carry the idea of imago, why not my sprightly Burmese alpha male feline? I sense the existence of his imago as much as I sense the existence of my own, but I suspect he may do a better job of living the idea rather than pondering it and getting himself confused.

Serious-minded Neurologists search for the location of will in the brain. They have experiments in which people are choosing to press this or that button. Just like cockatoos and clever crows. We can all do it. Button-pressing defines us. Does my imago include the process of button-pushing? I think not. Neither do I think it includes crosswords and chess in its overall program; but I suppose it might. How would I know?

Which leads to the question, at what level of consciousness does the imago idea operate? In Almaas's world-view, where in the levels of consciousness does essence work its magic? Where does any coherent form of being exist in the human psyche. The old quarrel between realities makes it impossible to be sure of anything, so why should I pick out imago as a special case? I would like to do that, but that is not so different from picking out a god as a special case. If it is 'all in the mind', what credence is there in any idea beyond its own imaginative origin? The reality is that knowledge, (Big-Knowledge, that is, the giant edifice of accumulated and accumulating self-certain human presumption) doesn't actually know. It only thinks it knows and expects itself to be believed.

The Golden Secret

It is likely that I am giving the idea of the imago all the glamour of the 'golden secret', and all the energy of 'mystical experience'. Regrettably, these beautiful origins are just experiential. That doesn't mean they are necessarily invalid, but merely that they are beliefs. Imago is, therefore, also a belief, not a 'fact'. I like it, even love it, as an idea, but it is virtually impossible not to treat it as real. The term for this conversion of ideal to concrete fact is reification. To reify the abstract into the real is not a crime, nor even a sin, but it causes unlimited trouble in our world.

In the book, 'Imago', I conferred upon the boy, Jamie, the state of the 'golden secret', just as in my own life, I have nurtured the experience of 'mystikos', apparently direct contact with the mystical. It now seems to me that the idea of the imago is mystical. It is, to be open about it, my golden secret. I cannot claim to have avoided the act of reification. In the depths of my sceptical nature, despite all my protestations, I do need to believe in 'something'. I am rather ashamed of this weakness. I ought to know better, and I should be strong enough to stand alone in absolute innocence of any belief whatever. Such is my credo. Such is my dilemma.

It now occurs to me that the devil in my small print is that I want there to be truth in existence. I can accept that beauty and love are mind-products or emotions, i.e. that they do exist as human behaviours. Thanks for that, I say to my indifferent universe.

But Truth? I don't even know what the word means. Yet it is the unseen corner-stone of my existence. I thought I had given up the idea decades ago, and now, here I am, trying to find a truth in my own nature. I want imago to be real. Just as my friend and Almaas and Ichazo want essence to be real. Just as Christians and Jews and Muslims want 'God' to be real. Just as Atheists want disbelief to be real.

My World?

The Fifth Revelation has already come a long way from a simple need to drop fear and anger. It is now facing me with the need to abandon an entire mindset. I mean all of it: virtually everything in this chapter has to go somewhere else, out of my store of 'knowledge'. I can't quite throw it all away because the amputation might kill me before I die. Cold storage is an option. Whatever that might mean in terms of consciousness. But why would I do this casting away? The reason is that I need to restore and develop my 'golden secret'. No, it isn't just one more reified idea to plague myself with. It is the need to be in my being. It is the need to be present. And here there is a beautiful irony.

On the first page of the first chapter of 'Essence', Almaas defines 'presence' and he needn't have said any more. Indeed, had he stopped there he would have had me as a convert. He wrote:

We want to inquire into the meaning of presence by contemplating and analysing the actual experience of presence. Let us examine a familiar situation, the aesthetic experience. My eyes catch the sight of a beautiful rose. Suddenly my sight is clearer, my smelling is keener. I seem to be in my seeing, I seem to be in my smelling. There's more of me here, seeing, smelling, and appreciating the rose.

Precisely. I would only add to that a personal caveat about my own ability to be present. In such a state of being, a state of exceptional awareness, I often ruin it by becoming aware of my heightened awareness. I try too hard to retain the feeling of presence. That is the first fatal step into reification. Almaas writes these simple words and then goes on with a great act of reification. The secret is how to stay with the 'presence'. As Gurdjieff is said to have said, the key phrase is 'I am here'. And it all depends on what I mean by 'I'.

Exit: imago reified.

Enter: being present.

Chapter Eight
In The Presence

In the sixth essay of this book, the author describes his typical mystical experience:

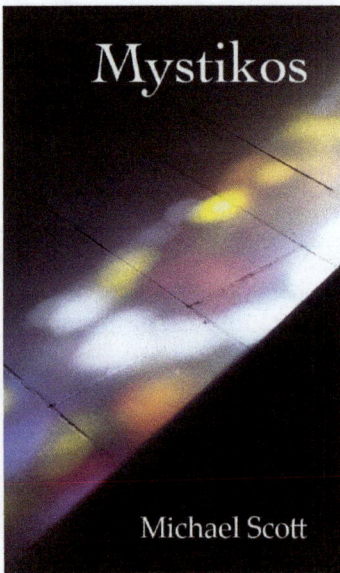

Mystikos

Michael Scott

I feel removed from the immediate, mundane world, although I stay aware of it. I experience a strong connection to other living things, trees, flowers, animals, and, more rarely, people, who tend to be the very young or the very old. This connection is usually suffused with strong emotions such as grief, joy, anger, bliss, or fear. There is usually a recognition of being where I belong in the experience, but the situation is not necessarily well understood by me. The existential flavour of the experience is typically isolated in time and space, super-real, suffused with dense but rooted super-energy, as if holding me still. The energy is transformative of myself, and of others if they join in to the connection. Sometimes, the love, sympathy, sadness, or desire to help another person or creature is unbearably powerful. I am aware of a power of an ineffable kind, in myself and my surroundings, in mystical experiences, but it has no defining characteristics whatsoever. My responses, on the other hand, are highly characteristic and move my consciousness to new positions.

The Mystical Mystery

All those 'mystical experiences', all these mystical experiences (as they haven't stopped), have given me less fullness of being than they could, or should, because I have tried to understand them. Picture the scene: the opportunity of presence surprisingly occurs, and I am egoic enough to want to know background, meaning, and purpose, in effect to validate the experience. I ask the ultimate inane question, 'What's going on here?'

Not that I fail to appreciate my good fortune. My consciousness is replete with many images and memories of great power, some beautiful, some painful, and all suffused with the light of the 'golden secret'. The error I have committed, and still tend to commit, is to treat these gifts as information rather than states of being.

For example, there's the picture hanging on my bedroom wall, a mixed media work. It shows an aspect in my memory of the fish-ponds in the village of Uley, about two miles from the housing estate in which I was raised in the 1930's and 1940's. Although far from being the only 'golden secret' of my childhood, this place was the most powerful one in my early teens, before I fell in love more extensively and sometimes more dangerously.

By Almaas's 'presence' criteria, never mind the accepted 'list of mystical encounters' that I used retrospectively for validation purposes in my middle age, the fish-ponds were almost unbearably vivid to me as an eleven-year-old. I was so 'present', for much of my time in that place, that I felt on the edge of ecstatic madness. As I remember it, that is.

Water, in the fields and woods, was the key element in my extreme of excitement. I couldn't resist it in any form, in any season. I don't think I ever tried to 'understand' the emotions then, but simply gave myself to them. By the time I began to set my mystical life alongside my spiritual scepticism, probably in middle age, a dual condition afflicted me that had never bothered me, I think, as a youngster. This duality of consciousness is common enough in my species, I know, and I am just becoming aware of the damage it does to the possibility of being present. Indeed, not merely duality is fatal to true being, because all our divisions of thought interfere with the 'golden secret' I once took for granted and now regard as the ultimate blessing of existence.

Gradually, while the elements coalesced (trees and flowers, animals, hills and sky...) into a vast panoply of golden secrecy in my growing consciousness, I moved simultaneously further and further into thought, ambition, and the desire to possess the slippery creature, knowledge. The 'golden secret' was clouded and suppressed by my busy intelligence. Thus the duality became bigger and more stressful. Like Parzival and Feirefiz, I became two aspects of myself engaged in heroic combat rather than in brotherly love. Madness, yes, but madness endemic in our genes and in our culture, an entire, magnificently intelligent, race of control-freaks.

So it came to pass, as some put it, that the absolute value of life, the presence in being, gave way to the relative value of existence, doing and winning. The presence in being became an esoteric hobby, hugely and wonderfully important, and in a way still supreme, yet deferring to the power of systematised reason. The most ironical, indeed comical, version of this schism is the human attempt to give religion a position of systematised reason, whereas if it belongs anywhere it is in the wild land of the 'golden secret', beyond the use and interference of humankind.

Religion and science have been the accepted duality for centuries, apparently the global manifestation of my minuscule duality. But I think this is false. Religion and science both deny the 'golden secret' by their obsession with knowing. Science is perhaps more obviously denying, in that it purports to discover the truth about existence by experimental procedures. Religion is more subversive in that it assumes the revelation of truth by a supernatural process. In other words, religion, of one sort or another, makes truth appear out of thin air.

Unfortunately, anything that is not scientific, i.e. logic-based and evidence-based, can claim 'divine' credentials. Herein lies a massive pile of question-marks.

Pure Presence

This is the 'golden secret', and it is overwhelmingly important to protect the 'golden secret', the majestic metaphor, from both religion and from science, for they will corrupt it. Of all paradoxes, it has to be admitted that golden though it appears, there must be doubt around the word 'secret'. In other words, the 'golden secret' contains the seeds of its own corruption. This is because the human mind cannot abide being deprived of knowledge thought to be 'secret'. We feel, as a species and as individuals, that we must get access to it by hook or by crook.

So we finish up being hooked and crooked. Religion is the process by which we fool ourselves that the universe (in some form) loves us, which would be very funny if it wasn't so profoundly harmful. Science is the process whereby geniuses in white coats tell us to wait for their cosmic messages: even worse than the religious scam because it seems to make a crazy sort of sense, with all the machinery, formulae, and experiments, like the pitch of a brilliant foot-in-door salesperson. The 'golden secret' becomes the secret that is ousted and busted by the time each of us is an adult. The Enneagram and other systems try to explain this collapse. Maybe there is some deep imperative to give up on the inner child; (e.g. 1 Corinthians 13:11, King James Version. 'When I was a child, I spake as a child, I understood as a child, I thought as a child: but when I became a man, I put away childish things.') Maybe each of us feels that children are aliens or abnormal, somehow inferior however cute they may be. To be a parent is to patronise. Grown-ups are bigger and better than kids.

The so-called research into the first five years of childhood can hardly avoid an adult bias. Yet this is the source of our apparent knowledge of that state. By the time each of has lived past babyhood and childhood we have only two sources of information about the very young: observation and memory. We are no longer in the childhood state. There is no possibility that we can rely upon observation to give us a true picture of being a child, but only what it looks like to us. There is no possibility that we can rely on our memory of our own childhood because it has gone past us and we are thinking from a new standpoint.

I was transfixed by a report on work being done (by adults, admittedly) on one-to-five year-olds. The findings cannot be reliable because of the points just made, yet what was seemingly discovered was astonishing. And now I can't find a trace of that report. It seems that the human child up to age five is virtually a different species from a human being above that age. There is even a different morality in place. As it is generally acknowledged that about 90% of brain-development in the human occurs in the first five years of life, we are effectively a different civilisation as children because of the sheer speed at which the mind is growing. In a sense, the child-mind is necessarily in continuous revolution.

For an adult to act as trainer of this young creature is a tragic waste of opportunity, if the adult has completed its mind-growth and is now merely passing on the adult mindset, however infantilised it may be to make the process appear genuine. In the child's mind there must be, at least, a perception of falsity, or of blackmail, or mere brainwashing, and it must be storing up contempt or scepticism for its own adult existence - even if it convinces itself that it must conform to the social mores operating at the time. By the time the child has added another ten years to its experience of the adult-dominated world it must be in deep turmoil. The world is simply not as it is remembered or expected. Adolescence is, therefore the first great crisis of trust and untruth for the typical human aspiring to full membership of the species. The adults then rub salt into the wound by laying on a special rite of passage in which the young human is expected to pass through liminality and come out reborn into adult conformity. Thus it happens, perhaps, that anything golden or esoteric about the child-state is obliterated by the experience of growing up.

The Hidden Mind

There is an underground resistance to the process I have described. Essence, soul, ground of being, whatever, is still down there in the shadows of the mind. Most of us let, or encourage, our depths to manifest in a way that is acceptable to the society as we perceive it. Usually this is a half-hearted surrender to cultural fixations. By this process, the mutilated essence suffers further damage and the unfortunate, average, normal, human being lives a life of wretched half-submission to a jaded rule of law, unwritten or spelled out in officious gibberish. To some extent, whereas hobbies, holidays, rebellions, flights of fancy, games, and love sometimes, are powerful placebos or panaceas. We manage to struggle along, even being happy, but that blazing experience of presence, glorified by Almaas et al, never, or hardly ever, puts in an appearance.

My desire is to bring this hidden mind into the open sunlight. Now I realise that heroism is at best a dangerous illusion, and that fear and anger are inherently preposterous states, I am perhaps ready to turn to the way of mindfulness, the innocent exploration of unjudged existence. Is there any chance of doing this? Are my bad habits too deeply entrenched by decades of submission and compromise?

Yes and no, respectively. I feel that it is possible and, in some ways, already happening.

The Inner Child

Like its near relatives, the inner woman (anima), or inner man (animus), I am very sceptical of this presumed entity, which, according to Wikipedia:

'...includes all that we learned and experienced as children, before

puberty, and denotes a semi-independent entity subordinate to the waking conscious mind.'

This is adult thinking; reifying, fixing, explaining, making a thing where no evidence of a thing actually exists. I am weary of metaphors made of concrete. I love metaphors, but as illustrations not as objects. And the *idea* of an inner child may be delightful but the body of an inner child would be a serious and pathological intrusion. Except, presumably, for a pregnant woman. Which I am not nor ever have been.

What I do have, however, is a (metaphorical) video-album of my childhood experiences. They are vivid and most certainly outrageously inaccurate. But they are strong particles of my essence or soul. Whatever may be inadequate about them in terms of historical accuracy there is no gainsaying their sublime power. The make a sort of reference point. They are distinguishing features of what presence can be. In themselves, they are *presence in aspic*. I have never fully acknowledged their power and I apologise to them for this lapse of attention.

Nevertheless, this personification of the hidden mind is just as false and misleading as any other form of reification. The concept of a 'mystical experience', the words, may seem innocent enough, but, like the much more invasive tenets of religion, something intangible is made crassly material. It is much like the phenomenon labelled 'consciousness', indeed it is the phenomenon called consciousness in the 'golden' sense, yet as the human mind is not apparently able to understand this phenomenon, and gets very disturbed as a result, the subject is either hotly debated or ignored altogether.

To my surprise there appeared yesterday, 21st January, 2015, a long article on consciousness in The Guardian newspaper. It seems appropriate to mention it because much of the article addresses the issues in this and preceding chapters of this book. It is almost as if the editor of the paper has had a 'revelation' that resembles mine. It stands out as an oddity, if a most welcome one to me. The heading is, *The I in mind* and the writer of the article is Oliver Burkeman. I recommend it. A key phrase, that seems relevant to my theme is as follows:

Consciousness, according to Dennett's* theory, is like a conjuring trick: the normal functioning of the brain just makes it look as if there is something non-physical going on. To look for a real, substantive thing called consciousness, Dennett argues, is as silly as insisting that characters in novels . . . . must be made up of peculiar substance named 'fictoplasm'; the idea is absurd and unnecessary, since the characters do not exist to begin with.

*From Wikipedia:
Daniel Clement Dennett III (born March 28, 1942) is an American philosopher, writer, and cognitive scientist whose research centres on the philosophy of mind, philosophy of science and philosophy of biology, particularly as those fields relate to evolutionary biology and cognitive science. He is currently the Co-director of the Centre for Cognitive Studies, the Austin B. Fletcher Professor of Philosophy, and a University Professor at Tufts University. Dennett is an atheist and secularist, a member of the Secular Coalition for America advisory board, as well as an outspoken supporter of the Brights movement. Dennett is referred to as one of the 'Four Horsemen of New Atheism', along with Richard Dawkins, Sam Harris, and the late Christopher Hitchens.]

I love 'Four Horsemen of New Atheism', and maybe I qualify as one of their horses.

Anyway, I find the Dennett approach on consciousness much to my taste. His hostility towards unnecessary reification is most refreshing. I intend to read one of his books. Or two.

Parsing Presence

Obviously, and most necessarily, presence is not a thing. That's the whole point of this excursion into beingness, which is also itself not a thing. Presence is itself not a thing. Beingness is itself not a thing. Consciousness is itself not a thing. Even that is too much. These states are not 'itselves' either. They just are. We have to jettison 'itself', along with all the other archetype-like baggage. When I was first trying to become awake I made the mistake of treating 'awakeness' as a thing to be achieved. That was an identical error. Being awake is being awake: that's it. There's no product, no objective, i.e. awakeness is its own reward, so to speak.

When Buddhism first met Taoism, centuries were consumed in trying to define 'emptiness' compared with 'void'. We Occidentals are not the only mad humans. Imagine spending valuable ages merely trying to get the thing named properly. Well, maybe they were better than that, perhaps only wanting to know what they were talking about. But it's still a big mistake. Knowing is not possible nor useful when being is an option, as it always is.

As this is to a degree mere word-play, what is the semantic relationship between 'presence' and 'consciousness' and 'awareness/ awakeness'? That is to say, is there any difference between the ideas carried or projected by the words? I have, to my own satisfaction, recognised that my so-called mystical experiences are not obviously different in kind from the rest of my consciousness, or presence, or awareness, but certainly different in intensity. But that leaves a universe of questions unanswered. My own experiences may be different only in degree rather than nature, but what about other people, other animals, other life-forms generally, and even non-living systems? And even my own experiences have different emotional or intellectual impact upon me.

The Uley Matrix
Therefore, are we, all beings or things, living a single experiential continuum or a vast range of quite different sorts of consciousness? And, all-importantly, does it matter? To keep it as simple as possible I will return to the Uley fish-pond experience in my memory. Here is

an experiential matrix, I assume. In one 'section' of it there is the fact that it is a memory. So it exists, as far as that section of the matrix is concerned, solely in my consciousness. In that consciousness it is existent at the aware level, but presumably it also exists at the unconscious level. (That raises the question of whether a human consciousness can also be unconscious. There seems no doubt at all that this is the case, but it makes the very word 'consciousness' bizarrely incorrect, does it not? No wonder scientists and other pundits are having difficulty with understanding a 'process' that has not even been named properly.)

The child that I was, entered the matrix with a conscious desire which was also a mini-matrix. Or so I think it may have been. I was not merely motivated by a need for fish. (The roach were inedible.) But there was a need for *fishing*. I don't understand that, now. I assume it was an atavistic drive, which would be another section of my consciousness-matrix. I was also in love with the tackle and the shop in which I purchased it. (Many shops, then, in the small town of Dursley, were full of enticements for me, too.) I also liked riding my bicycle along the narrow country road, which was almost free of other vehicles as I remember it. Another section, this, because an entire series of children's mobility 'toys' (scooter, roller-skates, pedal-car, mini-bicycle, home-made trolley) had obsessed me in my small-boy years. Incidentally, that consciousness-matrix seems to have overcome our entire species, the transport-phenomenon now being an overwhelming presence in human existence whereas the other great apes are stuck with moving by legs and arms, as quadrupeds generally must be. Is this a triumph of human consciousness or merely an out of control habit that will destroy us?

Arriving at the fish-ponds on a summer evening stimulated a surge of consciousness. It was an invitation to be present, though I'm not sure how far the juvenile me was able to experience presence. I remember strong emotions, as I have recorded in 'Mystikos', but that may be in my adult consciousness as deep-set memory. The physical presence of living organisms in and around the fish-ponds are also very clear memories, however inaccurate. I can imagine that I felt strong animistic feelings and it's possible that I did. Nature, as it is called, was in full spate and I think that I often struggled to contain it and myself.

This struggle was both good and bad, a Manichean world, which was very real to me as a child. Or so I remember it. I was often afraid. I was often ecstatic. That is the way it was, as I remember it. But that was true of my life in general. It still is. My consciousness at the fish-ponds was under constant pressure, but from where that pressure came was and is a mystery. Indeed, as far as the 'mystical experience' is concerned, it is a mystery of bewilderment about all that seemed to happen to me. It still is. I am driven to the viewpoint that it is all a matter of 'isness' and quite beyond comprehension, whatever religion and science try to tell me.

In my paintings of the memory-fish-ponds there is a great degree of colour and zest, the water and reflections are very vivid, the trees seem to have personalities, the reeds and bullrushes heave at each other for space and light. That small painted world seems more alive than it could possibly be, yet it probably was like that for anyone who wanted to experience it in that way.

Which raises the question of will, or intent, as an aspect of consciousness. It is an entire section of the Uley-matrix. Did I just happen to go there, mindlessly, or was I driven by an inexplicable compulsion? How does intent fit into the unknowable phenomenon of consciousness? How would it figure in the peregrinations of a chimpanzee in a rainforest?

The 'Hard Problem'

I don't think this problem exists, but a lot of philosophers seem to think it does. Their argument goes something like this: there must be an extra, so far unknown, factor in the brain or mind that makes us aware that we are conscious. No-one knows what that factor might be, but it must exist otherwise we would be 'zombies', i.e. perfectly ordinary humans who don't know they are aware. We do, it is asserted, look out at the world and know that we are looking out at the world, which means we have this special gift, the gift of being conscious.

I refute this because consciousness for me includes the looking out at the world. It seems to me that philosophy has this ingrained habit of wanting to find Russian dolls, whether they exist or not. Like the famous Snark, or the Yeti, or the Loch Ness Monster, you can look for it in case it exists, and get a lot of fun out of the futile chase.

I also refute it because it is so anthropocentric. We, as a species, have this mind-set: human is the climax, and transcendent, species in the world/universe, so we can forget the other organisms and focus on ourselves as the one living organism that really matters. This ridiculous arrogance has disastrous consequences. We easily overlook the immense range of qualities in human beings. So imbued with the sense of our climactic uniqueness, we edit out the worst features of ourselves when taking a global philosophical view. We ignore the reality of the previous, extinct, human species. The other great apes are significant to us only as major pets, like super-intelligent horses or dogs. We do not recognise our mundane biological reality.

Many humans are far from wonderful examples of consciousness. Political correctness conflicts with 'racist' attitudes but even now, in the apparently civilised West, we sideline individuals or types as below par. We are still tribal. And still warlike and bloodthirsty. Many human beings are very stupid or pathological. Belief systems dominate regardless of lacking factual evidence. Some human consciousness hardly seems worth having.

Yet, if we avoid these value-judgements and simply regard consciousness as a phenomenon, we see that is everywhere. It doesn't, surely, figure as a special gift to the human mind or brain, a special 'substance' that makes us self-aware. We have made this mistake with essence or soul, let us not make the same error in regard to consciousness. The most obvious fact to me is that consciousness exists in every organism and maybe in reactive non-living systems.

It depends largely on how we define this inadequate term.

David Rosenthal, a professor of philosophy and expert in cognitive science has said:

'The term "consciousness" is used in several ways: to describe a person or other creature as being awake and sentient, to describe a person or other creature as being "aware of" something, and to refer to a property of mental states, such as perceiving, feeling, and thinking, that distinguishes those states from unconscious mental states. Distinguishing these different concepts of consciousness is crucial in evaluating the major theories of what it is for a state to be conscious. Among those are first-order theories, on which a mental state is conscious if being in that state results in one's being conscious of something; global-workspace theories, on which a state is conscious if it's widely available for mental processing; inner-sense theories, on which a state is conscious if one senses or perceives that state by way of a special inner faculty; and higher-order-thought theories, on which a state is conscious if one is aware of that state by having a thought about it.'

'Being aware of something', a phrase in the second line of Rosenthal's definition, could be applied to all living organisms. Indeed, 'consciousness' could be used in the definition of a living organism. Consider a bacterium: it grows, reproduces, varies its behaviour according to changes in its environment, changes its susceptibility to antibiotics or presence of nutrients, moves if it possesses flagellae, in general it behaves as any organism does in its attempt to stay alive and procreate. In a limited sense, this is consciousness because it means being aware of external conditions.

As we look at more complex organisms, the evidence accumulates. A microscopic slipper animalcule avoids obstacles in its swimming path. Water fleas react to sundry changes in the aquatic conditions. Earthworms have a busy life which depends on a range of external factors. Snails and slugs negotiate complex manoeuvres in the small jungle they inhabit. They are aware of where they are and what they are doing. As we get to cats and dogs and crows, we see a vast range of behaviours that could only be possible in a conscious creature. Even the humble octopus is a genius of responsive behaviour.

Then the plants. I am not suggesting that they think like a human or even a 'lower' animal. But they certainly respond to external events and internal changes. If it were only the phenomenon of flowering in trees and herbaceous plants, we are witnessing an awareness in action. But the preparation in a tree for winter and the response to spring again shows an organism aware of changes in its world. Algae suddenly 'bloom' in certain marine conditions. A house-plant moves its flowers to follow the sun. Mimosa responds to touch. Pitcher-plants catch and kill insects.

Panpsychism

If we stay with philosophy for a moment rather than stay on the relatively solid earth of science, we begin to wonder how far consciousness reaches in the universe. If the responsiveness of water to temperature, the reactivity of chemicals generally, and the formation of stars and galaxies, are seen as some form of response to external and internal events, then why not see the whole cosmos as conscious in some way or another.

This approach erases the 'hard' question: if consciousness is just a feature of the world and the universe, then we can stop worrying about the symptoms and nature of human consciousness - it's just a bit of the overall consciousness matrix. I must say that this really appeals to me as a coherent theory. It is satisfyingly Ockhamish. Human egomaniacs will not like it, I guess.

Quantum Theory

The idea of consciousness being a cosmic phenomenon comes into a very different field and one that I hardly fear to enter. This is the perplexing and fundamental mismatch between classical physics and quantum theory. In this split in the scientific mindset there exists some opportunity to question everything that is claimed to be knowledge. That is very tempting, as Big Knowledge seems to me to be failing ourselves and the planet. Unfortunately, I do not understand the physics, being an erstwhile classical biologist. Yet biology also questions Big Knowledge if it is not also treated as Big Knowledge. I have long had the feeling that while physics (and chemistry) give an insight into living processes, they don't quite get into the almost miraculous nature of living nature. That is probably mere fantasy on my part, but it gives me pleasure.

Other people have new ways of questioning the scientific and philosophical status quo. For example, there is the curious case of Hugh Everett III, a maverick of the first degree. He postulated that the great paradox in physics was illusory and that the answer lay in the nature and effect of consciousness, itself a quantum phenomenon. Another interesting development comes from Stuart Hameroff, a medical specialist, who has worked with the physicist Roger Penrose to develop a quantum interpretation of brain function. Hameroff's website states:

My research involves a theory of consciousness which can bridge these two approaches (i.e. scientific and 'pan-psychic'), a theory developed over the past 20 years with eminent British physicist Sir Roger Penrose. Called 'orchestrated objective reduction' ('Orch OR'), it suggests consciousness arises from quantum vibrations in protein polymers called microtubules inside the brain's neurons, vibrations which interfere, 'collapse' and resonate across scale, control neuronal firings, generate consciousness, and connect ultimately to 'deeper order' ripples in space-time geometry. Consciousness is more like music than computation.

Consciousness Confirmed?

In sum, the idea of consciousness is under pressure. But not negatively. In this chapter I have moved into a more secure position on the subject while simultaneously liberating myself from certain limits. Beingness, or Presence, or Soul, and all the other pseudonyms, can rest easy in my mind. I have begun to glimpse the existential freedom that I instinctively feel is the ground-state of any creature, even a mere human one. My Fifth Revelation has a new dimension.

Chapter Nine
Daniel's Mind

The Source

Wikipedia says it well:

'In chapter 5 of Consciousness Explained Dennett describes his multiple drafts model of consciousness. He states that, "all varieties of perception—indeed all varieties of thought or mental activity— are accomplished in the brain by parallel, multi-track processes of interpretation and elaboration of sensory inputs. Information entering the nervous system is under continuous 'editorial revision.' (p. 111). Later he asserts, "These yield, over the course of time, something rather like a narrative stream or sequence, which can be thought of as subject to continual editing by many processes distributed around the brain,..." (p. 135.).'

I am grateful for the completeness of Dennett's account, more specifically it is joyous to encounter a great thinker who considers that the human brain makes the human universe using nothing but sensory data and its own processing equipment. It is all a product of the brain in the form of mind. It has been a long time coming to this in my own cranial processor. I have dabbled in mysticism, science, philosophy and semantics for decades and had been put off the idea that it is all in the mind because it seemed too absolutist to think such a thing.

Nagging at me all the while was the growing suspicion that the apparent universe was within the human skull, and only in there. Assuming that it is the human apparent universe which is being considered and that, given human variation, there were multiple human-conceived universes. Now I have reached that conclusion as the most likely scenario. As far as I can understand Dennett's most extraordinarily labyrinthine explanations, he has come to a similar conclusion.

Yet the master-stroke, for me, in the second half of the above extract, is the idea that the brain works as a publisher of a narrative which is endlessly edited and therefore changing. I was even ashamed of the way that my mind kept on correcting itself, as if I would never get it 'right'. I was ashamed as if there were any agency that would blame me authoritatively for being inconsistent. I didn't mind too much if people thought I was talking nonsense, as I knew I wasn't, but I hated having to admit to myself that I had made an apparent mistake.

So far, from the early part of Dennett's book, I have derived a spectacular relief, which is that my brain makes consciousness for me and I have to dwell in that consciousness because it is all there is. It is my home, whether I like it or not, and it is the only, though infinitely variable, 'reality'.

'It Doesn't Matter'

The first intimation of actual mental freedom, which is, of course, also the product of Dennett's reasoning, was when listening to a recording of Adyashanti talking to an audience. His voice is a very potent input to my brain, because he has stripped away so much flimflam from his own mind. I should explain, here, that I use the word 'flimflam' advisedly: my brain postulates that virtually all human discourse is suspect, including its own naturally. Our minds are inveterate swindlers. I mean this in the nicest way. We produce a narrative that is primarily intended to influence the minds of others. As I am writing this, I want the reader to be influenced, do I not? However hard I try to be open and neutral, my intent is set upon persuasion.

Adyashanti is a very effective persuader. If he intended to corrupt or suborn his listeners, he would do it superbly. Fortunately, his impulse is as honest and loving as his mind can manage. As I listened on that particular occasion, I saw through him in several ways. I saw his truth, I think, and loved it. I saw his mind working, as I might watch a humming-bird hover. I admired that. Thirdly, I saw his need, the best thing of all. He needed freedom above all else. He was defying the vast army of injunctions, guilts, pomposities, faiths, greeds, terrors, etc which crush each of us into a stunted victim, and he was rejecting the malign products of millions of human brains over thousands of years that we treasure as if they were wisdom. I cried out excitedly, 'It doesn't matter'. I meant, I guess, that *they* don't matter.

How does my brain deal with that? How does my behaviour respond to that? How does that change who I am? I can feel the whole inner system grind its teeth. My brain says, 'Good idea. Let's see you do it. Correction: let's see me do it.' The best I can do at present is to accept that I am the Void, or a quantum wave/particle of it. But that is merely to accept the methodology of my brain/mind. These concepts are also part of the vast army of inputs and I can't really 'trust' them any more than, say, 'god' or 'heroism'. In some sort of truth, the 'Void' is no better than 'God', they are merely outputs from the central neural publishing industry of the mind. Meanwhile, while I live, I have to live, somehow. I need, as previously recognised, to shift focus from analysis to behaviour. At least, with Dennett, and Adyashanti, I have a clean sheet, a cleaner sheet than a year or so ago. So, first I'd like to see where Dennett takes his freedom into action. I think I know how I need to enact mine but it would be nice to compare and contrast narratives.

Another Calvin

John Calvin, born 1509, was (according to Wikipedia) influenced by the Augustinian tradition, which led him to expound the doctrine of predestination and the absolute sovereignty of God in salvation of the human soul from death and eternal damnation. His writing and preachings provided the seeds for the branch of theology that bears his name. The Reformed, Congregational, and Presbyterian churches, which look to Calvin as the chief expositor of their beliefs, have spread throughout the world.

So, that Calvin was an enemy of reason and of reasonable morality, as far as I am concerned. It is no small irony that another Calvin, William, born 1939, should be as much an authority for me as Dennett, maybe even more so. Somewhat to my shame or chagrin, I find that my pet subject, evolution, has been applied to human consciousness in a way that is both ingenious and immensely to my taste. Here's Wikipedia talking about William Calvin:

Calvin writes as an advocate of the idea that brain-based Darwinian processes are what provides brains with what are called "consciousness" and "intelligence". Calvin starts with the division of brain processes into two types, those that depend on "cerebral ruts" (hardware) and those that dance more freely through the brain and so are able to function like "software"; Calvin usually calls these "firing patterns".

Alongside this is Dennett's interest in the extraordinary expansion of the human brain in the very short period between 2.5 million years ago and 150 thousand years ago. He calls it the Great Encephalisation, and emphasises that it happened before the development of agriculture, cooking and language. This explosion of brain growth is inexplicable as is the product, in Dennett's words, 'An enormously complex brain of unrivalled plasticity, almost indistinguishable from our own in size and shape'. Furthermore, it is in the twinkling of a geological eye, a mere 10 thousand years, that 'civilisation' has appeared, an evolutionary moment in time. This meteoric advance must, according to Dennett, be due to the harnessing of the brain plasticity, virtually similar to the creation of software.

Why did our ancestors' have the equivalent of a cephalic big bang? Lot's of theories seem to circulate. Calvin (William) postulates:

'...the pattern of action potentials in any particular neocortical minicolumn can be replicated and spread through the cortex like a piece of software code and be "played" on the millions of other minicolumns in the same way one can play a million copies of a compact disc (CD) on a million CD players – the key difference being that while all CD players are designed to do basically the same task, the various cortical minicolumns can all have their own unique "ruts" and the copies of the firing patterns are not exact duplicates. This allows for a "cerebral symphony" rather than just a million-fold amplification of the same tune and a "survival of the fittest" process whereby those firing patterns that resonate best with the existing pool of "ruts" will dominate one's consciousness and generate intelligent behavior. ("Our long train of connected thoughts is why our consciousness is so different from what came before.")'

Presumably the cranium grew to make space for the expanding brain? If so, we have had very, very, fast evolution in those few million years. But why? The contemporaneous and closely related shaggy apes, e.g. the chimpanzees went on with their divergently evolutionary journey, of course, but it was minor compared with ours. Now my view on evolution is that it is a non-purposeful, chance process and the great expansion of the human brain is in no way a teleological miracle for me. It seems more like autonomous technology gone crazy. Yet it so happened that the resulting 'accident' involved a massive shift of 'intelligence' in the animals we then were. It also let loose an immense variety of behavioural patterns.

Inner Evolution

In other books, I have already played around with the notion that we humans could undo a lot of the damage to ourselves and the planet by a process I called Envolution (for want of a better word). I suppose I was thinking of memes rather than genes. In Dennett and Co. we have inner evolution, i.e. the brain has taken on an evolutionary role on its own accord. If true, this implies an ability to change behaviour, awareness, consciousness, in a specialised, algorithmic manner. It is not so much a process of rational development, but rather one of playing complex games or behaving quantum- like. In effect, we could take the intentionality and pointfulness out of the activity called intelligence. If this makes humankind look like machines, so be it, if that is how we already operate.

On the other hand, anything could come out of the process. We've had gods and science, morality and aesthetics, law and academia; we might ask, what next? Is anything and everything possible since nothing is ordained? Could we become a new species from the inside out?

Me Me Evolution

Ah, but it has been happening for millennia, it appears. It is obvious once the fact is allowed to show itself fully. When I first met the word 'meme' in Dawkins' Selfish Gene, I confess that I dismissed it as a sop to compensate for the loss of 'progressive' evolutionary comfort. Until recently, we humans could, and did, congratulate ourselves for being chosen as the 'image of god'. Now I realise my error, so obvious, so inane. The facts are stark and simple, it seems, human apes separated off from chimpanzee apes six million years, and then, three million years on the human ape's brain began to get bigger. It grew until recent times, about 150 thousand years ago, when it was four time its original size. Dennet calls this the Great Encephalisation. He emphasises that this huge, and actually rapid, change (in evolutionary terms) preceded language and agriculture. Why it did this is anybody's guess. (But see comments above regarding William Calvin's work.) It may have been a mechanical miracle of organic computer technology. In any case, it only took a blink of an eye for the complex, changeable giant of a brain to reach its climax, a mere ten thousand years ago. I feel that this change is like the brain ceasing to serve the body and, instead, becoming the master of the body: a kind of rebellion of power, maybe.

At least, the new brain in Homo was more informative to its subject. It has a more developed awareness of the world without and within. More significant still, perhaps the ultimate developmental significance, is the appearance of 'ideas' rather than mere 'reflexes'. My own human brain is having difficulty with this, as my stumbling prose indicates, but it, my brain, is telling me that all this accidental, rebellious cortical development 'gave' our race geniuses like Mozart, Einstein, Turing, and, quietly modest, the great Darwin himself. It also gave us Abraham, Genghis Khan and Hitler, neutrally inventive as it was. Just as the world of animals contains swans and crocodiles.

The brain is evolving in a new way, too, which is what really excites my curiosity. It has a new kind of replicator, very fast and hugely powerful. It makes the gene look slow and clumsy. This is the meme, the bodiless and invisible invader of the human cerebral cortex. At the beginning of this volume I poked fun at the hero-fixation. At that stage I thought it was a ludicrous and dangerous complex. Having followed the band for decades I was disinfected: Shane was rather a figure of fun. But I didn't see why we were so vulnerable to such myths. Why should a brainy biped be such a fool, I wondered. Now, at another layer of the Fifth Revelation, I see that memes make fools or geniuses of us without caring what happens, the power is all-important. Memes must rule.

Must they? Or is it merely that once they come out of the cerebral matrix, they just have to go public in a big way, as if they are powered by cerebral aviation fuel. The word 'craze' carries that implication. That is a mad enthusiasm. Though memes are often amazingly long-lived. Take the meme, 'god', an idea that has virtually overwhelmed the earth for the ten thousand years since the cerebral rebellion began. It is a craze that never seems to die a natural death. Fortunately there are those that are beneficial, such as 'beauty' or 'kindness'. The thing about memes, like the plodding genes, is that there is endless creativity. My worry about Big-Knowledge must be tempered by this new premise, i.e. that knowledge is just a bunch of social genes which arise and skid about as if they owned the place - which they do. I don't know whether Dennett would agree, but it occurs to me that memes have the benefit of being as unherdable as cats. Unlike the humans that promote them, as the individual human brain is utterly credulous, snapping up stray memes like a street pigeon.

Who Is Boss?

So the brain, or the mind, or individual consciousness, is just an astoundingly complex but 'democratic' and utterly machine-like electronic matrix? Its products are memes, which come and go, yet control us? That is a very rough summary of what I have been reading. It fits well enough my conception of the human body, including the brain, unavoidably, as a vast army of semi- independent cells, some human, most non-human, operating as a single functional unit. Like the brain, as described above, the body, the brain's 'vehicle', couldn't possibly work like this, but it does.

The 'consciousness exploration industry' is a strange scene: here we have brain-minds, in universities and laboratories all over the technological and philosophical world, trying to understand brain-minds: a very weird picture, when this (my?) brain-mind looks upon it with mixed admiration and distaste. How can all this extraordinary effort possibly succeed? And it is a sort of mind/mind incest, too. In any case, accepting that the brain is the source of mind, and consciousness, it is clear that all the brain/minds have done is to paint themselves into a corner: they have no 'boss in the brain-system', only a range of names (e.g. homunculi, yet again) and possible arrangements to suggest how the mind process gets done. My own brain/mind (if it is mine) is troubled, not so much by the interesting confusion, but by the arrogantly persistent attitude that science will solve it eventually. I am happy with the confusion and mystery.

One phrase in Dennett's book stands out, for me. In the last paragraph on page 258 there's an anxiety expressed that perhaps the brain is not really designed (hard-wired) for 'such activity' as he puts it.

Oh, yes, I cry, that seems right: the brain, after all, is just a zoological organ among the many and we are asking too much from it.

A Snark?

"Just the place for a Snark! I have said it twice:
That alone should encourage the crew.
Just the place for a Snark! I have said it thrice:
What I tell you three times is true."

The crew was complete: it included a Boots-
A maker of Bonnets and Hoods-
A Barrister, brought to arrange their disputes-
And a Broker, to value their goods.

A Billiard-marker, whose skill was immense,
Might perhaps have won more than his share-
But a Banker, engaged at enormous expense,
Had the whole of their cash in his care.

I suppose they have to keep on hunting. It seems to be hard-wired into the brain, this search for something in itself. But we all have our Snarks. It took me a long time to realise that my Snark was the great delusion of my selfness, and all the fuss associated with it. Then, after knocking myself unconscious in the garden on a cold, wet, November afternoon a decade or so ago, I discovered that I hadn't got a self. That's how it seemed, when I looked for it. Not that I can be sure that I had one before, because I hadn't looked for it, specifically. The self is generally the favourite Snark of most people, if not all. In my case, I eventually divided the self I might have had into three parts:

1.   The basic animal self. There's no doubt this exists. I just live that one. As my cat lives his.

2.   The made-up self (or imaginative self). The projected, special me, writer, poet, artist, egoist. This self is the personality, the archetypal being, the soul, the personal void, inner god etc. etc.

3.   The transcendent self. Unknown but sacred, a mystic entity, shamanic, even more unlikely than the second self. At least I do paint and write. But I don't really know how or whether I transcend.

The basic self is no Snark. It is born, it eats, it dies. It is real, in its way. But selves 2 and 3 are dubious, if not downright delusionary. They are central to Dennett's exploration.

His book is dense and seems endlessly investigative. Is this much effort really needed to dispel the illusions that constitute consciousness and attitudes to it? I suppose so, especially as the entire human condition is permeated by them. Dennett give many a fine bravura performance as the destroyer of delusions but one paragraph attracts me particularly (p. 416)

'But the strangest and most wonderful constructions in the whole animal world are the amazing, intricate constructions made by the primate, Homo sapiens. Each normal individual of this species makes a self. Out of its brain it spins a web of words and deeds, and, like the other creatures, it doesn't know what it is doing; it just does it. This web protects it, just like the snail's shell, and provides it a livelihood, just like the spider's web, and advances its prospects for sex, just like the bowerbird's bower. Unlike a spider, an individual human doesn't just exude its web; more like a beaver, it works hard to gather the

materials out of which it builds its protective fortress. Like a bowerbird, it appropriates many found objects which happen to delight it - or its mate - including many that have been designed by others for other purposes.'

Where has this taken me in my pursuit of the Fifth Revelation? A long way, I feel. But maybe there's more to come. The meanings of 'I' and 'me' and 'my' have been shredded, which leaves a new kind of void, by no means unpleasant, though more extreme that any existential doubt previously experienced by this brain/mind matrix or whatever it is. The self-referential terms are too useful to jettison but I must find a way of making them de-reified. Perhaps the 'royal we' could be used, but the brain/mind is the ultimate democracy, so that won't really work. This seems a good place to end, with a poem about wisdom, written by 'us' for a poetry group,:

Mount Wisdom

Looking at myself, I see
How fortunate I am to be
A specially intelligent kind of ape,
Sapiently, the only animal to escape
The existential limits of this planet:
Nothing can compare with this, can it?

Turquoise bacteria, I must confess,
Made earth alive, which does impress
Me, as a very late arrival on this sphere,
For, otherwise I would not even be here.
I am not sure when, exactly, I became
World Dominator, but that is now my name.

I have billions of helpers in my global realm
A diversity of powers, with one at the helm:
We make knowledge out of thin air, or find
It as gold created from the alchemy of mind.

I, and my helpers, are suffused with sapience
I teach them, and they me, with wise deference

If there is a dipterid in our mindful emollience
It is our rather limited, even variable, tolerance
Perhaps we are too intelligent, too inventive,
And competitive thought is a great incentive.
We appoint advisers and teachers, with a role
To keep us within bounds, to keep us whole.

It has been growing for many a thousand year,
Our great mountain of wisdom, but there is fear,
In our great intelligence, that the Wisdom Mount
Is not all that it should be, not a dependable fount
Of benevolence, all-healing, of gentle progression,
But too often an excuse for untypical aggression.

I have now met a Maverick who gave me advice:
That the human race has cost an excessive price.
'To what and whom', I asked. 'It depends,' he said,
'On your version of truth, the stories in your head.'
'At the best,' he said, 'Humans are just a nuisance;
'And worst-case, well, we are a universal pestilence.'

I felt so insulted that I wanted to kill - to erase him.
Then another thought made my incandescence dim:
I looked up to the overwhelming knowledge mountain,
And desired it to crumble into dust, to let me start again
Upon my appointed quest. But, then, who appointed it?
What authority was using me as an excuse for it to quit?

Or is the mountain breaking apart with internal strife,
Unable to stand the argumentative explanations for life?
Or does the cosmos regret the introduction of mankind
Into a world of nature untroubled by the ever-itching mind?
How could evolution have made such perverse wrongness
When it seemed to be doing so well, making steady progress?

Maverick says evolution isn't progress, just chancy grind
The human experiment was mindless even in making mind.
And to cap it, my mind is not at all efficient as a benefit:
It is not at all evident it will help in our reputed attempt to fit
The world environment, probably the entirely opposite effect,
Because everyman's thinking has so much inherited defect.

'Wisdom? What a conman's word!' said Maverick, 'Think tall,
Taller than the mountain, wider, taller, till you can't think at all.'
Suddenly I saw myself infinitely small, hardly visible to the eye,
And I saw all species on this little speck of earth, and saw why
I'd made those stories, and collected all that knowing, and cried.
Wept for my ineptitude, all that assuming. And this, my world, died.

They have come to take Maverick and me away. The un-minded
Are cleaning the thought-strewn stage, and I shall be blinded,
Chemically cleansed, imbued with normal wisdom, made to see
Again, how it is and how I must learn to be, fully wise, unfree.
Maverick is hanged for treason of opinion, his skull still bright,
On a spike, on the mountain-side, confirming he was a right.

Shall I take up his sword of light, flashing in the morning sun?
What advantage lies in truth that defies the law of General Run?
The blue-green microbes do not heed me, they live fortuitous,
Complicated lives, as well as I do; no, rather better, circuitous
Reasoning makes me false: I almost envy the Cyanophyceae,
At least they haven't built a pseudo-mountain in the sky. Hee-hee.

The idea of self as a pseudo-mountain in the sky is persuasive to
someone trying to shed the trappings of false personhood and the
ruinous Big-Knowledge from the last few thousand years. Like the
termites, humans have a compulsion to build a superstructure, but
unlike the industrious insects,

*(National Geographic quote, 'A single termite can be barely bigger
than the moon of a fingernail, its semi-transparent exoskeleton as
vulnerable to sunlight as to being crushed by a child in flip-flops. But in*

groups of a million or two, termites are formidable architects, building mounds that can reach 17 feet (5 meters) and higher. The 33 pounds (15 kilograms) or so of termites in a typical mound will, in an average year, move a fourth of a metric ton (about 550 pounds) of soil and several tons of water').

Humans make buildings of belief and dogma as well as skyscrapers and shanty-towns and have egoic consciousness-creations to match any known constellation of fantasies. But how do they, the humans, identify their being, who or what do they think they are? Is madness their only defining feature? Is beauty, truth, and love a trio of delusion? Where can a human stand, in terms of being, and living, an identity that makes any sense at all? How should or could a human identify and define its own form and nature, as it tries to describe that of the mighty termite? Is it just a plain impossibility and does it matter anyway?

Chapter Ten
We, Us and Ours

We are a human brain.
We think, therefore we probably are. We used to tolerate the fiction that we were a 'person', a fantasy entity that issued edicts about its selfness. We didn't object, particularly, as we were generally able to continue our practice as an intricate organisation living its own complex existence. This was not entirely satisfactory, however, because the false entity we had allowed to emerge from our organisation, the 'person', was evolving into a nuisance. It claimed, for example, that it was the point of our existence, rather than a vastly overbearing side-issue. We were indulgent, however, letting the pseudo-being play its games and fret itself over its alleged suffering. We had to accept that it was one of our mistakes that had, unfortunately, become a preponderant characteristic, making alleged humanness far too important and causing some extremely serious effects on the outside environment. This is a feature of many of our billions of associate brains, i.e. that their 'human fictions' all seem to do a similar thing, smugly naming their transgressions with all kinds of grandiose words, unaware, apparently that these memes were also figment entities.

We are, therefore, troubled by the behaviour of our 'products'. By which we mean the bipedal animals that regard themselves as divine and heroic because they have us as brains, unaware that it is we who have them, mores the pity. They still see the brains in their skulls as servile mechanisms, and are unable to make the imaginative leap into recognising the actual situation. Of course, to be fair, it is us who would have to make that leap on behalf of the bodily vehicle. We have been remiss and lazy, and too absorbed in the business of being a mind-structure. It seems, too, that we don't have a programme for reframing the operating criteria. It seems not to have evolved in the course of the brain's changes over time. Some of us have come to realise that we, as brain-minds, are only half-finished, or, even worse, fundamentally flawed: unfit for developing a purpose.

We, this particular brain, expressing our narrative sequence as words through a computer keyboard, do have problems. Perhaps the most intriguing of our problems is that we are an unpredictable labyrinth trying to find our way in our own labyrinth. A double labyrinth, it might be said. It is altogether too similar to that famous fictional double labyrinth, Frankenstein and the fabricated monster. If Frankenstein represents us in unitary form, silly as that is, the monster represents the human creature that we have allowed to manifest out of our complex depths. We, this brain, do not really understand what we have done, and we are also harbouring a meme that might be guilt.

What Are Brains For?
If it is impossible for us, a brain, to possess a unitary identity or a figurehead leader, as seems certain, can we see any purpose in our existence? We, and our fellow brains, over a long time, have wondered about this. How did the algorithm of purpose ever come into our circuits? It is a very subversive question. What, actually, does the word mean? We exist, so how does anything else matter? Oh, yes, that fellow Dennett says our purpose is to persuade other brains of our wisdom, which is simplistic nonsense. But it is nevertheless true that our narrative does keep reverting to the idiot question, 'why'? Quite often, our great collective, this brain, asks what it's here for.

While it would be as foolish for a herd of elephants to discuss their meaning, there is, fortunately, no evidence that they do so. Yet we human brains do, via our products, discuss our meaning, one way or another. We discuss our purpose, too, as there is some case for saying that meaning and purpose belong to different narrative sequences.

Some of our constituent circuits say that the whole idea is a human error. This 'self' entity, which we have allowed to parasitise our systems, is said to carry the blame for asking the ultimate and egotistical questions about its value to the living world (which means, in human terms, 'itself' because our human by-product doesn't really acknowledge any other beast but the bipedal ape). We, the brain labouring under the spurious identity 'Michael Scott' (spurious for many reasons, not least that there are thousands of brains in human vehicles labelled with that 'name'), are in great confusion about everything. We are not clear, for example, whether so-called emotions have a real or relevant part in the whole brain-process. Putting this another way, are emotions just effusions of the self, a falsity dependent upon a parasite? The self-calling itself 'I' in our brain complex is prone to emotions. For example, in this moment, as it types the words on this computer, this 'I' feels sad and anxious because its 'soul-mate', a self made by another brain and thus linked to our brain-person for sixty years, is in a hospital being 'ill', as they say. Our brain is barely able to function as a processing system (not that we are ever that good at it) because of the emotional interference to the normal electronic process.

An interesting alternative would be that thoughts and emotions are the same, as against the conventional wisdom that says emotions are of a different ilk altogether. Clearly, memes are ideas or feelings, which does imply basic similarity. In our earlier experience, this brain (aka Michael) thought that thinking involved emotion and vice versa. It's tidier to admit that they are the same thing, though logic and passion may vary in the contents of each.

Some authoritative brains (i.e. those with persuasive or influential parasitic selves) have asserted (for millennia) that the ultimate purpose of the human biped, and even its brain, is actually to suffer. By this odd thesis, suffering is purported to be good because it raises 'consciousness' to greater heights. On this basis, we, the brain, have the job of managing the pain and misery of the bodily vehicle, and the objective of creating transcendent bliss. We, i.e. this brain, are aware of a number of other brains which are dominated by this meme. We are not free from the same electronic impulse. But is this really what we are designed to do (if we are designed to do anything but merely blindly follow the think-algorithm)?

On the other hand, there are other, quite distinct, memes circulating within, or between, brains. So there is a choice of purposes and meanings, it seems. This is not to say that we as a brain have 'choices', as we merely create the memes through the meme-algorithm (an automatic and purposeless set of instructions for making memes), while it is the parasitic-self that regards the memes as choices. Not that it seems to do much good for the self, as a fantasy doesn't have much power over itself. Typically, the parasitic self does attempt to induce its brain-host to function in ways that ease the pain or confusion of its passenger. Memes exist for 'self-healing', by meditation, drugs, or praying to the supernatural. There is the gigantic meme called 'medicine' by its aficionados, in various sub-meme varieties, whereby the tortured self-homunculus attempts to overcome its inherent limitations. Generally speaking, both the brains and the passengers tend to be ambivalent about the benefits of this particular meme-system, partly because there is suppressed recognition that everything ends in the entropic state the suffering-self calls death.

Another widespread and long-established meme aims in a different direction. It has many labels in many languages. We will, for the sake of simplicity, call it 'bliss'. In fact, it has a vast range of variants and philosophies. But we, as a sophisticated brain-matrix, will start simple and let complexity take care of its own vagaries.

Follow Your Bliss

From Wikipedia:

'One of (Joseph) Campbell's most identifiable, most quoted and arguably most misunderstood sayings was his admonition to "follow your bliss". He derived this idea from the Upanishads: "Now, I came to this idea of bliss because in Sanskrit, which is the great spiritual language of the world, there are three terms that represent the brink, the jumping-off place to the ocean of transcendence: Sat-Chit-Ananda. The word 'Sat' means being. 'Chit' means consciousness.

'Ananda' means bliss or rapture. I thought: I don't know whether my consciousness is proper consciousness or not; I don't know whether what I know of my being is my proper being or not; but I do know where my rapture is. So let me hang on to rapture, and that will bring me both my consciousness and my being. I think it worked."

He saw this not merely as a mantra, but as a helpful guide to the individual along the hero journey that each of us walks through life:

"If you follow your bliss, you put yourself on a kind of track that has been there all the while, waiting for you, and the life that you ought to be living is the one you are living. Wherever you are - if you are following your bliss, you are enjoying that refreshment, that life within you, all the time."

Wherever you are - if you are following your bliss, you are enjoying that refreshment, that life within you, all the time.'

The circuitry of this brain (we) quite resonates with the quoted effulgence from the brain carried by the vehicle called Joseph Campbell, though with reservations, considering the romantic bias of the meme in this form. We have difficulty understanding the key phrase:

'If you follow your bliss, you put yourself on a kind of track that has been there all the while, waiting for you, and the life that you ought to be living is the one you are living. Wherever you are-if you are

following your bliss, you are enjoying that refreshment, that life within you, all the time.'

Is this nonsense, like the Snark poem, or is it intelligent, like the best memes we have created from our own matrix? It appears, in any case, that enthusiastic followers may have irritated the sensibility of the Campbell self-construct which has said it wished it had said, 'Follow your blisters', as a corrective to excess memes of hedonism arising from the original reference to 'bliss'. If so, what did bliss actually mean for the Campbell-self? Are we, the brain-system whose parasite is writing this, in a state of bliss? Because we are most assuredly interested in our activities - whatever the sufferings of our parasitic Michael.

According to the Campbell brain-product, bliss is a kind of true or right path, which has been available always. That is a very common, and long-lived, meme. It's another version of the old adage, 'The kingdom of god is within you'. There are umpteen versions. No brain can be entirely free from some version of this fundamentalist certainty, this apparent god in the brain-machine. But is it, and in what sense is it, real? There are photographs of religious 'persons', such as popes or archbishops and lowlier prelates. They can be met as bodily manifestations. They speak and say prayers. They bless or excommunicate. They are, therefore, as real as our meme, Michael. But aren't they also false, as is Michael? We are trying to say that they are all mere narratives from brains like us. Therefore bliss, or divinity, or whatever, is a fiction made by brains such as we. It follows, therefore, that we, as manufacturers of memes, must own up to ourselves that we have made ideas that are not substantiated by actual evidence - unlike the popes etc. who stand resplendent in their ecclesiastic finery, mouthing our memes.

Campbell, too, was real as a body, like a bishop, but he spoke brain-generated fantasies. In his case, ironically, he made a career as a great mythologist, i.e. an expert on myths, unaware that as an meme-oracle he was, himself, a myth.

Bliss, therefore, as an inevitable and eternal track endogenously provided for the journeying 'self', is without any foundation beyond the brain's inventiveness. But all we brains agree that the brain is real. It is there in the vehicular skull: it can be seen and held in the vehicle's hands when the skull is cracked open. Is it reasonable, then, to regard the brain's products as fantastical just because they are not as physically evident as the brain that made them? We, the brain, refute this, at least to the degree that our products are not to be so casually dismissed, especially as they constitute the only consciousness in existence. (We mean, of course, human consciousness, of which we brains are the sole manufacturers and purveyors. Other consciousnesses have other sources, the brains of non- human animals, presumably, or so we are informed by our parasitic processes.)

The incarnated meme, Dennett, or at least the brain that has generated 'him', seems confident that its manifold processes have a ring of truth, if only because the famous ancient tool, logic, has been applied to the consciousness-investigations in laboratories all over the globe called Earth. The Dennett meme-brain processes are exceedingly clever, as this brain, the agency behind this writing, can barely keep up with them. What, if anything, can we, the brain owning Michael, do to settle our mind on these matters? Should we pretend that Michael really exists and let him tell his story? He has worked assiduously to tell ours (and the Dennett-brain's story), so why don't we give 'him' a temporary franchise to weave 'his' magic carpet, as if he were an authentic brain-product?

The Meme's Story

I am the meme, Michael, a product of the brain occupying this old man's skull. It is absurdly obvious that there are many, perhaps millions, of Michaels, all telling different meme-anecdotes about themselves and their physical kith and kin. Such is the profligacy of the mythical Mother Nature. I am grateful to my patron, the brain in my head, for allowing me to speak as if I actually existed. I say that to abide by the rules, whereas I do, of necessity, behave as though I actually do exist. It is what we meme-vehicles can't help doing.

I have experienced bliss, I still experience bliss occasionally, and it does rather feel as if it has been a companion, on and off, for my whole life up to now. My problem with the Campbell-meme is that he doesn't seem to acknowledge the complementary 'reality' of misery. Was it all bliss, in 'his' case? Surely not. 'He' was one of the world's fastest half-milers for only a very short time. Never mind, 'he' was heroic and multiple-talented. He had a lot of bliss, in the ordinary sense of the word. The bliss of the Campbell-person was not just the ordinary kind, I suspect. I think I know what it's like. It seems to resemble my impulse towards biology and painting, inexplicable life-long enthusiasms, coupled with an attachment to the kinder side of the biosphere. I have even viewed myself as a nature-mystic, especially as a counter-culture to theism. Does all this add up to a Campbellian bliss, I wonder? Post-Dennett, post-Dawkins, I recognise a powerful meme here. Had I made a good career-choice I would have been a naturalist, but I didn't know how to be that and became a biologist instead. Worse still, I morphed into a business-person. What a path of error that was. What did my brain-lords think they were doing? Russian roulette? Come to think of it, having ideas is rather like that game.

If it is all in the brain, as seems increasingly likely, as a few members of the Homo species begin to wonder about memes like god, self, purpose, morality, love and ambition, as they wonder about these things not as given absolutes but as dreamed up ideas, then the brain looks more and more like the human Big Bang and the universe that is alleged to have resulted. Of more personal interest is the individual brain and its big bang as it explodes into activity in each child-head. I see the Big Bang as a metaphorical meme dreamed up by frantic physicists. But it's a useful metaphor in the sense that anything can happen from that kind of singularity.

The two people who engendered me, the physical child they

named Michael, were 'simple peasants' as the patronising saying goes. They didn't do very much lofty wondering, their brains being almost wholly absorbed in the physical problems of survival in a deprived layer of the society, although they were provided with a council house, an immense benefit to people in the bottom stratum of the species. One of them, extraordinarily, desired my elevation to a higher level. The other didn't. My brain had some difficulty figuring that out, and gave up trying early on; but I followed the ambition and escaped my lot. Except this weird passion for other life-forms which sometimes manifested as a natural brutality to them and sometimes soared into delight at their beauty. I have no idea where that came from. Except, of course, that I blame it on the brain that made me.

Is there, then, a Naturalist Circuit in the gigantic matrix of the brain and its mind? Is it one of the really big memes of humankind, or at least a sub-circuit of the immense meme that holds the idea, 'Nature'. At the least, it might be expected that a super-intelligent mammal (if that is what man is) would be obsessed with its environment in every conceivable way. This obsession would go beyond mere survival, into fascination about the nature of Nature. Is Homo the only animal that thinks about Nature? Is this our super-meme?

Moving on, there's another book by Dennett, 'Darwin's Dangerous Idea', in which the enormous significance of Darwin's work is deeply considered. Here is another grand scenario in which one human brain considers the extraordinary vision of another human brain, particularly concerning the haphazard and wonderful making of the definitive human brain in the first place (about a quarter of a million years ago).

Daniel and Darwin
Here's a flavour of the book (page 123):

'The R and D done by natural selection in the course of creating actual trajectories in the Vast Space of possibilities can be measured to some extent. Among the important features of this search space

are the solutions to problems that are perennially attractive and hence predictable, like forced moves in chess. This explains some of our intuitions about originality, discovery, and invention, and also clarifies the logic of Darwinian inference about the past. <u>There is a single, unified, Design Space in which the processes of both biological and human creativity make their tracks, using similar methods.</u>' (My underlining.)

This reminded me of the Campbell quote about 'bliss' and his odd remark:

'If you follow your bliss, you put yourself on <u>a kind of track that has been there all the while, waiting for you</u>, and the life that you ought to be living is the one you are living. Wherever you are - if you are following your bliss, you are enjoying that refreshment, that life within you, all the time.' (My underlining, again.)

Perhaps it is a totally different sort of track in the two quotes, but the coincidence seems to say, to this brain's creature, that the nature-meme was in me from the start, set by the minute detail of the 'Design Space'. If that sounds as if Michael thinks he was predestined to be passionate about plants and animals, well, he's thinking of an algorithmic design (not a god's intent, perish the thought).

The brain within the skull of Charles Darwin seems to have been the crucial equipment for opening a new and more sensible account of human behaviour. Nothing in the religions, nothing in the other sciences, nothing in any other branch of the human knowledge-tree, nothing can compare with the overwhelming majesty of Darwins's 'bliss', for that is what it was and is. Dennett's value, as apologist for the Darwin masterpiece, is that he warns us against the simplistic confusion of evolution and progress. Michael infers (from us, the brain in his skull)) that the really dangerous idea, which the human selves deny and detest, is that the evolution of man is purposeless in origin - even if there is the brain's creation of purpose in the form of memes of human behaviour as well as everything else it manufactures in its circuits. This is seriously worth pursuing, says Michael's brain.

Evolution by Algorithm
Is the human brain an algorithm machine? Flippantly, Michael might (does) say: 'What else would it be?' Only the brain can answer this multi-trillion dollar question. In fact, the brain of Charles Darwin has already answered it. The algorithm responsible for everything (certainly for everything that is, was, or will be, living) is Natural Selection, although it is very badly worded and even worse-understood. (Michael is now deep into the ramifications of the Fifth Revelation, in a territory he never imagined or anticipated, the Arena of Absolute Chance. Such is the power of the brain.)

In The Beginning
The most delightful problem concerns how life started on this globe. In Darwin's time, we guess that the general mindset (even his, maybe) was that a great power had seeded the earth with life, some god or goddess being a popular choice for the job. Then, in the last few decades, the scientific bias was towards a soup of reactive proteins or to alien cells or spores on a rock from space. Neither the human brains nor their parasitic protégés could go the extra distance and think of life as a mere molecular event of staggering complexity. Today there has been little growth of awareness for most of us, brains and parasites alike, and even if we can accept evolution as a natural biological process there is still obscurity around how it kicked off.

Here, we brain and its Michael, are glad to quote an answer from Daniel Dennett:

'Fortunately for us, the laws of physics vouchsafe that there are, in the Vast Space of possible proteins, macromolecules of such breathtaking catalytic virtuosity that they can serve as the active building blocks of complex life. And, just as fortunately, the same laws of physics provide for just enough nonequilibrium in the world so that algorithmic

processes can jump-start themselves, eventually discovering those macromolecules and turning them into tools of exploration and discovery.' (p.163/4, Darwin's Dangerous Idea.)

At the end of this paragraph Dennett adds an ironic, *'Thank God for those laws!'*, and goes on to explain that 'God' is the last entity to thank. Our brain and this Michael are enthused to take apart the sophistic lunacy of the 'Anthropic Principle', probably the most popular of the theories of specialness used to protect our species from the truth. Oh, how plausible it must seem, to whoever needs to be reassured that the universe cares about minuscule humanity. It so happens, goes the fable, that the universe provided exactly the conditions, down to the finest detail, for human life to be possible. Therefore, that story continues, there was a plan and an agency behind the appearance of our species on earth. Elaborating the myth, it is said how even a minute difference in the speed of light would have prevented human arrival, and how odd, it goes on, that the constitution of air and water are exactly as required. There is no doubt, the anthropic mindset asserts, that the universe needed and wanted human beings to come into existence and arranged itself accordingly. Hence Daniel's ironic reference to the laws of physics as God's equipment for making our species as the most special of special cases.

Well, this is all too typical of the brain in absurd-person-ego mode. The logical flaw in the anthropic principle is that while it is true that had the universe not been as it is humankind would not be here, but it does not follow that the universe is as it is *so that* humankind can be here. A different universe and no humans, certainly, but so what? A parochial version of the logical error might be that Darwin's evolution produced apes, therefore man-apes became possible, is turned into: Darwin's evolution produced apes so that man-apes became possible. The difference between <u>therefore</u> and <u>so that</u> does not seem so great, yet it results in mind-boggling foolishness. Take an even more parochial version of the same error: Elizabeth Bowes-

Lyon existed on April 26th 1923 and therefore became available to marry Albert, Duke of York, and therefore was available to be the mother of Queen Elizabeth II. All true, but it cannot be argued, by a royal version of the anthropic principle, that Elizabeth-Bowes Lyon existed so that she could be the mother of Elizabeth II. (Though there might be nutters who'd think that way.)

Why Is There Something?
Right on the back foot, the stoical defender of the anthropic conceit asks the last-ditch question: *Why is there something rather than nothing?* Now isn't that just one hell of a clincher? It isn't even anthropic, because its stretching a poor case to its limits by supposing that the something/nothing argument has any relevance to us, particularly? The implication proposed is that there's got to be something because we wouldn't be here if there was nothing? Is that the excuse? Michael's brain is steaming, Michael is laughing.

All right, let's go back all the way to the phantom quantum. For starters, nothing is an unstable state - it is questionable whether nothing ever exists at all (for long, anyway). It is not just the microscopic question of human origin but at least the question of how the universe(s) came into existence. (If the brain is right in thinking that a cosmos does exist.) The Big Bang is predicated on a pre-existing something, even if it is ludicrously tiny, or, for some sort of 'steady state' the universe has always been there, a significant something. But all these ideas are just brain-products and they don't fit very well with another supreme brain-product, the baffling quantum and its physics. In the old days, Aristotle coined the aphorism, 'Nature abhors a vacuum', which is neat considering that some brains, today, assert that 'nothing', being unstable, is as much as 50% likely to turn into something spontaneously.

Now, considering that all this lofty debate comes out of the human brain, itself an enigma, Michael observes that we parasites of the brain had better avoid any absolute notion. Instead of the big bang or the steady state or (even) the multiple universes, why not just admit the possibility that a universe could come out of nothing, not even a singularity, just as life arose out of non-life, a considerable something out of nothing if it is accepted that non-living is a nothing compared with living?

Staying with biology, then, how sure is it that life came into existence in a non-life environment? In other words, the thing that matters most to the parasite of the brain, me, is whether living organisms actually did arise from non-living matter. Necessarily this would have to be autonomous, spontaneous and utterly without godlike things manipulating the manufacture. Well, as previously stated, our guide, Dennett, thinks there is clear proof of life coming out of non-life, something out of nothing.

Let us look at this in slightly more detail (not too much, otherwise this brain and Michael will fall out with each other from sheer failure to communicate).

Molecular Evolution

Dennett's spruce definition implies the way 'non-life into life' occurs. Michael's brain insists that we show Daniel's brain's first salvo on this subject (p.155/6 of 'Darwin's Dangerous Idea') which is, in turn, a quotation from Bernd Olaf Küppers, 'Information and the Origin of Life' 1990:

The smallest catalytically active protein molecules of the living cell consist of at least a hundred amino acids. For even such a short molecule, there exist 20 to the power of 100 (or, nearly equal, 10 to the power of 130) alternative arrangements of the basic monomers. This shows that already at the lowest level of complexity, that of the biological macromolecules, an almost unlimited variety of structures is possible.

These macromolecules are not 'alive' by most current criteria, not even as 'alive' as viruses, which become 'alive' when parasitising a living cell. But that's jumping the gun because there were no living cells to give life to virus molecules. But viruses are, or were before they had living cells to invade, extremely interesting intermediates in the evolution of life. They are, as Daniel says, 'just' huge, complex crystals, 'but thanks to their complexity they don't just sit there; they do things. In particular, they reproduce or self-replicate, with variations'. As he puts it, meaning the very earliest non-parasitic viruses, 'a virus travels light, packing no metabolic machinery, so it either stumbles upon the energy and materials required for self-replication or self-repair, or eventually it succumbs to the Second Law of Thermodynamics and falls apart.' That sounds pretty 'alive' to me, justifiably described as 'quasi-living things'.

Before these half-developed, half-alive prototypes, there were 'macros', some of them were just macros (it was a long time ago so it's all rather vague), mere programs or algorithms, only able to self-reproduce - a bit like computer viruses today. These viral ancestors were able to evolve because of the facility of self-reproduction, but they 'half-lived' for about a million years before true living things came from them.

Michael's brain is insistent that it is made clear that these replicating macros were not inherently 'simple', but were made of thousands/millions of 'parts'. Maybe they were even too complex to serve the imperatives of evolution. Some simple form might do it better. They could have been silicon-based self-replicators, forming ultra-fine particles of clay swirling in the turbulence of ancient waters. It was, as it is, a cosmos of limitless and exquisite organic chemistry.

The Brain Speaks

That's enough. There's no end to the story we have been allowing, sometimes encouraging, Michael to tell. It's all true, of course, but we are getting bored with the attempt to prove the obvious. We wonder why we are continuing to do this. We want Michael to change tack, to go on to something more interesting. We have, as far as we are concerned, made clear why a substantive divinity figure is not a option for us, unless it is given a very different definition from the hundreds that circulate within the human species. In fact the present chapter is rather a good meme for divinity. It puts us where we belong, at the heart of things. Things that matter to this brain, anyway. It has to be admitted, perhaps lauded, that we, Michael's brain, are entirely solipsistic: there is no universe but us. We are all there is. If there were such things as gods and unicorns, they would be in us and nowhere else. The universe is in us and nowhere else. Until that fact is accepted and embraced, as true of all brains, human life, at least, will continue to be bloody awful.

We also wish to back out of the limelight and let Michael appear as our definitive voice again.

Chapter Eleven
Practice Makes Perfect
(Or the Invention of Intention)

Before this bit of life, the life behind this book, I wasn't sure how I came to intend anything. Nor was it clear to me whether I ever had a real purpose, as opposed to a mere behavioural meme. I accepted the Existentialist orthodoxy that meaning and purpose did not exist and, further, that we are all scared stiff about it, therefore making up gods, etc., to fill the unacceptable gap in our needs.

A Surprise, Therefore.
The least that any living organism has is the intention to live. Its purpose is to live. The non-alive, then half-alive, macromolecules, aeons ago, invented this intention and this purpose. A sort of meaning came into existence, macromolecule-engendered meaning. It is not, of course, uniquely human intent, nor meaning, but belongs to everything that lives and even to some that do not. It is the unique human intent or purpose that we humans venerate, as if we think we deserve a special version just for us. What ingratitude and arrogance that is!

Yet the brain has its own ways of making purpose and intent. We do have a second bite at the cherry. In fact many bites, in that the brain is endlessly manufacturing intent. The brain that owns me, for example, is almost like a super-sized, mega-mega-molecule, self-replicating and intelligently designing the memes that will dazzle me and make me feel special and grateful to be its parasite. It is a surprise, then, to discover that I am full of meaning and purpose after all.

It is the wrong kind for many people, it seems. What do they want? Miracles? Perhaps. But they, the miracles, are what we already have. Algorithmic miracles, processes and designs arising from nothing, have been on earth for billions of years. Why isn't that enough to satisfy the collective human ego? In my own case, as bad as that of anyone else, I grew up with the notion of specialness, requiring a specific purpose and meaning in life. That would have been all right had I not, at least unconsciously, nurtured the feeling that I somehow deserved these things as gifts from above somewhere. Well, it now seems to me that they were there all the time and that I just failed to recognise them.

The Two-Edged Miracle

The problem is that, as a servant of the magnificent brain, each human being simultaneously aggrandises and underestimates the algorithms that determine ideas and behaviour. The 'books of instructions' are there, in the glove-compartment of the phenotype vehicle, i.e. mind and memory, and no-one understands quite how they have got there. This stage of my fifth revelation has revealed a lot to me that I didn't know before, which is both interesting and exciting. The next stage is beginning to appear. It seems to be that new appreciation is needed of what is called perfectionism or its lowly relative optimisation.

Somewhere in our nest of algorithms we each nurture a concept of excellence, in ourselves or in our life, or both. We strive for that excellence or we sink into despair if it fails to materialise. The specific instruction seems to be that there is a pot of gold at the end of the rainbow if only we have the wit or luck to discover it in reality. The ego is the horseman that rides this unicorn. I now understand that macromolecules were acting under a similar biochemical mandate billions of years ago. And they still do, witness the resourcefulness of bacteria outmanoeuvring the antibiotics and their sheer dominance of the environment:

One of the most famous of these living macromolecules, *E. coli*, is often referred to as 'the *best* (my italics) or most-studied free-living organism', which is a flagrant example of skewed rainbow- thinking. More prosaically, *'Escherichia coli (abbreviated as E. coli) are bacteria found in the environment, foods, and intestines of people and animals. E. coli are a large and diverse group of bacteria. Although most strains of E. coli are harmless, others can make you sick. Some kinds of E. coli can cause diarrhoea, while others cause urinary tract infections, respiratory illness and pneumonia, and other illnesses.'*

No question, then, that such organisms are excellently successful at what they do, and this is why the word 'best' is carelessly applied to outstanding examples. Exactly the same might be said of Homo sapiens, if we didn't know better. It might be more accurate to say something such as: *Homo sapiens* and *Escherichia coli* are examples of extremely prevalent organisms, which in some ways are the best that evolution has contrived, and in other ways, the worst, depending on the viewpoint.

Adaptationism

This is a good example of rainbow-thinking. In my book, 'Creatures of Power' (2013) p.27, I made the following statement:

'Hence the minefield of ideas concerning the evolutionary effect of genes and phenes. Is it just a layman's error to assume that it is the organism, the container of the genome, that is running the show? And has it been transmuted into a scientific "conceit" called adaptationism. This may be described as a concept of evolution that assumes without further proof that all aspects of the morphology, physiology and behaviour of organisms are necessarily the best possible. In other words, they are optimal results. The idea here is that it is theoretically

impossible to do a better job than an organism is itself doing in its own environment. But plants and animals, as a practical fact, are not necessarily optimal. Nor do they always protect their own interests, as we would expect of an optimal phenotype. Witness the birds that succumb to the cuckoo's devious practice.

While not trying to negate the idea of perfection by evolution, the devil may be in the detail if it shows that optimisation often fails to occur. In layman's terms, it would show how the 'work of nature' can be a 'cowboy job'. It could also be an explicit and persuasive demolition of any idea of benign 'mother nature' or, even more, of a 'benign deity.'

If I had written that today, I think I would actually have said that the 'idea of perfection by evolution' was wrong. I now accept that evolution is not a progressive process, but merely a change process. On the other hand, while I previously subscribed to the orthodoxy that evolution was purposeless, I now concede that it has purpose and meaning in a limited and rather mechanical sense. This is the two-edged miracle built in to the evolutionary algorithms.

What is the 'purpose and meaning' in evolution, however limited compared with our grandiose (or outraged, creationist,) view of it? There is the individual, personal, will to achieve, gallantly, often absurdly, rainbow-shaped. Then there is the broad view, whereby humans see the process of evolution in supernatural terms, as if it is being guided to do something wonderful. The guide, in their imagination, may be 'god' or 'cosmic intent' or the 'thrust of consciousness', and we have difficulty in accepting that the whole thing is just a chance process. But what is it actually?

Fortuna

(From Wikipedia): *Fortūna (Greek, Tyche) was the goddess of fortune and personification of luck in Roman religion. She might bring good luck or bad: she could be represented as veiled and blind, as in modern depictions of Justice, and came to represent life's capriciousness. She was also a goddess of fate: as Atrox Fortuna, she claimed the young lives of the princeps Augustus' grandsons Gaius and Lucius, prospective heirs to the Empire.*

Again quoting from my 'Creatures of Power' (p.172), a few words about 'chance':

With Fortuna/Tyche, what you got was the luck of the draw. Now that is definitely not a proper deity. You might as well say that it was all down to the vagaries of nature, indeed, that the goddess was nature. The wonderful Baruch Spinoza, the seventeenth century philosopher, created and continues to create controversy by his profound understanding that God and Nature were the same process. Fortuna/Tyche got there first.

Such a deity is obviously nothing of the sort. A real god is supposed to control things, is it not? What is the point in praying to something that hasn't any intention of listening, or if it does listen, it leaves everything to chance anyway. That's as bad has having a god that lets massive catastrophes happen and merely says 'whoops!' We wouldn't trust one of those, would we? (Even if we do.)

Evolution is an algorithmic process replete with unlimited gambling possibilities. It is almost a gambler's charter. It is also ruthless. And it is conservative. These paradoxical instructions make evolution the most powerful imaginable manifestation of change as a process. The human brain, and its vehicle, have no choice but to obey this complex algorithm. It is necessary to reiterate that algorithm, in this context, is a body of instructions (itself originating by chance, from an ancient, more primary algorithm than itself) that controls the machinery of the human brain - and, therefore everything we do and everything we are.

The Romans were no more fools than we or anybody else: they got the measure of chance, even if they were rather muddle-headed about its supernatural guise. The words are important, in that they define, by a mysterious implication, who and what we are. If I say humankind is the product of a chance algorithm in the universe or solar system, people may disagree but perhaps not too angrily. If I say humankind is a cosmic accident, the hackles may be raised. But why would anyone, brain or vehicle, be so disturbed by knowing they were accidents? Millions of people alive today must be actual biological accidents if only in the sense that they originated from a random sexual encounter, or a failure of contraception. I know people who feel blighted by being told that they were an 'accident'. Well, it might help them, at least, to realise that all people, all creatures, everything living, are also accidents. So, what is wrong with an accident per se? Surely it must be the result of the accident that matters; and that can be good or bad, depending on the operative value-system.

The Meme-Machine

This is the 'operative value-system', as I have dubbed it. The human brain makes memes, from prototypic ideas, which it has all the time. Everything in our world is a brain-product, in the sense that what we perceive as our world (or universe) is a narrative supplied by the brain. That is how I have become obliged to see it, largely because of the biological and neurological and cognitive 'evidence' I have learned from the narratives I find most persuasive.

Yet, as this 'fifth revelation' of mine unfolds, my uncertainty burgeons. And my uncertainty is at a maximum in regard to 'intent'. Which is what this chapter is trying to be about. What a word it is. What do I mean by intent? What do I intend to convey by the word? How is intent different from intention, for example? I suppose intention means a general frame of mind compared with intent as a specific, focused, goal. But how is it that a brain-narrative, a meme in the making, say, becomes something like a purpose or a goal. What is the 'drive' in this and how does it arise?

I have said that intent/intention is basic in all organisms, in that they all intend to live (except for humans who are heroes and martyrs and suicides, which is a whole other nest of intentions). So intent is written in to the algorithm of life. As it was, apparently, written into the algorithm of not-yet-alive molecules. And, interesting thought, maybe still is.

Does that mean that the universe is also characterised by intent, and if not, why not? Has it an intent, perhaps, to exist and grow and replicate? Is this the fundamental universal algorithm? How could it be otherwise? What, then, is the difference between this fundamental universal algorithm and the alleged author of the universe, a being, a *personified* algorithm, 'God'?

If they are the same thing, all we need to do is to reframe the concept 'God' and maybe we will get a truth from that. Let's examine the phrase 'personified algorithm', and see where this meme takes us. First, does it make any sense to describe an algorithm as 'personified'? On the face of it, this is quite nonsensical - maybe the whole trouble with religion, in fact. Or is it a disease of the meme-system? A disease of meaning, in effect?

A disease of meaning it probably is, in the way that muddled language falsifies existence. I, Michael, the author of this book, behave as though I am a personified (or personalised?) algorithm, i.e., like most people, I behave as though I am lord of my microscopic universe. And that is the way we seem to regard 'God', or any other supernatural myth, in terms of the universe writ large; whereas I, and we, are algorithmic narratives made by our brains.

It looks increasingly to me that the whole intention-debate is a product of muddled language, in turn a product of misinterpreted brain-narrative. What humans want is to be certain that they are intended denizens of earth, and that they have a divinely inspired purpose. There is no possibility of this certainty existing, except in imagination. In the limited sense of macromolecular algorithmic information systems, of course we are intended and purposeful, as much as any mosquito or earthworm or maple tree. In that limited sense, of course the universe is characterised by intent and purpose. But it's no big deal. It just happens to be that way through cosmic algorithms or some such device which you can call 'God' if you want to, as the Romans called chance by the name of a Goddess, Fortuna.

Whatever name we decide to apply to whatever process or narrative, the essential mystery remains unassailed. The human parasite, the self or person, following the neural information flow of its indifferent but controlling brain, is no better off for this semantic conceit. We are half-finished animals of unusual intelligence who have absolutely no idea what we are doing on earth and, worse, we have unlimited freedom to behave badly. Even our good behaviour is ambivalent in its nature, as we have no certainty who really benefits. Therefore, my Fifth Revelation takes another leap into unexpected territory: as we probably don't, as a species, count for much (being less successful than a bacterium such as E.coli and more nuisance to the biosphere than most other big mammals) we could do worse than make a gigantic reappraisal of what we do individually and collectively.

I know that my books show that I have been in this mind-set before, and already, and that there is a numberless throng of my fellow-humans who are similarly troubled. But what is actually going to happen to us? Do we really realise that we are seriously liable to become extinct? If this is so, what price all the talk and thought about the cosmic or the personal intent that has so laboriously been created since the half-alive macromolecules? In other words, are we not fouling up the modest intent and purpose that the macromolecules have conferred upon us? Further, much as we may love our babel of memes, do not they require a complete overhaul before anything can be done about our behaviour and therefore our destiny?

The Imperfection of Practice

We are not very good at being living organisms, as you can tell by comparing us with any other wild animal, ape, mammal, lizard, fish. A case could be made for saying we are the worst organism on the planet in terms of muddling up our intent and our purpose and how we enact them. It almost appears that this truly wonderful intelligence of ours, (of our brains, anyway,) is a curse amounting to a disease of existence, not just of meaning. Maybe it is 'actually', not 'almost', looking at the mess we are creating around us.

Another viewpoint could be that it doesn't matter because the universal intent-algorithm will go on its way undisturbed by our failure. We may be absolutely free to do our worst. What does the wonder-brain say about that? I am asking mine, or any other one, to answer that question. I ask it as if it were a directionless prayer. I ask:

'What, O brain, would be the appropriate narrative for this lack of cosmic grace in your beloved parasite, me?'

Squadrons of memes advance like the armies in 'Lord of the Rings': the brain is Gandalf, I am Frodo. Or maybe it is the absurd adventure of Alexander the Great or the solipsistic maniac Genghis Khan pointlessly conquering 12 million square miles of territory. And I am one of a billion Adams who believe that the universe exists for us to appropriate it into our knowledge-bank. The brain overwhelms its vehicle, a giant riding on a mule. Or maybe it is Rocinante, the willing, faithful, worn-out nag bearing the burden called Don Quixote.

How could the brain answer a question that cannot exist? There is no appropriate narrative. Every narrative is possible except this one. Why? Because the brain cannot parse 'cosmic grace'. Nor can the human self comprehend it, however much it rants on about it. What is there to understand about the super-meme, Cosmic Grace? Does it even exist, as so many human creatures seem to suppose? The brain considers: can something possibly exist even though it cannot be parsed? That seems a more interesting and even possibly answerable question, it seems to say.

Yes: Cosmic Grace could be parsed providing you know the algorithm for it. Yes: you do have to know the set of instructions for making Cosmic Grace. Then it would be easy to parse it. You could start by parsing the two parts separately, as there are probably two sets of separate algorithms involved. But it is the brain (or brains) that should do it, complains the human self. But the brain never parses itself, obviously. How could it? 'You', i.e. the human self, have to do this without recourse to your master's machinery. 'But I only exist as a by-product of the brain, apparently', protests the disempowered self.

The brain is playing games. I, its parasite, know what it's up to: it loves to be clever, its great weakness. It will eventually become more interested in the problem than in merely gazing at itself in the electronic mirror. Then we may learn something. Maybe.

The Intention Algorithm

There must have been this, or many of them, when the world began. Otherwise Nothing would have remained in control. The almighty Nothing was overbalanced into an almighty Something. It must have happened quite often to get life going as well. All this is pretty obvious, says brain (and therefore me too). For practical purposes, brain says, Cosmic Grace is just a fancy way of saying Intention Algorithm, so we will stay with that. (In any case, it says, 'grace' is a meme made almost useless by its semantic vagueness, though cosmic is reasonably precise.)

So, this intention algorithm so-called. The big difficulty is resolving the question of whether 'intent' can ever be a real thing. As everything is in the brain, that is where intent must be along with everything else. Being scrupulous, my brain asserts that as 'intent' is a product of its machinery, as is the complementary phenomenon of 'cause' we are back in Snark-territory. How gracious of brain it is to admit this. So the questions of intent or (prime) cause are mere narratives, or ideas, or memes, fabricated by porridge in the skull? This means that the universe was not necessarily 'caused' at all and has no purpose whatsoever? The 'Big Bang' is a fiction because there's no certainty that the universe actually started and that 'cause and effect' is just one more meme and a fatuous one at that?

This is revolutionary: a brain admits there is no basis for any of its narratives and that means that the apparent somethings all around us are at least illusions if not outright delusions. After all, we do know for sure that algorithms are just chunks of information, self-made instructions, so anything goes, or not, as the case may be. Also, if meaning means anything, this revolutionary admission makes almost all living processes, including human ones, entirely suspect. They have no basis in the meme called 'fact'. What a relief, I hear myself think. Yet I know it's not that easy. If only because the brain and its products do actually exist (a modified Cartesian certainty) there is most evidently actually something in existence. The question is, what is it?

Generally speaking, human brains seem to latch on to the idea of existence in its peculiarly human form and adorn this with ideas of god, essence, void, and many other narratives or memes. It seems to be genuinely experiential, but that proves nothing except that the human brain has the experiences. Is that enough for us? Do we really need to know whether there's actually anything in the ideas, anything *valid* or *real*? The brain of Martin Heidegger, for example, seems to have had no doubt as to the reality of its narratives, like those of so many philosophers, prelates and even scientists. The Heidegger brain speaks for the human masses when he says, 'Dasein', the meme meaning all sorts of things but prominently such states as 'being there' or 'presence', though it could mean just 'existence'. Does it differ from the brain narrative of A.H.Almaas or the Dalai Lama or any humanist psychologist? This particular lingua franca runs as follows:

Dasein refers to the experience of being that is peculiar to human beings. Thus it is a form of being that is aware of and must confront such issues as personhood, mortality and the dilemma or paradox of living in relationship with other humans while being ultimately alone with oneself.

Is this anything more than poetic metaphor purporting to be somehow real without any evidence except that the Heidegger-type brain manufactured it as a narrative? Most important, does it matter? Should I, the parasite of Michael's brain, care whether there is an actual intent concerning human existence? Can I not be satisfied with a vague universal intent to exist? Can I live happily within the fact that there is no Cosmic Grace to make my life glorious? Or, more practically, can I live a civilised life knowing that the intention to do so is entirely the product of my brain engineering?

The New Autonomy

Put it this way: my brain is in charge of me and everything I think I experience. There's no particular reason to suppose this is not true. How do I, the parasite of my brain, feel about it? The answer is that I feel really good about it. In a new sense, I am all of a piece: I am actually whole. The Fifth Revelation may be just this, the climax of the experience so far. It concatenates exquisitely with Revelations Three and Four, making a neat series, I am relieved to note. In fact, I am back on track, after a long detour. Here's the chain of three:

Revelation 3. I saw that I was being absurd to be so angry about the botches of nature (evolution) including the crazy experiment of the human mind (brain). Nature is after all just a mass of blind intentions and countless failures as well as 'successes'.

Revelation 4. My own errors, my personal crazy experiment and blind intents (memes) yet why not credit me 'self' with some successes and be happy to have had so many failures, just like nature everywhere.

Revelation 5 (so far). My brain and I (its parasitic narrative) are all of a piece and we owe nothing to anyone or anything. Our wholeness is written in to the algorithms that begat us. The macromolecules, a million years ago, kicked in the processes that made us. We now create our own meaning and purpose, this brain and I, according to our developing brain narratives. What could be better?

Chapter Twelve
The Riddle of Meaning

LOVE: what else?

Looking for meaning as something inherent on the universe is a mug's game, by which I mean that it is a very poor gamble indeed. Purpose does exist, or intention, because evidently the human brain, as a mirror mechanism of the universe, is purposefully busy on its narratives and memes. And those macromolecules were driven by a need to develop just as unicellular organisms needed to survive, an intention handed down to multicellular organisms. So, yes, we are pulsing with intent and purpose. But *meaning*, what I suspect most human beings yearn for, is an elusive idea even before considering whether it does, or should, exist.

Ordinary meaning is obvious, mundane and undeniable. This sort of meaning is virtually identical with intent. It is common-or-garden desire or need. It says 'I want' or I 'matter'. No argument here, it is just an expression of human ego or ambition. Ordinary meaning is also semantic, in the context of asking for clarification. Or explanation, as in, 'What is the meaning of this?' asked as an aggressive question.

Extraordinary meaning enters in when we ask 'What is the meaning of life?' As if it were obvious that there should be one, a meaning of life, that is. I contend that it is not obvious. Once again,

I quote Dennett on the subject:

'Real meaning, the sort of meaning our words and ideas have, is itself an emergent product of originally meaningless products - the algorithmic processes that have created the entire biosphere, ourselves included. A robot designed as a survival machine for you would, like you, owe its existence to a product of R and D with other ulterior ends, but this would not prevent it from being an autonomous creator of meanings, in the fullest sense.' (p. 427, 'Darwin's Dangerous Idea')

Instead of the word 'meaning', with its inherent ambivalence (i.e. not being able to decide between 'cosmically given' and 'man-made'), I would prefer a word that elevates intent to a truly aspirational level. That word is 'love'.

I will open up the subject of love by quoting from the end of my first novel, 'The Halcyon's Nest'. In this excerpt, the two young men, Ossian and Ariel, are struggling to find a way of repairing and developing their relationship:

'Ariel had gripped Ossian's wrist with surprising strength. He peered hard into Ossian's face, as if trying to read a response. Ossian's stockade seemed to close in around him. He suffered a mixture of alarm and embarrassment. But he was also ashamed. He knew that Ariel was right. There could be no doubt whatsoever that nothing else mattered so much as this, this human connection. But his wall was holding him in. He wanted to get outside it. But how? It had been there a long time, and had served him well in adversity. It was a good wall, doing its best to protect him. He could not simply dismantle it.

'Ariel, I must tell you something awful. I'm sorry, but I think I am locked in a prison of safety. I am afraid of you. I am afraid of loving you at the human level. I am afraid of losing my immunity.'

'Oh, yes, of course!' shouted Ariel delightedly, 'absolutely right! Me too. You are the Other, aren't you, and you cannot be trusted. Of

MICHAEL SCOTT

course. Ergo: you are really an enemy. How could I love my enemy, the terrible Other? But it is not just an external relationship, even though it's with an apparent outsider. Isn't it also an internal journey into self-forgiveness? Even more so, isn't it a life and death struggle with one's own ego? Is it something we could do? Are we going to try? Are we, Ossian?' (The Halcyon's Nest. 1998. p. 397.)

I am surprised to see that I wrote this nearly twenty years ago. I am a slow learner. I knew the truth then but I am still trying to live it. At least I am really trying now, instead of merely knowing it, a useless position. Love is probably both an algorithm and a meme, which is consonant with its enormous power. Love also contains its opposite, hate, otherwise the algorithmic and the memetic qualities would be incomplete. The words, love and hate, are grotesquely inaccurate simplifications, but to have a complete set of instructions and a universal meme, there must be a comprehensive applicability of each. This is one way in which we fail to follow either algorithm or meme, i.e. we expect to swamp the reality with our own simplistic fantasy. Thus, the Buddhist 'poison', hate, is set against its opposite, love, but the assumption is that love can somehow overcome hate. This would require a distinct algorithm or meme usable to destroy part of the basic love/hate unity. That's not impossibly, I suppose, but it is very confusing. It's rather like the absurdity of pulling oneself erect by one's shoelaces.

As they are professed experts, how do Buddhists deal with the inherent ambivalence of the love/hate algorithm? (Or how do Christians, for that matter.) I found something on the internet that seems to clarify the Buddhist approach:

The definition of love in Buddhism is: wanting others to be happy. This love is unconditional and it requires a lot of courage and acceptance (including self-acceptance). The "near enemy" of love, or a quality which appears similar, but is more an opposite, is conditional love (selfish love, attachment).

The opposite is wanting others to be unhappy: anger, hatred. A result which one needs to avoid is: attachment. This definition means that 'love' in Buddhism refers to something quite different from the ordinary term of love which is usually about attachment, more or less successful relationships and sex; all of which are rarely without self-interest. Instead, in Buddhism it refers to de-tachment and the unselfish interest in others' welfare.

I think this is a very rational concept. I also think it is mistaken. Remaining un-attached, which is a major mindset in Buddhism, is a very self-protective device. Theoretically, the love is pure and without strings, but where is intimacy, the ideal of being connected? It is also hard to understand the emotional content of 'unselfish interest' in the 'welfare of others'. I can see where these impulses come from, but I wonder if there is too much aloofness in the posture. The intended result is perfect, of course, in that it is aiming to put others in a benign state of being. But is the human brain, and its parasite, really able to be so magisterially unsullied? Aren't each of us complex 'narratives', which resemble the apocryphal 'cartload of monkeys'? Could we really be so morally tidy as to love in the Buddhist manner? Isn't there a risk here of treading the 'road of good intentions' and finding oneself in an icy hell?

So, what has Christianity to say about this? Another strand of the internet offers an answer:

The Greek language (the language of the New Testament) uses two different words to describe and define love. The most commonly used Greek word translated "love" in the New Testament is "agape." This love is represented by God's love for us. It is a non-partial, sacrificial love probably best exemplified by God's provision for our rebellion: "For God so loved (agape) the world, that He gave His only begotten Son, that whoever believes in Him should not perish, but have eternal life." The gift of God's son as a provision for sin was given to all humans, regardless of who we are. God's love is unconditional.

In contrast, our love is usually conditional and based upon how other people behave toward us. This kind of love is based upon familiarity and direct interaction. The Greek word "phileo" defines this kind of love, often translated "brotherly love." Phileo is a soulish (connected through our emotions) kind of love - something that can be experienced by both believers and non-believers. This is in contrast to agape, which is love extended through the spirit. Agape love requires a relationship with God through Jesus Christ, since the non-regenerated soul is unable to love unconditionally. Agape love gives and sacrifices expecting nothing back in return.

Whatever else it may be, this Christian love is certainly not unconditional: you have to believe in 'God' and 'Jesus Christ' to 'get it', even if the unfortunate Jesus did die to save each of us regardless of what and who we are, thereby giving the impression of unconditionality. The so-called agape love is, apparently, conditional on having a 'relationship with God . . .' which also makes nonsense of the claimed unconditional nature of the love. That's not to say that Christian love lacks certain merits. There certainly seems more 'passion' in it than in Buddhism. It feels warmer. But it does also have some barbed psychological and emotional hooks. The theism unavoidably makes it a private club rather than an advanced meme.

As for Islam, the following shows a range of comments on the internet concerning love and this religion:

1. No religion urges its followers to adopt mutual love, affection and intimacy like the religion of Islam. This should be the case at all times, not just on specific days. Islam encourages showing affection and love towards each other all the time.

2. Dear brothers and sisters, the guidance of Islam is the guidance of love. The innate, natural and ancient religion that is Islam is the religion of love. The Prophet came to guide us to love and to make clear the love that is at the core of all religion. Our purpose as human beings is to consciously manifest Allah's love in our lives.

3.   Muslim scholars who talk about love as the heart of Islam and of religion generally take the position that God's love and compassion motivated him to create human beings so that they could love him in return. The goal of creation is to bring lovers into existence, and the goal of lovers - that is, you, me and everyone else - is to escape false loves and return to what we really love. This, for them, is the key message of the Quran, "the story of love and lovers."

4.   We believe that Islam is the origin of true love in all its dimensions (top-down, bottom-up, and horizontal) and forms, quite independent of any other faith, except inasmuch as both come from the same source, as established by historians. Many Quranic texts and Prophetic hadiths undeniably prove the fact that love, in the broadest sense, is an intrinsic ideal of Islam.

Although Islam has many unique features, it does tend to fit into the Abrahamic mode. There is the same idolising of a creator-being who is thought to originate everything, including, love, and require unconditional devotion from humankind. As with Christianity, there is an overpowering sense of absolute certainty and a great deal of aggression towards 'non-believers'. Consequently there is a recurrent risk of hatred being generated and enacted where threats to the religion are perceived. The Crusades are still with us, one way or another.

I am also bothered by the obsession with rules in all the Abrahamic faiths, as well as the draconian reprisals against rule-breakers. Is this remotely characteristic of real love?

To round this off, what would Atheism know of love? Assorted internet comments again as follows:

(I have given this greater space than the religions because these opinions show an attempt to comprehend rather than merely espouse doctrines.)

1.   *Recently, I've discussed the topic of love with a few atheist friends. All of them claim to discredit a God because religion is based on 'experiences' which can be rationalized with biological processes. However, I am perplexed as to why they, as atheists, don't believe in a God (and regard him as just a series of experiences with no concrete evidence); yet they do believe in love, which is also really just a series of experiences with no convincing scientific/physical evidence. How does love fit into atheism? Why is lack of evidence sufficient to discredit a God, but not adequate to discredit love?*

2.   *Love can't be precisely measured or even precisely defined, but it's still a very real emotion. Just as it is possible to love someone/ something that doesn't exist, it's also possible to have a real belief in something that doesn't exist. For instance, we still feel love for others who have died. The target of our affection no longer exists, but our feelings for them are still there and still real. Taking it one step further, it's possible for someone to love a fictional character, to feel a great deal of affection for them, even though they never existed. The character was never real, but their love for them is. That love doesn't prove the character exists. If someone believes in a fictional character and loves them their belief is a very real (although unquantifiable) thing. It doesn't prove that the character exists, though.*

3.   *Love is an abstraction, a label that we put on a set of emotions or frame of mind. It doesn't have physical existence. When somebody says, 'I'm in love with you', they aren't speaking of the existence of a physical thing, they are speaking of their internal state of mind – it's shorthand. So, if you want to equate god to a feeling that has no physical manifestation, I'm fine with that.*

4.   *God is usually defined as some sort of intelligent being existing*

independent of humanity. God is not a series of experiences. Belief in god is a series of experiences, but the object of that belief is not the experience of believing. The key issue is that love is a feeling whereas god is not. To prove that love exists, all you have to do is find a single loving person. Defining love is tricky, but once you have some sense of what it might be, your job is easy. Defining god is also tricky, but finding a believer doesn't prove that god exists, merely that faith exists.

5.   Extraordinary evidence for extraordinary claims is the name of the game. Though I accept the existence of love as an emotion (along with all the others: hate, anger, envy, jealousy, lust, fear, greed, etc.), I do not accept any emotion as being a force that can magically effect change by its very existence (certainly emotions can indirectly influence events). In order for me to accept that form of love, I would need extraordinary evidence. In addition, the expression of emotions, a very interesting topic indeed, varies from culture to culture (sort of like religious beliefs, whose existence I also accept though not recognizing in themselves as being reflective of truthful reality). Some cultures emphasize responsibility as a major proponent of love. Others, emphasize the romantic aspects of love. Despite these differences, we are still dealing with a real emotion – no matter how subjective – an emergent property stemming from our nervous system. And though we can be sure of our own emotions (if we do not repress them that is), we can be terribly wrong regarding the emotions of others.

These Atheistic observations are particularly interesting because they show the human brain actually making narratives 'on the hoof' rather than merely parroting received opinion. This doesn't make them 'right', or true, of course. Indeed, there is little attempt to go deeply into the nature of love in the way I want to do it, i.e. as the only worthwhile form of meaning. This aspirational intent, as I have called it, does, in fact, figure in the Buddhist and Abrahamic religions, though without any serious analysis or inspiration. 'Love' in these religions, tends to be a mantra rather than an expression of inspired intent. Love should be given greater status than being merely a buzz-word. Where can we look for evidence of this kind of love in practice?

In the last Atheist quote it is stated:

'I do not accept any emotion as being a force that can magically effect change by its very existence...'

This is an important standpoint, because it dismisses the human brain as a true inventor of algorithms and memes (I consider emotions to be part of the brain's creative activity).

The Love Meme

You can say that love is an instinctual emotion, an evolutionary step whereby civilisation was made possible. I could say that - in fact, I think I do. It is evident from the behaviour of female mammals towards their young, for instance, and that is an obvious adaptation that favours survival. Love, of a kind, can be observed between animal siblings, and even unrelated species. But the main power of love for humankind is in its function as an algorithm or meme, an ideal brain narrative. The main interest, for me, is how weak it is in practice as a positive force in facilitating human happiness, especially good human behaviour. We manage love as badly as we manage all our less important talents and vices. Love is the one we can't afford to mess up. This meme needs to be redesigned.

If love, in its many forms, were removed from the human behavioural range, what would be left? Is it not obvious that human behaviour would be competitive, aggressive, and selfish without the slightest relief, in effect, civilisation would be impossible? Our existence, regardless of our intelligence and inventiveness, would be brutally savage. As it often is, anyway. In such an existence it would be absurd to even consider the ideal of 'meaning', unless that definition was concerned only with winning and destroying. It is this sense that love is the basis of meaning, because it makes possible the building of co-operative relationship, in effect a connected community.

How, then, could the human brain transform the existing situation, had it the mind to do so?

An Epicurean Solution

As far as we can tell from so long past, especially as his works were almost wiped out by the Christian censors, Epicurus was the slave of a brain that had mainly the right ideas for our times as well as his own. As far as I can tell from the pitiful remnants of his vast written output, Epicurus distinguished between love and friendship, so that two millennia ago he was chary about sexual love and enthusiastic about friendship. It is a key feature of his narratives, his brain-made memes, that friendship was the best route to happiness. This gives a clue as to what we need to do to reorientate ourselves to make love the global force it should be.

The fact is that 'love' has been debased in many aspects of our lives by being equated to erotic passion or romantic attachment. It has also been put to extraordinary use by being applied to 'King and Country', or to sport and luxury and consumerism. Hence we 'love' a wide range of things and actions that are far removed from the ideal as I see it. Unfortunately it is not clear to me that any other word will do. 'Friendship' is not a powerful word, and it also suffers from the same looseness and varying range of definition as 'love'.

Maybe the words matter less than the chaos of the emotions and actions that they label. In terms of meaning, the word love, and its weak sibling, friendship, are as meretricious as they are all-embracing. We behave as though we believe that the ingredients of love do actually bring meaning into our lives. I have no doubt that is true. But the quality of the meaning is very often as poor as the poorest actions of love. Epicurus tried to solve the complex problem by creating a state of being in which friendship and close collaboration prevailed, where his friends were self-sufficient rather that employees, and where communal living in peace and tranquillity was achieved. His methodology still finds expression in our culture, but only as a minor sideline to the miserable orthodoxy that runs our lives. This orthodoxy is rarely questioned directly, as if it is accepted that it is basically good, while there is endless complaint about the actual elements in our lives - which are blamed on scapegoats such as the casuistic politicians, the 'Powers that Be', and random acts of stupidity, violence, or avarice. We are consumed by hope, despair, neediness, jealousy, and insecurity. We are falsely comforted or exhorted by the religious authorities, where 'love' is a mantra-word without much substance.

As against all that, there are magnificent attempts to put love/ friendship into practice. I need only mention the NHS to make the point that we are capable of a high degree of caring, even if it is often undermined by bad judgement or personal failure of medical workers. We try to teach our young, with something approaching love/friendship, but it is a mixed performance. We do try to make life meaningful in a patchy way. The trouble is that there is so much in our world that points entirely in the opposite direction. It seems unavoidable that the most appalling behaviour goes under the pseudonym of 'love', some people love to fight, to compete, to abuse the young (and the old), to steal, to bully, even to kill, and especially to make a fetish out of food and sexuality. No wonder we are a confused culture as far as love and meaning are concerned. What are our brains up to? Why do they initiate so many awful memes? What is the meaning of these outrages?

Editing The Memes

If Dennett (and the large amount of work he describes) is right, the fault lies in the basic information system operating in our inherited algorithms (and the ones constantly being formulated as memes). In a sense, we can't help being as we are: the programmes direct us. Yet these directives have come out of the brains occupying our skulls. They are partly the result of genetic evolution and partly the outcome of recent human brain development - the sheer size of the this brain enabling it to carry out extraordinary electronic invention.

It would be nice to think that our brains could sharpen up their act positively and make our memes globally meaningful and happiness-promoting. Why not, one might ask? After all, they made the world as it is, they could unmake and remake it, surely? Well, I am afraid that the biological imperatives make that unlikely if only because, despite memes, that every man is, to a degree, an island. More hopefully, there is some chance of individual people, or small groups, editing the memes controlling their lives.

Even that minimal amount of re-creating meaning has enormous obstacles. We, as individuals, claim authority for a miscellaneous collection of beliefs and actions. To edit our individual, or locally collective, meme system would entail a drastic sceptical approach to everything we hold dear as well as everything we don't. There's a wide range of intensively held ideas and standards, if only at the 'intuitive' or 'gut' or 'heart' level. Some things are so firmly embedded that there must be doubt as to whether they could ever be changed. Yet everything would need to be open to change. Could any of us do that? The best I can do is to describe one or two of my own efforts in that direction, which is why, I now realise, The Fifth Revelation ever got started. I will try to tell this narrative in the next chapter. It depends, of course, on whether 'my' brain is inclined to follow such a process. I can only ask it.

Chapter Thirteen
Edit Your Memes

Meaning of Love
This is a top priority. In examining the possibility of changing the meme that connects love and meaning, I will ask my consciousness to become aware of the global disaster that needs to be put right, if only in my own tiny backyard. So forgive me if my brain spills many beans. I hope it does. I have nothing to lose except my life and reputation, both of little worth.

My Little Grey Home in the West
If my family were not my friends, as I asserted in the first revelation (see Introduction), they were nevertheless the first people with whom I, as an infant, experienced love. As I also implied that, despite the vicissitudes of the relationship between us, I loved them till they died and I love them in memory still. But how much better could it have been for me and for them? The family is probably the principal love opportunity for most human beings and, therefore, it is where I would like to concentrate and try to see how a new conception of love might be forged in the smithy of home.

I am not sure how my magisterially neutral brain will turn this into a useful narrative for me, its slave/parasite. But I think it may be interested. It must be super-aware of the existence of the memes of love, indeed, it and its fellow billions of human brains, generated the very idea of love from its biological and genetic roots.

For my personal viewpoint, I must admit to a fragmentary recollection of love in my family. In this I am dangerously weak as a guide, but I certainly have very strong emotional memories however poor the historical detail. Overall, I feel that our family love was a long way short of ideal and of its optimal potential. Even the word, in any of its miscellany of meanings, rarely cropped up in our minimal conversations. It seemed as if none of us were very interested in love compared with other concerns, where finance, power, resentment, competitiveness and pride seemed paramount. And this was a family of the working-class, in which mere survival was a major issue. Love seemed a minor luxury and it, as a living meme, struggled to exist in our midst or our minds, as I recall the bleak atmosphere of our little grey home (provided by the council for a back-breaking rent).

I think I can remember a time when my father seemed to love me. I am not sure whether the duration of that love extended beyond my 9th or 10th year. I don't remember any physical or verbal expression of love even before then. On the other hand I was still unafraid of him at that stage, though fear became dominant soon after, until I disliked and distrusted him. How did love between this father and this son fail to thrive? And was it unusual? Judging by the work of Robert Bly (of 'Iron John' fame) men generally carry significant emotional and psychological wounds inflicted on them by their fathers. Asked what kind of room their fathers inhabited in their minds, Bly reported that the general view was a 'rat-infested attic'.

So, as advised by Bly, I put it to the personal test and, in consequence, conceived the kind of space I would like my father to occupy in my psyche. The result was very positive: what follows is a section of the poem I wrote to celebrate my father's relocation:

My father's house is also big enough for me and all my loves,
My gods and heroes, my fears and dreams. Now I belong
In the house of my father and my fathers and my ancient kings.

I take my leave of the lonely place I made for my orphan self
A bunker in the desert where I have grown old. I walk the long trail
To my father's house; full of music; old, old songs; love
Has been looking for its home for years as long as centuries:
I least expected it might rest within my father's bony arms

And from the safety of their strange embrace I look out again
At a world transformed by an unexpected vantage-point:
I see the one that battled fatherless against the fathers,
That raged kingless against the kings, godless against the gods
And needed too needily the sweet and bitter solace of women.
That poor man had lost his father - mislaid him, rather,
Put him beyond reach for failing to live up to presumptive glory.
Two poor men were now one, living tidily in my father's house.

We are orderly, the rooms are carefully arranged, neat
We are nervous of chaos, fearful of failure, we arrange
Ourselves in our house to keep alien forces away, tomorrow
Makes us anxious; we try to prepare, set ourselves up for it.
Morning comes, we meet in our great kitchen: eggs and bacon,
Toast, coffee, and imaginary cigarette. What shall we do today?
There's nothing to be done. In the new house of my father
We look out at the garden and decide to take each other for a stroll.

The love-battle with my mother was of a different order. Her love
was strong, even sublime, but dictatorial. She consumed me. Yet she
could not enter my world as I grew up. I needed her there, but she
could not, or would not, adapt to any new need of mine. So we split
up, as it were, and I married someone of my own age and she was left
holding a dead bouquet. I was angry with her, too, I must confess.
My poems to her are not very lyrical. For example:

Having wept a sea of salt and vinegar, my heart sings
Her praises. My bird-mind cocks his eye at me and asks, 'What of it?'
That struggling, striving, often frantic hen fed my craw and cleaned my
    nest.

If I could stand separate from my pride, my cock's comb, a moment
I could see the bird-bright vigilance of her brooding care and find
Her flying soul alongside mine, as it always was and always will.
As any bird she could only do so much, no more, no less, before
Her body and her spirit perished, broken by the indifferent machinery
That snaps and tears its way towards me also and to everything and all
The others I love and live beside. So, true, my mother did have limitations.
Hard for chicken-child to bear: a chicken-mother's imperfection.
Chicken-child is perfect - or rather might be - but for chicken-mother's
*   faults?*
She had ten, or fifteen, years to make me wonderfully invulnerable, to
*   make*
Of me a shining glory? This, I think, she tried to do: fortunately failed.
Fail she might, try she did, and how and who am I to ask
That it should have been otherwise? Why allow the backward glare
Of a fledged fool, seeing weary mother-bird culpable to infinity or more?
Is any new chick free to expect everything, to make a future dossier of fault
To warm itself to its own triumphant dying crash? Let me say, then:
I want none of it. That bird-mother is secure and sitting on her perfect
*   nest.*

But the landscape became a surrogate love. I was quite barbaric
as a boy, but love-of-nature was asserting itself increasingly, if
erratically. I didn't paint then, but I have painted that love since I
left the place and grew up into stereotypical manhood. I think the
paintings speak:

Pictures of my youthful love, 1.

The Pond

Pictures of my youthful love, 2.

The Way To Cam Peak

Pictures of my youthful love, 3.

Downham: farm, trees and hill under snow.

These paintings are products of my middle age; I had not learnt how to paint when I was a boy (though I did try). So the landscape paintings of my youthful love are from memory or imagination. They are therefore suspect information, but they do carry the emotion that I still have for that early place and time.

There were very many other loves associated with my little grey home, but they are not typically associated with my father and mother. Nevertheless, these two people were overwhelming presences in my first twenty years. There is a gulf between their importance as presences and their power as sources or recipients of my love. I was very dutiful to them. For a time I idolised both of them, especially my mother. But the force and source of my love was generally not focused on them. I was aware of that at the time, I'm sure, but it is only since they have died and I have become old, that I experience a retrospective grief for the lack of a great loving relationship with them.

Perhaps the truth is that I was too young, then, to know what love was. Maybe my parents were remiss in not introducing me more formally, or more concretely, to this vast emotion. As it was, I am not sure I knew much about it. There were in me plenty of desires, wants and needs, and some compassion here and there, though not much. I think it has taken me a lifetime to know love as an experience. As I experience it now, anyway. And I wonder how much more I could have known about it with more help from my many mentors.

The crux is that I just don't know if it was sufficiently elaborated to me. The religious variety was stuffed into me strongly and I soon spat it out as it seemed nonsense. I wanted human love and still do. Perhaps the culture then was that you got love from the surplice-and-cassock brigade - that was their job. Parents and teachers were too busy with life-essentials to bother with tacky stuff like love. So all I got was crooners on the wireless, and what good was that?

My One True Love

Portrait of Eileen

Other Young Loves.
It is easy to underrate the love of young people for one another. Adults tend to patronise this as a passing enthusiasm or mere eroticism. Or a parent may try to frustrate, control or even exploit the youngsters' desires. When I was fifteen or sixteen I felt intense affection for two people of the same age, an affection I would call 'sexual' in the case of the girl, and 'devoted' for the boy. I am sure these adjectives are both inaccurate and inadequate labels for the love I felt for these two young people. Such intensity was a shock to my entire being. Though the love was reciprocated in kind, it was stressful in my experience for reasons that seem to me now to have been typical human muddle: none of us knew how to optimise the state of being we found ourselves in. The two loves ended in failure as I recall it. I still feel the same warmth towards them as I did seventy years ago. But I ended the relationship with the girl and my friendship with the boy degenerated into little more than an acquaintance. So all my early experience of love, of family and friends, left me scarred and I don't know how they felt about me. What happens to love when it fails?

Just as mysteriously, the 'real thing' happened when I was twenty-one. How romantic? How appropriate? How difficult? This one lasted and still lasts, but to love this much is almost too much, at times, for the incompetent human mind and emotions to manage. There was no real danger of this love 'failing' but I rarely experienced mere peaceful bliss with my life partner. Whatever gloss I might put on it, the experience has been turbulent. So the question about this love could be: why did it keep going?

Honest Reciprocity
A simple formula, but hard to apply, if only because honesty is extremely hard to discover in oneself. In the two young loves, honesty was hardly attempted in the erratic interplay of emotions and motives. It was doubtful, therefore, whether reciprocity had a chance of happening. We were moving darts and shifting targets.

I sometimes watch young people interacting and it is obvious that they are gripped by a form of hysteria: they are playing at love. This habitual excitement extends into adulthood with often disastrous results. Erotic love is an extreme example of this inherent wildness and the experience of it can cling to the psyche for life. It even seems to remain as the typical manifestation of love in so much human behaviour and belief.

I am not surprised. My emotions at, say, seventeen, were an inferno. I knew nothing about life and presumed everything. I was not fit to love. Or even to be loved except by an indulgent adult. It was a bad time for love. Then when I met Eileen I had to change quite fundamentally to measure up to my ambitious need for her. This change was not planned or conscious, but in retrospect it was quite a personal revolution. It implies that for love to develop there must be appropriate change in the psychology and the awareness of the newly developing proto-adult lover.

Perhaps it implies that love might always require a basic change in any person's mindset, psychology or emotional structure. Further, that seems to suggest that the person's owner-brain has to come up with a new narrative or a new personal meme. (Extending this extravagantly, maybe love and purpose on this planet depend on the whole human species experiencing a brain-change. To be discussed later, perhaps.)

A New Narrative?
When I began to love Eileen must there have been a new narrative, or collection of circuits, or whatever, in the brain that owns me? Alternatively, was the potential already in place, just waiting for the right trigger? To explore this, I need to identify how it was experienced over sixty years ago. The point of this is that I would like to investigate why so much love fails to last the course in human behaviour. To build a world of love we'd need better building material than we have used as a species so far, would we not? Unless some other brain narrative is undoing love as fast as it is created. That is

certainly likely and, indeed, it can be seen all around us. Otherwise, why war, why crime, why hatred? At the personal level, i.e. my brain and I, what happened to make a wayward performance convert into devotion? I called it the meeting of soul-mates whenever I was asked how we stayed a couple. But that is mere poetry. A metaphor, surely? Wasn't it more likely that there was a deeper capacity for passionate friendship than I had tapped into before? If so, why? And what is the evidence that this potential for devotion already existed in my brain and me?

Why do fields of wild flowers, streams and hills, and cats and March hares enter my awareness at this point? Is the potential in the brain and me actually a strong tendency to love life itself? And is this applicable to a person who embodies the qualities that thrill in nature? It is a tempting connection. Thinking of Eileen I still experience the excitement, pleasure and longing that characterised my love of nature even allowing for its dark side. And the same for my feeling for her, too, I guess. I venture to suppose that it is a segment of the Great Continuity, this natural joy, and perhaps the Void also, even extending to a sense of the sacred. The evidence, such as it is, makes it seem that there was and is transcendence in the love I experience with this woman.

I should define transcendence, if I can. A narrative of transcendence. A transcendent meme. Why not? Just because I don't harbour ideas about gods, that doesn't stop me having inclinations toward ideals of beauty, truth, and kindness. The word often used for this transcendence is 'spiritual', which is also probably mere poetry, but it is a strong and powerful word nevertheless. I could confess to having a spiritual love for Eileen, but it would take some defining.

Fervent without Fixation
The human habit is to reify, to make concrete, to turn an ideal into a rule. It is making a rod for one's own back and the backs of others. Bearing in mind Dennett's survey of consciousness and its evolution, could it be that the brain of many creatures including humans are

already primed for love and not just as a polarity to hate? Love is a 'many-splendoured' and many-faceted nothing but a potential entire behaviour system, a complex algorithm which is self-mutating? The fervency of my love for Eileen, as for a wide range of other presences in my life, suggests to me that I am governed to a high degree by the love algorithm. The danger in fixing any love, as it is in fixing any hate, is that the governing power becomes incapable of adapting to changed circumstances. Thus, a major 'rule' is broken: any meme (or gene) may be destroyed by its own intractability.

Genes get round this by the process of mutation, i.e. out-of-date genes eventually disappear by natural selection (unless they are irrelevant and therefore simply ossify).

Symbiotic Change
To end this chapter, though not the subject, I want to suggest the most effective method of changing one's love/meaning process. The idea already exists but it operates in a less than effective manner. It used to be called mediation, as in 'Relate' or 'diplomacy', where a specialist counsellor helps putative partners to come into line with each other. Therefore, the memes for relationship-change do exist. However, my focus is on a more vital and engaged symbiotic engagement. Love, and the meaning inherent in love, depend upon a mutual urge to create beauty or happiness. If the urge is absent, the effort is useless. If the urge is strong, full of good-hearted energy, then almost anything becomes possible. Not that it will be easy because both partners will have to change and change is difficult. Eileen and I have worked for over sixty years at the process. It only ends with death, as the exquisite lines of the marriage service declare.

In the next chapter, I will try to goad my owner-brain to helping me to give specific examples of the symbiotic process of love in a human relationship, in this case between two atheists who have always yearned for transcendence (beyond the 'short, nasty and brutish' baseline of human existence described by Thomas Hobbes in 'Leviathan').

Chapter Fourteen
A Case of Love

Time-line

Today, 19th April, 2015, we have been married for fifty-nine years, eleven months, and one week. The 'diamond' is nearly in our hands. And life is certainly ebbing away from us. So it is an interesting juncture in which to explore the course of this particular love - or, rather, this sequence of love-situations and states.

At times, it is agony. Love can be such agony. Perhaps this is an exaggeration, but not by much. The present situation, with Eileen fading away in a nursing home and myself a bit of a physical wreck, is very hard. The love part of it is in some ways the worst part. That is, speaking for myself, as I cannot speak for her. She waits for my long afternoon visits, from two to seven, with apparent eagerness and looks desolate when I leave. By myself, except for the cat, home is both a refuge and a prison. So this is love in somewhere-near-extremis?

I try to think, or feel, what may be good about it. That we still love each other seems wonderfully good. Why is that? Is it a moral good? Does it feel 'right' to still love so much at the low point of life? Does it redeem the lowness? I oscillate between anxiety and grief, which feels bad, very bad. What does she feel? I find it hard to know. I ask, of course, but there's not much of a reply, She says she is happy when I am there with her, but that makes be worry guiltily about the nineteen hours when she is without me.

On the other hand, there is the necessity of living in the 'now', the ever-moving present moment. I guess that should enable me to enjoy the love. It could mean that love need never be painful, so long as it is experienced joyfully. Oddly enough I find this a new and most creative thought, concerning love always and ever. Why, in fact, has it to be painful in any form or circumstance? Why can it not be unconditional in all ways, including the lack of need for security?

By focusing on the time-line rather than the moving moment, a shoal of negative feelings swim around the one who loves: regret, grief, guilt, nostalgia, loneliness, desolation and sadness, when love is being experienced as part of the past, or fear, anxiety, even terror, because love is felt as threatened by future disaster. This is to admit to the selfish or egoic experience of love, the extremes of conditionality.

Nothing Like The Present

It is a challenge to change my state of being at any time and in any way. There have been so many near-successes and near-misses in my efforts to reform or reframe my mindset and emotion-set during my long life. Mostly, I regret to say that I have considered myself changed and then found that I'm not. Not by much, at any rate. In the matter of love, more than anything else, this inertia of being is a disaster for me, as it must be for my partner.

Hence the unexpected fact that the present downturn in our health and strength is a wonderful opportunity. Not for the first time, but never as crucially as now, we have the starkest of choices: change or stay in hell. My situation, now, is hell if I stay in my long-established personality, the one that the Enneagram calls 'The Perfectionist', and I suspect for Eileen too if she stays imprisoned in hers, 'The Boss'. These categories are useful so long as their limitations are understood. Categorisation can never be trustworthy nor accurate, because the human brain/mind is too complex and mercurial to be safely held within a type. Nevertheless, to explore our present crisis the categories are a useful touchstone.

I can only speak for myself - I *should* only speak for myself (which is one of the changes I have to make). Thus I must admit that I am beset by perfectionist habits. Not all of them, but enough to make the point. So here goes: this is how I mess up loving and living. This is also where change could make all the difference to my chance of happiness. In explaining this to myself, hoping that my brain will co-operate, I also have to consider why this basic change hasn't happened long before, especially as I have been trying so hard to make it happen since I was in my fifties.

The difficulty is that the personality was constructed so early and so strongly entrenched that it is almost immovable. I guess it is the first and most stubborn of all the personal memes, so that even the brain is in league with it (if not actually the sole architect of it). In my case, a basic loathing of oneself is the driver of the process synergised by an only slightly less virulent loathing of the world. In this context, love has a hard time indeed, and in a most confused manner. It is not so much a matter of low self-esteem, so-called, as a rejection of any idea of worth or value in one's nature or being. The behaviour, paradoxically is a mixture of arrogance and compromise, and the primary personal reference is that one is *right*, and that one is moderate and superior. What a nest of snakes this is, though it is as well to remember that, in the Enneagram system, all personalities are equally awful.

The Trouble With Systems

The subject is love, but to understand it I need to see how it is connected to the personality and to whatever lies below, above or beyond this personality. In the Enneagram system, as in so many idealistic imaginings of the nature of being, there is supposed to be some kind of holy idea at the core of a human being. The holy ideas behind, or above, the nine personality types in the Enneagram are postulated as:

1.*Perfection*: the ultimate nature of everything is inherently perfect, good, and positive.

2.*Will*: the unfolding of the universe has its own drive and we're part of that (divine) will.

3.*Law*: the universe is a changing pattern and no-one functions separately from the whole.

4.*Origin*: true nature is the source of everything and we are inseparable from it.

5.*Omniscience*: we are all inseparably part of reality and our boundaries are not ultimate.

6.*Faith*: our inner nature is essence, allowing us to trust ourselves and reality.

7.*Plan*: the inherent logic of unfoldment of the human soul is towards self-realisation

8.*Truth*: everything is in (unitary) Being and all dualities are illusory.

9.*Love*: ultimate nature of all is beneficent and loving; we are all made of that love (Reference: Sandra Maitri, '*The Spiritual Dimension of the Enneagram*', 2001.)

Supposedly, the assault from the existential world upon these holy ideas, from infancy onwards, results in the construction of the personality as a means, or strategy, for protecting the idea but in a dysfunctional manner - i.e. the personality is a false design.

I find myself variably in dispute and in agreement with these postulates (dogmas). I will try to explain why by reference to Number

One, as I know it best and have to live with it. But I must start by pointing out that type Nine, 'Love' is said to be the touchstone for all the types, in other words I assume this means that love is the energetic power infusing the holy ideas in general. So, at some level, it is love that is damaged in the process of living, and it is love in one way or another that suffers as a component of all nine personalities.

How can this system have any actual relevance to human existence, particularly in the function of the miraculous human brain? Such a chicken and egg conundrum. I might ask, how can any system have actual relevance to the realities of human existence, particularly as this existence is apparently organised by brain-based algorithms that defy analysis by ordinary formal logic. At least, that's how it seems. So, love, an algorithm and a meme, presumably, rules yet doesn't rule our lives. Whereas we seem to think it should. It would be 'nice' if it did. That would be perfect. But it isn't so. Can we seriously look at our world, our 'civilisations', and deduce that love does rule?

My Perfectionist personality demands that it should. My intuition is that it doesn't. My psyche is riven by this incompatibility. My brain doesn't seem to care, except the emotional apparatus, which is in a kind of despair. My overriding narrative, at least that omnisciently produced by my brain, is desolation and despair: a waste land. Which is why T. S. Eliot's 'The Waste Land' has been my 'favourite' poem all my adult life. It is a poetic algorithmic meme for me, as it seems to be for many. The Perfectionist's Poem of choice. Tom Eliot's brain worked overtime on this for years and it is a work rich in allusions and references. Wikipedia helpfully offers the following information on Eliot's sources for the poem:

'The style of the poem overall is marked by the hundreds of allusions and quotations from other texts (classic and obscure; "highbrow" and "lowbrow") that Eliot peppered throughout the poem. In addition to the many "highbrow" references and/or quotes from poets like Baudelaire, Shakespeare, Ovid, and Homer, Eliot also included a couple of references to "lowbrow" genres. A good example of this is Eliot's quote from the 1912 popular song "The Shakespear-ian Rag" by lyricists Herman Ruby and Gene Buck. There were also a number of lowbrow references in the opening section of Eliot's orig-inal manuscript (when the poem was entitled "He Do The Police in Different Voices"), but they were removed from the final draft after Eliot cut this original opening section.

The Waste Land is notable for its seemingly disjointed structure, indicative of the Modernist style of James Joyce's *Ulysses* (which El-iot cited as an influence and which he read the same year that he was writing *The Waste Land*). In the Modernist style, Eliot jumps from one voice or image to another without clearly delineating these shifts for the reader. He also includes phrases from multiple foreign languages (Latin, Greek, Italian, German, French and Sanskrit), in-dicative of Pound's influence.

Sources from which Eliot quotes, or to which he alludes, include the works of: Homer, Sophocles, Petronius, Virgil, Ovid, Saint Au-gustine of Hippo, Dante Alighieri, William Shakespeare, Edmund Spenser, Gérard de Nerval, Thomas Kyd, Geoffrey Chaucer, Thom-as Middleton, John Webster, Joseph Conrad, John Milton, Andrew Marvell, Charles Baudelaire, Richard Wagner, Oliver Goldsmith, Hermann Hesse, Aldous Huxley, Paul Verlaine, Walt Whitman and Bram Stoker.

Eliot also makes extensive use of Scriptural writings including the Bible, the *Book of Common Prayer*, the Hindu *Brihadaranyaka Upa-nishad*, and the Buddha's *Fire Sermon*, and of cultural and anthro-pological studies such as Sir James Frazer's *The Golden Bough* and Jessie Weston's *From Ritual to Romance* (particularly its study of the Wasteland motif in Celtic mythology). Eliot wrote in the original head note that "Not only the title, but the plan and a good deal of the incidental symbolism of the poem were suggested by Miss Jessie L Weston". The symbols Eliot employs, in addition to the Waste Land, include the Fisher King, the Tarot Deck, the Chapel perilous, and the Grail Quest.'

I wonder what really motivated Eliot to create this extraordinary masterpiece. He was strongly inclined to fame and societal importance, clearly, and he was also in some mental distress apparently. Well that sums up a lot of men, including myself. I write poetry and dyspeptic books about dystopia, so there's another similarity. But, at some deep level, I suspect that Eliot was suffering from a love-need that caused him sadness and some panic. Of course, this is projection: that's my self-diagnosis - T. S. himself may have been perfectly jolly all the way through. Another factor is the problem of transcendence in, or of, the waste land in which we live. Eliot's poem was written soon after the First World War, understandably. I was born just before the Second World War and, as I grew up, anything to do with the First War moved me to tears while I more or less escaped psychologically unscathed through and after the Second War. It is as if the impact of the 1914-1918 apocalypse marked me for ever and nothing subsequently did anything but merely confirm the potential for absolute agony in human existence. I grew up lacking faith in humankind and the universe that had spawned it. Whereas I yearned for beauty and love. This was my personal waste land and Eliot's overwrought muddle of a great literary tirade fed into my desolation. I should not need to query his motivation for the poem, the same cry of pain is constantly echoed in my consciousness.

Marriage, The Love-Bond
I married for love, as the saying goes. Unwittingly, at twenty-five and not very self-aware, I foisted myself upon a beautiful and clever young woman who happened not to be very happy. We leaned upon each other gratefully because we were lost and lonely, if that isn't too schmaltzy a way to put it. We stood hand in hand in our joint waste land. At university, of all places. When we left academia we got jobs and married. It should have been 'love's young dream':

Oh! the days are gone, when Beauty bright
My heart's chain wove;

When my dream of life, from morn till night,
Was love, still love.
New hope may bloom,
And days may come,
Of milder calmer beam,
But there's nothing half so sweet in life
As love's young dream:
No, there's nothing half so sweet in life
As love's young dream.
(Thomas Moore, 1779-1852.)

Well, it actually was, for me. And, I believe, for her. But love's young dream has to grow up, and that process can be very challenging. After all, what is intended, if only implicitly, is that love's old dream will be even better. How can that be achieved?

I think the mistakes we made, especially mine, were definitive. Although committed to each other, we had little idea how to balance self-love with other-love. There was unrecognised confusion within me and I think in Eileen as well. Not only that, but parents and relatives and friends we also involved in the confusion. Which mandates should we serve, how to prioritise, how to achieve maximum conjugal happiness? It was a serious muddle. Yet, 'Beauty bright' somehow pervaded everything, just as the charm of nature still rides above its chaotic pain. Though we were each used to illness, there was now a much sharper fear and misery enforced by the medical problems of each other. Never had I so agonised over the sickness of another human being as in those first years. That has continued until the present day, as if love is the sworn enemy of self-absorption.

As practised by our species, it seems to me that we are using the wrong memes, as couples though it is equally wrong for collectives. We are following a deep-set biological pattern, of course, in that sexual reproduction is fixed genetically and mimetically on pairing and mating, followed by some degree of caring for progeny. This process, practically adapted for species survival, was amplified or emphasised by a strong emotional bond, at least in most species of vertebrates. So breeding and love became entwined, particularly in the extravagantly conscious human races.

To a varying degree, the two elements, breeding and loving, could exist separately, as in the practice of friendship for example. In my own relationship with Eileen, after unproductive miscarriages, the breeding factor was allowed to lapse. But the love factor took on its own momentum and the lack of progeny was probably our good luck. I say 'probably' because there are some aspects of parenthood which seem most appealing. Anyway, for some four decades, this particular childless couple lived on a diet of one-to-one love only, and this love veered gradually towards platonic devotion. We were, and still are, very fortunate in the number of close friends.

So, love for me, has been truly 'many-splendoured', especially in the way it has grown and matured as if fed by a deep subconscious stream. In the way it has changed I think it is appropriate to suggest that a new meme has been created, presumably via the co-operating narratives of our two brains. To some extent, it is possible that our two brains have joined together in making one joint narrative. Sometimes, we have been shocked to find we have two separate narratives, we wonder how it is possible to think so differently. For several years we argued hotly about differences in our experience or opinion of 'spirituality', and we are still somewhat adrift in our views of purpose or meaning in life.

I hope it is not too romantic an idea that for us, love has been a process of discovery rather that a fixed jewel in our shared crown. Now, as our lives fall apart with age and infirmity, the discovery continues. There is the entropic change of our biological structure, but there is also, almost as floating free, a development of love and the understanding of it. Biology is, in effect, separating us, from life and from each other, which is a peculiar agony. But consciousness is forging new connections. I suppose this is the process that encourages people to think they will have an actual 'after-life', in which they will meet those they have loved and lost. I am unable to sustain that idea for myself, but I do recognise the impulse that drives the idea. As I have said before, our minds are not perfect instruments, and they will concoct all kinds of placebos to give us false security. But we also have a capacity for intelligent questioning. We should exercise it more. We won't necessarily achieve absolute rightness but we might avoid absolute wrongness.

The Right Love-Memes

As I suspect we all live the wrong love-memes, have I any inkling what might be the right ones? To some extent I have implied what they might be in the previous section. Essentially, I think it requires a revolution in our approach to knowledge, especially that which we call intuitive or innate. I suggest these forms of knowledge are merely atavistic biological imperatives with no more 'value' than the innate desire to kill, or possess, or dominate. That they are inevitable components of the basic animal mind, which we share with all mammalian species, is indisputable. But do we have to let them manage our lives now that we are fortunate enough to share our individual lives with a brain of astounding profundity and complexity? Further, do we have to accept as absolute the various narratives turned out be this magnificent machine? Do we have choices, in fact, i.e. freedom to decide which is largely under-utilised? Our deep-set emotions, especially those bound up with ego and personality, will fight tooth and nail to stop us making existential changes, and particularly in emotionally charged consciousness as in the case of love.

I have been experiencing precisely the internal combat that I am trying to describe. The last few months have been very turbulent for me. Basically it is the love-test at it most acute - at least in my experience. The test has been whether I can disentangle my two greatest needs: the need to feel safe and contained in my relationship with my beloved one, and the need to feel safe and contained in my relationship with myself. Gradually they are disentangling, but neither of the needs are receiving much satisfaction. So the test becomes to make each need, so far as it is clear and susceptible to alteration, a sustainable and even enjoyable experience.

Somehow, I have to guide these needs towards a new definition supported by new memes. In simple language, I have to find a way of being happy with having a wife sequestered in a care-home and myself imprisoned in an empty house. I will not attempt to list or analyse the range of feelings and miseries bound up in this arrangement, but it should be possible to indicate how the struggle can be sustained and even successful.

The first step is to realise that though the detail of the new situation seems novel, the fact is that there is much in it that has existed, even festered, for decades. To reframe my present mind, even if I regard the past as done with, means that I have to look at my long-established personal memes. In general, these are the stories I tell myself. They may even include the fresh thinking of recent days or months or even years. All the books I have written need to be taken into account. All the attitudes of mind should be questioned. Even and maybe mostly, the ways of my loving have to be re- examined. Then there is dealing with fear, a predominant emotion now, and one which may have controlled my past. Can I deal with fear in a new and successful manner?

If Dennett and his collaborators are right, and I am inclined to believe they may be, then the human brain is the universe as far as we are concerned. Ideas such as 'gut instinct' or 'knowledge of the heart' or 'intuitive understanding' are metaphors whereby the brain is by-passed in favour of some other supposed bodily function. Fear, or love, or hate, can thus be placed outside the brain-based mind, just as ideas of self or archetype or even consciousness are suspended in space rather than being brain-products. The mind and the brain are, in effect, denigrated when they are described as 'intellectual' (or even mere intelligence!) as opposed to emotional or instinctive or even intuitive, as all these functions must originate in the brain and, if not, where else?

Hence, fear is a mind product, a brain-narrative, indeed an algorithm as a well-rehearsed meme in the general mentality of all sentient creatures. So, my brain makes my fear. It is created on my behalf by the brain that, in effect, owns me. This, if there were no other brain-products, would be enough for me to argue (admittedly another brain-product) that the human brain is preposterously undervalued by the human animal that it orchestrates. We are, in effect, traitors to our cranial lord. How the brain lets us get away with that can only be because either it doesn't actually care, any more than the universe does, what we do with our lives, or it is itself governed by a stand-aloof algorithm that evolution has devised for it. On the other hand, my intuition is that the brain may actually care but doesn't possess the algorithms necessary for correcting the errors arising in the programs it constructs. Or none of these ideas are true. How would I know?

One thing is certain, fear may have its uses and yet still be abusive to anyone who feels it. It is a wild card in the pack of consciousness. We can readily understand why it exists as a survival mechanism, yet it puzzles us by the way it shatters our peace and quiet with hysterical raving for no apparent purpose. It is hard not to conclude that fear is a dysfunctional function. But thinking further, is it not also obvious that all the functions of consciousness are riven with dysfunction? What part of my consciousness is aware of the dysfunction present in all my consciousness. Is there actually a set of algorithms in the brain that keep watch on the internal mechanisms? Am I, as it were, wired with a fire-alarm? If so, then fear is a double whammy, it is itself dysfunctional, and it is also afraid of dysfunction.

But a moderate degree of sanity would require a control-mechanism that is not immediately obvious. How do I manage to be relatively free of terror (guilt, anxiety, grief, sadness etc.) most of the time? Is there a governing mechanism in my brain that stops me overheating or freezing? There must be something, otherwise I could not have survived for eighty-four fraught years. This 'something' has inestimable value. I wonder what it is. Uncommonly, it may be what people call 'common-sense'.

Let me try to take this seriously. Am I suggesting that in the colossal complexity of my brain there may be a psychological thermostat that protects me from exploding most of the time? Of course I am. It must be so. But what is it? I need to augment it in any way I can. So does the entire species, it seems. Maybe I am doing better than my species: wars, famines, criminality, drugs, crazy ventures everywhere, wasting the planet. My madness is to be sitting here at the computer, writing this, at 4 a.m. because I can't sleep. Bad enough, in itself, but not really big time. On the whole I am moderate and well-managed. Even in some distress, I still remain fairly civilised.

My species is not as good as that. Sounds smug, but that's the last thing I am. I am thinking of human excesses that shock me to my core. The search for Higgs boson, for example: what an idiocy that is. The Hadron Collider is a lunacy. Worst of all, in the recent past, was the absurd trip to the moon. Why? These are not massacres, pogroms or holocausts, but serious searches after knowledge by responsible scientists, yet they are still extremes of collective madness. Thinking further, of course I am just the same. I am absurd too. The moderator in the brain doesn't work that well for any of us.

Yet it does something, even if it is imperfect. The big desires or fears seem to unhinge this mechanism, though. Just as my love for Eileen makes me behave most eccentrically by normal selfish standards. Even my bad sleeping is a symptom of love, even at my advanced age. I am immoderate in my concern and actions. The excessive, or obsessive, compassion is relatively useless, yet I keep at it as if it were necessary. That's what love is like, it seems, a well-intentioned insanity. Like going to the bloody moon.

Coming Awake

This is the alleged solution, and I have proselytised it more than most. Ironically, suffering from debilitating insomnia, I still sing the praises of being awake. An inebriated man extols the virtue of sobriety? That doesn't seem quite right. But it gives the essential picture of dysfunction. It suggests that being asleep in my love keeps me awake in my bed. My internal wires seem to be crossed. The most likely explanation is that this love of mine is too self-directed while pretending to be devoted to the precious other. I appear to be cheating somehow and may be suffering for it? Can I stir myself sufficiently awake to get a bead on this from my lordly brain? Please, O mighty brain, give me a hand here. Will I get any help, I wonder?

Oddly enough, within a day or two, a response seems to have wheedled its way through. My beloved and I had ridiculously wrangled about how to 'celebrate' the sixty year wedding anniversary. I had become exasperated, unnecessarily and stupidly, and had a 'night of the long knives' as a result - self-blame, self-disgust, sorrow for my beloved - the full works. This became the open door to a new edge to the love-revelation: I saw that my insomnia and general wretchedness were the result of wanted to control the world for my benefit. I wanted to 'cure' my darling wife to make me feel better. The sheer self-obsession appalls me - which is yet another trap, also based on hyper-self-importance. My brain, has made a small narrative, perhaps, to reveal the abject megalomania of its parasite. Well done, brain.

As the beginning of this section, around a dozen lines above, it is obvious that I already knew this from previous brain-promptings, but it had not penetrated deeply enough into my psyche. The shock of my bad behaviour pushed the awakeness further, it seems. But the next problem, or question, appears: what use is this on-going revelation of personal muddle? What a revelation, again: so there has to be a use, has there, in this whole process? Do I assume I am going somewhere with it? Is this awakeness-work really pointful? Another trap, set by my self-importance: it is the man-trap of self-importance, again.

No, definitely not, I am not going anywhere with this, if 'anywhere' means sunlit uplands of aware nirvana where I can be happy ever after... *all that's happening is that I am trying to cope with the problem of just being.* Isn't that a revelation?

Coping With Love
This is an ambiguous heading. And rightly so. There are various meanings in it. In fact, it is the opening to another dimension of the love-meme and its relevance to existence as a whole. The overriding question must be whether love is a means of progress of some kind, or whether it is a state of being rooted in the present moment. I think, or my brain does, that this book has been like the others in that it has an implicit interest in improvement of the human condition. Its title, 'The Fifth Revelation', while not overtly an 'improving-manual', as in 'How to become a Brilliant Exister', its tenor has been how to do a better job of being me, with loving as a primary ingredient. This now seems misconceived. A new narrative looms. A new chapter, then.

Chapter Fifteen
Myths of Improvement

Heroic Love

As in heroism itself, the heroic aspect of love is an ambivalent power. It is particularly so when we consider the need to be happy. If this were a clear and absolute desire, then much of heroism and heroic love would have to be revalued. I am not saying that love and happiness, nor love and heroism, are necessarily incompatible. But I am wondering if neither of these pairings are necessarily compatible. This is especially the case in a time-context. Heroism or love can begin, or even end, I suppose, in happiness. But the course of heroism, like love, even when true, will generally not run smooth.

The results of evolution, popularly understood as a progressive process, do not run smooth either. The mutations which introduced great apes to the biosphere have, in my opinion, been very sub-optimal judged on whether there's a successful and balanced population of any of them. The smaller-brained apes, for all their physical power and cerebral ingenuity, have been spectacular failures, now barely clinging on to habitats being destroyed by the single species of big-brained ape, the human. On the other hand, while most humanoids became quickly extinct, the huge brain of Homo sapiens seems to have worked for that species in helping it to spread over the whole globe, whilst probably dooming it too by the wreckage it is making of the earth. In other words, it is very intelligent for an animal, but not intelligent enough.

Similarly, some of the human memes have also been less than useful. Many of our characteristic behaviours are of dubious worth, and my concern is that our capacity for heroism and love are nowhere near their vaunted usefulness or desirability. The ideas may be fine, but the practices are often anything but. Sometimes, that is, in some cases, or in some traditions, or in attitudes bordering on insanity, we would be best advised to drop the pretence of having such superior tendencies. This would probably be too depressing for most people, and it certainly depresses me. Having been quite gung-ho for most of my life, whatever my inner doubts, it is hard for me to realise that nature is not particularly on my side, my own nature as well as nature in general.

To cope with existence, to face honestly the five horrors (death, isolation, lack of meaning, lack of purpose and the terror of taking full responsibility for oneself), requires a strong will and a sound strategy. I quail at the mere thought of creating such a strategy and putting it into practice. My excuse would be that I am too old and too weak for such stern measures. When I was younger, I behaved differently: 'gung-ho!' was the war cry and my innate fear was placated with whatever placebos I could lay my hands on. Smoking and alcohol were favourite buttresses for the basic human frailty, as if they really helped. I have never tried cannabis, but I am told that it can be a powerful support for psychic frailty - unless it takes on a destructive role, I suppose. However we weave the cloth of life, the fact seems to be that it is not an easily improved process. As I think that evolution is also not inherently a program of improvement, I am not surprised that human endeavour to progress is at best a mixture of success and failure - the ultimate inevitable 'failure' being dear old death itself.

What, if anything, can I do about my predicament? My first thought is that I have to revert to the ancient Greeks, the Stoics and Epicureans, for answers, as two thousand years of Judaism, Christianity and the more recent Abrahamic form, Islam, completely fail to offer me anything. Buddhism is less flawed, but is too optimistic in its recipes for happiness. Taoism is slightly better, but rather excessively vague and intellectual. Is Greek Existentialism then, if I may create this strange amalgam, the most obvious cure for my malaise?

The Internal Predator

This is a metaphorical invention, mainly attributable, I think, to the fecund imagination of Carl Jung. For my purpose it is a convenient way of rolling together the various ways in which we increase the unhappiness in life (our own and that of others) by allowing the proliferation of obsessive ideas in our own psyche. To some degree, the development of the so-called Enneagram Personality-Type typifies the process. As a result, each of us may live according to the Predator's directions. 'Bluebeard', for example, is an excellent representation of the Internal Predator in women, while people like Hitler or Stalin are actual examples of the internal predator on a mass- scale. So-called 'archetypes' such as the 'Evil Mother;' or the Bad Father', or the (malign) Trickster are Jungian inventions of this kind.

Therefore, one way of tackling my 'predicament' is to identify the kind of internal predator I have created for myself. It can then be an arena of battle, in which I at least confront it and maybe defeat or weaken it. As it is something attacking me from within, it is a matter of perception and willpower to fight back. Fortunately, while on the subject of internal metaphors of power, I should mention that there are also Internal Helpers in most of us. They should become involved in the battle for happiness.

The Epicureans took a rather different line. They actively pursued friendship and joy, presumably believing that these benign elements were available within, as if 'internal helpers' perhaps. For example, a good and close friend of mine has written to me about my 'predicament' and he seems to me to be taking the Epicurean line. These are his (edited) comments:

'Thank you for your reply and kind words and for taming for a moment your Internal Predator, to feel the Love that seems to permeate the Human Psyche and perhaps underpins our search for a meaning to existence. I think our natural state of consciousness is a feeling of joy... babies are full of it provided they are not hungry or sick. Also when I look at Spring in all its fulgency and see the flowers in full bloom under a shining sun they seem to be in joyous rapture as their colours and scent titillate our senses. It would seem we create the stresses and strains that detract us from our joy or contentment with just being...

...work, wages, mortgages, bills, lifestyles, dysfunctional relationships, and "wrong thinking" for example take us away from our inner sanctum wherein there is a well and wealth of wellbeing.

I know you are suffering a lot at the moment, and so it must be hard to feel any Joy... probably very fleeting moments and so when we are stressed fear stalks our hearts and thinking, I guess that is why I put so much into meditation because it does at least switch off the internal chatter, even when our emotions are all churned up.'

He doesn't mention his formidable internal predator, an introjected figure from his real life, that dominates and disturbs his existence. It seems that he manages to keep it in a separate compartment. That may be a good stratagem. But it won't disarm the predator - indeed it might actually empower it. There is also an Epicurean compartmentalism in the separation of 'natural' joy (babies, nature) from 'life-habits' (work, wages etc.). They are all natural or are all life-habits. Then there is meditation, a way of separating a part of one's consciousness from the rest. I am sure he accurately describes the way we make our own stresses, but this is exactly internal predator behaviour. A final word on segmentation, the internal predator is not for taming, it should be extirpated or at least diminished. The point here is the difference in dealing with difficulty, and I am happy, in principle, to borrow any of these stratagems to ease myself into greater happiness. Nevertheless it is important to recognise the degree to which all these ploys are just brain-products. In a way they are not real or serious.

Joy Of Being

This is undoubtedly available amongst the many brain-products, indeed it is almost as if we have an internal benefactor bearing this gift whenever we are able to receive it. As it happens, I have today experienced this in action, apparently, and am very, very, grateful for it, whether or not it is real or serious. It has manifested in four connected happenings:

Visit to a doctor. I had not consulted her for a few years, which was a mistake as she is a splendid person and a wise medic. I knew I needed her help for my mental state, my almost useless lungs, and an inguinal hernia, in descending order of importance. With remarkable speed, yet unhurried, she attended to all the issues. Then she asked me if I was still painting. A good doctor.

Anniversary party. Ten of our friends were able to visit the Care Home where a party had been arranged. We, the old couple who have been sixty years together, were shilly-shallying about having any celebration. I am sick, she is more or less immobilised, and we are both feeling low. How could we have a party? For a mere £72, the staff set up a party for us, with brilliant 'nibbles' and excellent sauvignon blanc. It turned into a seminar on the Enneagram, not inappropriately as most of the personality types were there. And there was some joy amongst us.

Going for an X-ray. Eight a.m., in out-patients, is my idea of one of the many hells available on earth. But the good doctor wanted to be sure that I was only suffering from chronic bronchitis and emphysema (renamed Chronic Obstructive Pulmonary Disease; COPD), as I shouldn't be going downhill so fast - that is, my ability to cover quite shallow upward gradients has become almost non-existent in a few months. The X-ray results are still to be revealed, though, as the nurse said, they were not sending me immediately to A& E. I shall be surprised if there is no abnormality, given the miserable state of my breathing.

Taking a walk. After assembling and using the new treatment (antimuscarinic inhalation)) prescribed by my good doctor I set out to do the walk I used to achieve a year ago (about 3 kilometres with several gradients), suddenly feeling I might manage it. I have a fine walk and return to my home to make a large brunch for myself. To my great pleasure, I find that people have planted English bluebells and cowslips in a small patch of dedicated land, and that volunteers are attending to it. An exquisite skipper butterfly completed my small trip. Joy at last. (That was yesterday. Today I tried another walk and it was a bad experience. I had to crawl home defeated. There are no miracle cures.)

Head is where the Heart is
It is relevant, I think, to insert a poem at this point. The subject for this month's poetry-group meeting was 'Sun and/or Moon'. I was not inspired to rush into composition, and was surprised to realise how little I now care about these astronomical features. But they are such powerful symbols. Surely there must be something loitering in my brain and its slave-psyche which could make a poem about these heavenly presences? Then I remembered my recent painting called 'Sun Setting Through Trees' and felt how it embodied the sadness and distress of the decline of my wife and myself. A poem came quickly into existence, I combined it with the painting, as follows:

Sun Setting

Through Trees

Is This It?

Yes, it cannot be any other metaphor for me,
There it is for all to see, a painting on the wall:
The dying sun, trying very hard to be set free.
Absurd to see us mirrored in a minor stars fall.

In my prime, in my pride, I bathed, a fool in sun
And have the skin to show for it, tan long gone,
But the bliss of photosynthesis is still the one
That wise old plants enjoy, all said and done.

My love and I sink hand in hand, falling, failing;
We've 'had it good', a life to celebrate, so they say
Well, say they may, but we are not plain sailing;
Two old sea-dogs unready to call a day a day.

But that old sun will die one day, a burnt out star
And this planet with it, or long before, all dead
In this neck of the galaxy, it can't be all that far
In light-years - if longer than six decades wed.

To my surprise, this was received with approbation. And one member of the group explained to me that she was so 'moved' because I was 'speaking from the heart', whereas my poetry tended to be generally 'from the head'. This made me wonder where people think that joy is experienced. Is calling it 'heart' a metaphor or an evasion (often the same thing)? I am troubled by this dualism. Is it a way of downgrading the mind and elevating feelings? As in the person who became agitated (in a conversation a fortnight ago) when I said intuition was merely an 'atavistic biological imperative' centred in the mind as is everything else (see pages 143 and 144). There seems to be a human need to place some mental events, including even consciousness itself, outside the mind. While it is obvious to me that human experiences are restricted to the human mind, many people deny this and prefer a supernatural world from which we are receiving external narratives.

Thus, joy could be considered an external phenomenon in which we may partake, rather than an emotion centred in our own brain. I regard this as a denigration of our primary 'organ of consciousness', however imperfect it may be. (I say 'primary', just in case there is intelligence operating in the body apart from the brain - you never know.) It also means that we futilely seek external solutions to our internal problems. It also means that we harbour unnecessary fears and hopes.

Skilful Will

How, then, could we achieve improvement in our life-experience as, in effect, an act of 'skilful will' rather than looking for non-existent visitations of bliss? I suspect that it is possible and, indeed, the only way to secure our position as happy beings. This was the Epicurean standpoint, as I understand it. As an Enneagram One I have access to Enneagram Seven, the Epicure Personality Type. This doesn't mean that any of the Enneagram lore is profoundly true, but it does illustrate a process that does seem to exist. Neither the One nor the Seven are anything but aberrant fossils of behaviour, or armour forged on the anvil of cultural trauma. But they illustrate, if not prove, how we live an illusion with occasional shafts of coherent intelligence. This intelligence is, in my opinion, the only machinery for making and operating a skilful will. It is grotesquely underused or sadly misused. The important fact is that it can be properly used to achieve real improvement in the human condition.

Yet I dislike the phrase 'skilful will', as much as I am put off by the word 'psychosynthesis' in which Roberto Assagioli postulated this specific kind of will. A few years ago, deeply imbued with high-minded humanistic psychology theory, I attempted to help some friends with the notion of will as an enabling, aware, nurturing influence, a way of managing one's life for maximum wholeness and happiness. I explained that the idea of will as a force associated with the ego, dedicated to imposing behaviour on self and others, was generally toxic, therefore will was usually regarded as a negative agency. I put forward the psychosynthetic form of activating skilful will. It was essentially, as I saw it, the identification of what one wanted to achieve in one's personal existence, then absolutely promising to work to that end, and then actually doing it.

A nice idea. It still rumbles around inside my psyche. But how does it fit with this fifth revelation, which has led me to a far less coherent, integrated, and knowing realisation of my being? Why, indeed, do I dislike it though still harbour it? In a way, it seems that the skilful will has become my internal predator. Or part of it. I feel a malaise of guilt and panic, which I have attributed to the decline in health of myself and my partner. But what if that is not it, not it at all?

Assagioli and his ilk are *improvers*. They want to make humankind better. So am I, and so do I. In my case it could be said to be my Enneagram 'personality-purpose': one of my type-titles is The Reformer. I am a teacher-preacher, of all things. As it now appears to me, the skilful will is a primary tool in the Improver's box of tricks. At the very least, this equipment suffers from being simplistic, at worst it is fascism. And how does it relate to Daniel Dennett's brain-based version of reality? If Dennett's picture is true, then all the improvement-cults are merely memes, and memes of dubious effectiveness. If he is wrong, where is this 'will' located, what is it made of, how is it programmed, and how come it seems rather ineffectual judging by human behaviour in general?

Where does this leave the ideals of Greek Existentialism I mentioned earlier? Regretfully, I think (We think, the brain and I) that the Greek ideals, as practised then, will have to stay in ancient Greece. I cannot borrow from the past, two and a half millennia ago, if only because I don't remember experiencing it. My existential situation is now. And joy is hard to find. Or maybe it's just hard to cultivate, being a rather wild phenomenon.

Does Entropy Always Win?

Hard as I might struggle to improve, is failure inevitable? Put like that, the only answer seems to be 'yes'. I will die, after all. Isn't that the ultimate existential failure? Dress it up as much as we like, we still regard death as annihilation. And might this be the way I stifle joy? Or the way the whole human race makes joy into a fatuous ritual of collective egotism? Entropy is the collective internal predator of our species, an ugly creature bloated with the false narratives of how to improve to an infinite degree. Entropy inevitably engenders dreams of heaven. We must have consolation to offset inevitable disappointment. So it seems. I am one molecule of panic in the huge babel of human hysteria. I object to this assignment. What must I do about it?

Therapy Versus Entropy?

When all else fails, try healing. But seriously, I have really been 'in therapy' since 1987, when I attended the first group led by Eric Cassirer. After twenty-eight years of therapy I am still unhealed?

This is nonsense, of course, even if it is the nonsense we tend to live in this culture we have concocted. I am just in the process of entering another turn of the crazy screw; I am going to ask for help in a straightforward way, no longer under the pretext of wanting to be an Improved Reformer. I feel it is appropriate, here, to explain why there is this new slant on my fifth revelation. It is not the first time I have felt desperation, but it feels unique in the nature of the 'suffering'.

For a start, ironic as it is considering how this book began, fear is now the primary emotion in my suite of experiences. It lurks all the time and overwhelms frequently. The good doctor immediately latched on to depression, as they do, but it's only half of it. Still, they have to have their ritual labels to keep everything tidy. Then, a new field for me: loneliness or maybe isolation. This book was never intended to dig down into the black depths of my psyche, it was to be an all-out assault on the twin goblins, fear and anger. But the biter is thoroughly bitten. What does my brain think it is doing? Is this what it deems appropriate, an algorithm of despair, a meme of the inner waste land? Apparently so. Therefore, here is the sort of 'narrative' I offered to the good doctor:

(A Meme of Misery: Eileen says I should pull myself together. Very wise, I'm sure.)

Insomnia, Panic, Depression, and Grief because I have COPD and swollen ankles and discoloured skin on my lower legs and Eileen has been in decline for five years and is now in a care home and less reachable week by week and we've only death to look forward to and at 4 a.m. it seems intolerable so how can I cope with this bloody scenario? On the other hand, I do want to celebrate and be happy, because I am extremely fortunate in every way except for the items mentioned above. This, apparently, is DEPRESSION and if I don't want yet more pills then I can have something cognitive with somebody. Some time. Meanwhile, it is 3.55 a.m. and I am writing this as if it will somehow help. I think I will just take some more paracetamol for my slipped disc. And wait for the morning to arrive, assuming it will. Goodnight dear brain.

Still Here

Why? A serious question. On the face of it, I am remaining alive on behalf of someone other than myself. That's my story. I am laying the blame for my continuation upon Eileen and a few friends. She, particularly, insists that my presence is necessary to her. I cannot be sure that isn't true. How do I feel about her continued presence? So much has her presence changed that I am very confused about that question. If she 'disappears' into the void of old age altogether, not necessarily by death, but just by forgetting (for example, who I am), I anticipate my aloneness as terrifying. Yet people cope with that. Why couldn't I?

Is it really my own death that is the problem? As the song goes: 'Tired of living and scared of dying.' That is a song about black slavery, written by a white man with a Jewish father and a British mother, namely Oscar Hammerstein II. But am I also a slave? I must be, in the way that I feel trapped and frightened, yet in the depths of the sleeplessness of last night I thought of how very free I am. Is it actually the freedom that is bothering me so badly?

It must be the case that I could do as Eileen says and just 'pull myself together.' There must surely be the freedom to do that? I look at Stephen Fry, for example, and see how strange it is for him to be so depressed when he is so blessed. Is it that his brain, and mine, are feeding on the wrong diet of chemicals? If so, are we actually free to feel differently? Doesn't brain chemistry rule everything?

Most of all, I ask myself how much any of this actually matters. Is self-importance infecting the whole body-mind, so that anything wrong becomes everything wrong? Can I learn to live with chronic and acute personal imperfection?

Thanks to the internet, I have discovered (with some difficulty) that the treatment prescribed for improving my lung function, which I have been using for a week, actually causes depression in some people. I also discovered that I could side-step the depression by meditation. So I must now stop that medication and see if my depression eases.

To add to the confusion, the chest x-ray shows a large 'bulla' in my right lung, which has been there without my being told after its discovery nine years ago, so with COPD I can hardly expect to walk briskly again. Finally, the anti-depressant, Mirtazapine, that I inveigled the medic to prescribe has apparently the most scary side-effects and I will not use it.

This all adds to the relevance of learning to live with 'chronic and acute personal imperfection' (see above). It is a time for letting go of old standards, except perhaps the sane old practice of meditation. And I will just sleep when I can and not care when I can't. This is all very embarrassing if I take it very seriously. Can I learn not to take it so seriously?

Chapter Sixteen
Revalued Revelation

Surrender to Mirtazapine

I said I wouldn't but I have. Why? Because I was afraid I might succumb to suicide after one night's anguish and thought I should report it to somebody. I got an appointment with a female doctor who supported the prescription of the first one, saying it would have immediate effect on sleeping and therefore ease the anguish. However, she says I must stay on this medication for six months to get real adjustment to my depressed mood. This means that I, and the brain that owns me, might be expected to start behaving differently from how we have up to now, and that this book will also change its nature.

It takes two weeks for the long-term effect of this drug to start appearing so, that is some days away. The *immediate* sleep-benefit has not exactly happened. So 'we' are still in the anguish state though maybe a bit less desperate. I am, anyway, but not sure about my brain - I don't even know whether it ever feels desperate. It must, surely, generate the narrative of desperation, I suppose? It is sad and frightening that this most probable source of human experience is shrouded in mystery. Or is it just as well? We might try to fix it if we knew what was actually going on. Though, of course, that is what we already attempt to do, with very mixed consequences.

Presumably my brain, with its vast resources, must realise that it hasn't long to live. In what way or sense it might have that realisation is a fascinating question. Can and does the brain 'care' about such an eventuality? Does it experience fear or resentment? If it only makes narratives and memes and, presumably, algorithms, which its slave/ parasite then uses as best it can, it could be argued that the brain is only the messenger, a neutral information system. I find that hard to accept. I see no reason why the brain should not be in its own version of pain, unless, of course, the brain and I are sharing the same pain. Or joy, or whatever is there to be experienced.

Therefore, in moral issues, or problematic emotional questions, does the brain, with or without its symbiotic human person, decide what is important and what course of action to follow, or does the slave/parasite have to make those decisions? In a way, this is an irrelevant matter, because the fate of the 'partnership' is immutable. The question's relevance, if any, is in the nature of evolution and the meaning or purpose of existence. It is interesting that Tom Stoppard should have chosen the so- called 'Hard Problem' of consciousness for his latest play and that it has more or less disappointed everybody, because there are, of course, no answers to the 'problem'. Like anyone else, and philosophers over the centuries, Stoppard's actual focus seems to be on issues arising from consciousness, which is certainly fair enough, but who or what is driving the consciousness-chariot? Why, to be trivial, am I giving my brain a cocktail of chemical toxins? And who am I, to be making such decisions. Is this surrender or vandalism? I do not know. The best spin I could put on it is that I am experimenting, in conjunction with my brain master, to explore whether my life has lost its point or whether some new paradigm is possible. Just being happy would seem to be the greatest outcome, but it's hard to see that happening. The improvement myth is under personal scrutiny and love has proved more of a hard taskmaster than a relief. My only hope is that I am in a temporary slump - and to some extent I can see that as the reality. And I can't imagine what else I can or should do. There is a sense, however, of a deeper surrender being possible if only I knew what and how. If I could really accept my fears and ills, would life be better? Am I suffering from the stress of hope? More likely, am I suffering from the abandonment of hope? It is true that I have long ago put down the idea of hope as an absurdity in a world with an unknowable future. I have tried to avoid the error of hoping. Was this wise? Could the effect of hoping be to strengthen the resolve to live happily, while remembering it is a gamble? Maybe I have been too cynical. Maybe it is time to indulge in the permissible error of hope?

I Hope I Am Wrong?

More than this, I seem to have been wrong in abandoning hope as a credible approach to the future. I have argued that as the future is unknowable it is a mistake to have hopes about it. But this attitude is flawed if it dismisses the possibility of something in the future. My approach has been to assume the worst, in effect, which is to indulge in the error of negative hope. It is a good thought that the future might bring better rather than worse events. I have missed an opportunity in thought and therefore in feeling. It is high time I took advantage of this loophole in the existential fabric of life.

I remember feeling sorry for a friend who had just lost her husband and thinking how inexplicably foolish she was to cherish any hope after that devastating blow. We briefly argued about it. I was utterly convinced she was wrong to go on hoping about anything rather than staying completely open to what many happen. I ridiculed the part of the burial service that includes the words: '...in the sure and certain hope...', because of its insane double-think. I was right and I was wrong.

I have hamstrung myself emotionally and psychologically. I have limited myself by pedantry. I had assumed that because the future is unpredictable it is wrong to cherish hopes about it. This was, I now realise, an act of logic-chopping, an arid interpretation of existence. The reality is that although the future in impossible to anticipate accurately, the only rational approach is hope. Or, to be fair to myself and to reality, it would also be rational to anticipate the worst. This apparent oxymoron is due to the uncertainty rather than the inherent weakness of the logic algorithms.

It is more a matter of emotion than thought anyway. The best way of dealing with the future must be by means of intent, the formation of goals. Then we by-pass the absurdity of equal and opposite desires and become realistic. This revelation is nothing less than life-changing for me.

I Am Not Wrong?

My brain and I can, in fact, *act* into the future. It is so simple and I made it so complicated. There are two realities involved. In one, the one I had chosen pre-mirtazapine, was the depressed reality, in which the lack of certainty about the future activated pessimism. The other reality, post-mirtazapine, is one in which I do my best to secure a satisfactory future outcome. They are, of course, the same reality, and the difference is only in my *attitude* to the unknown future. The revelation is important: I *choose* whether to be a pessimist or an optimist. How unbelievably odd that such an intelligent pair as my brain and I failed to realise that elementary fact.

The question then becomes much more precise: how do I decide whether to be optimistic or pessimistic about any question of future possibility? Where, in the brain, does that question get answered? I have no idea. But I bet that some neurologist in some laboratory somewhere has a clue to the process involved. He probably uses pigeons or rats for the experiments. Because if pessimism and optimism are narratives in the human brain, it's an odds-on favourite that this engaging pair of opposites exist in vertebrate brains generally.

The question of the rightness or wrongness of my opinions has lessened in significance as the mirtazapine-days increase. Only ten days into the treatment I am experiencing reduced concern for what I think and increasing interest in how long I will continue to exist (in symbiosis with my brain, presumably, although even that meme is beginning to weaken). Therefore, the qualitative assessment of my life also changes because I now take less for granted. Maybe nothing much has actually changed, but most things have begun to seem different. The change is not very attractive, either. I liked being stimulated and even excited by my experiences, and I am not enjoying this duller, more 'laconic', i.e. less interesting, world. I am not sure about hope, now that I accept its validity as an emotion. The 'situation analysis', a strategic term (meme), does not impress me as favourable. On a personal level, I mean, though I guess it extends to the general state of my species. I seem to be waiting for something to happen yet doubt whether I will like it when it does. It comes close to fear, in fact, in a rather dormant, dull, manner. And I am actually very weary of being afraid. Which is, of course, why I surrendered to mirtazapine. The jury is out on the wisdom of that.

Life With Mirtazapine

For the first two weeks of dosing myself with this drug, I recorded my struggles with it. Here are the notes for that period, edited to exclude names of places and persons:

22nd/23rd May 2015 from 8 p.m. Surprised by almost immediate lightening of mood. Surprised by heaviness of legs and difficulty of walking. Bed at 11 pm. No suicidal thoughts. But then surprised by vivid 'dreams', then amazed to wake up, as if time to get up, at 3 pm. Back-pain a nuisance, bed felt uncomfortable. Took 2 paracetamol, coped with discomfort, eventually back to fitful sleep. Got up at 10 pm. Took all heart pills. By 11.30 am. felt almost 'normal'. Mood still felt a bit lighter. Went to supermarket at 1 pm feeling very fragile. Bought sandwiches and took them to Care Home and ate without any relish at 4 pm. Feeling depressed and rather hopeless. Read to and talked with Eileen until 7 pm.

23rd/24th May. Delayed mirtazapine until 10 pm, hoping to have a longer sleeping effect. Took the pill immediately after light supper.

Little physical effect this time, just a bit drowsy. Ankles swollen as the night before. To bed at 11 pm. Perhaps two dozing episodes but no substantial sleep by 2 am. Back pains, as on previous nights. Took two paracetamol. Still more or less awake at 4 am. Walked about house for a while. Not really any serious suicidal thoughts and rather less depressed and panicky than I might have expected. Not happy, obviously. Slept for a while from 5 am. needed breathing relief at about 6 am. Bit worried about this but it felt necessary. Breathing laboured after more dozing, and occasionally heavier sleep, until 10 am. Less drowsy and weak than previous morning. Did some breathing exercise (with 'Powerbreathe'): surprised I could do it. Minimal walking - just a few hundred metres outside house. 2 pm. to 7.30pm., with Eileen, both sad.

24th/25th May. A bad day, feeling weak, walking with difficulty, needing 'reliever' inhaler twice before evening. 'Powerbreathe' not used. Worried about night, prospect of not sleeping. Will take pill at about 9 pm. before supper. Slight sense of more positive feelings trying to come through but body in a poor state. Ankles very swollen by evening. Pain down backbone and in sides of chest. No doubt will need paracetamol later - none taken all day. During the twelve hours from 10 pm. on Sunday 24th to 10 am. Monday 25th there were three different periods: the first, to about 2 am. was a wild and unpleasant sleep with an avalanche of images, almost a continuous nightmare. From 2pm. to about 5 am. I more or less slept, with paracetamol to help, with frequent breaks, one of which was to make a hot drink and write a few lines. From 5 am. to 10 am. I tried to sleep more normally, and was about 50% successful. Another slight reduction in discomfort and weakness as I started the day. Stressful time in afternoon/evening with Eileen but quite close.

25th/26th May. Felt panic about the day ahead, as yesterday was so awful. But walking surprisingly easier. Ate quite large lunch after some writing. Less shaky and fatigued at Care Home than yesterday.

A friend with us at the care home made the time together both easier and less satisfying. Ankles very swollen again. 'Salamol' reliever not used. Will take pill at 9 p.m. after supper. A difficult night: some light sleep at first, very awake at about 2.30 am. Felt some panic, got up and watched first part of 'Peter Grimes' on BBC iPlayer. Bad idea. Better, I think, to write and read a bit with a hot drink. Didn't do that. Tried bed again, took one paracetamol. Slept lightly for a while with half-awake nightmares from 5 am. Needed and took one puff of Salbutamol at one stage. Woke from deep sleep at 9 am. Breath-panic. Used 'Powerbreathe' instead of Salbutamol. Got up feeling depressed but not too unwell. Took all cardiac pills in morning.

26th/27th May. Still no joy in the day ahead. Writing, painting and shopping equally unappealing. Started a new painting anyway. Tried a walk and it was barely possible. Felt weak and awful. Had to take double puffs Salbutamol midday. Not hungry. Could hardly function from 1 pm. Slept in Eileen's room in Care Home till 5 pm. Aim to take pill at 9 pm. after supper, again. Ankles swollen. Mouth dry and taste unpleasant (an old problem). In bed from 11 pm. slept till 3 am. then stayed and tried to sleep but back pain and tension eventually made me get up at 4.30 am. Took one paracetamol and a hot drink and tried to settle again in bed, with a crossword. Needed and took one puff of Salbutamol and slept quite deeply until 10 am. Not particularly depressed. Nor very anxious. Something is working.

27th/28th May. Fairly relaxed about the day though rather doddery. No inclination to do anything. Wondering whether a walk will be possible. Ankles have not recovered. Wrote a piece for book. Revising 'hope'. No walk. Watered garden. Felt better than yesterday. Slept a short while with Eileen. Went to supermarket on way home to stock up. Very tired by time got home at 8.30 pm. Swollen ankles and bottom of legs. Plan to do same as last night it will be later taking pill and going to bed. A catastrophic experience: after the usual waking and tension at about 3.30 am went back to bed with hot drink and did a sudoko for a while - but felt something was different. At about 5 am I went back to sleep but a long nightmarish episode followed, a 'conference', in which the dream was repeatedly interrupted by hyperventilation, panic and depression until I could stand no more at 10 am. The 'conference' was a ghastly experience. Really frightened by the expectation that this would happen again on 28th/29th early morning. It hadn't occurred to me that I might need 'Salbutamol' but I tried sitting and meditating and the same distress occurred. One inhalation of Salbutamol seemed to put it right. Tomorrow morning should I try 'Salbutamol' again?

Shall be seeing GP today, will discuss this particularly, as it seems crucial to the success of the anti-depressant. (Can't face another 5 am to 10 am episode like the one just experienced.) Apart from shock and fear of tomorrow morning, I feel all right. GP said I looked much better and suggested I changed bedtimes. We agreed I would take the pill at around midnight and go to bed say 1 pm, then try not to sleep too late next day. Obviously I must use reliever when struggling for breath. Felt bad rest of the day (i.e. Thursday 28th).

28th/29th Overnight not too bad: went to sleep 1 am, woke at 2 am., semi-slept till 3 am, read in bed for an hour, took 1 paracetamol, slept till 5.30 am, half-slept till 7 am. Got up, made a drink, Horlicks, started the day. (Prepared to have further nap if needed). No reliever so far. Ankles unswollen. Felt quite good. Checked with pharmacist that a reliever isn't functioning if the aerosol is not clearly visible. Mine obviously often underperform, making things more difficult. Did walk in house and had a short sleep on bed at 11 am. Ankles swollen by noon. Friends visit to Care Home pleasant but felt pointless and unreal. Intend to take pill at midnight to minimise sleepless part of night. Didn't work this time...

29th/30th Stayed awake from midnight to 3/4 am. Made chocolate drink, 2 paracetamol, read article in bed. Got some sleep and woke 5.30 am. Went into doze till 9.30 am. Panic and breathlessness. Got on with day feeling really ill. Used Salbutamol, tried walk, got to top of nearby inclined street (just) back to unwanted lunch. Session with friend R, helpful. Slept in Eileen's room. Felt better. Home at 8 pm. Will try meditating if sleepless. Otherwise will cope as best I can. Useful to know friend R isn't scared of insomnia. A key question for me. What does it matter? I can sleep during day, regardless of skewing sleep-patterns. Just a neurosis? Make sure the Reliever actually works if I need it overnight.

30th/31st
Intermittent sleep with no clear pattern. Frequent urination, especially from 9 am onwards. Rapid and irregular pulse. Stayed in bed till 11am. Some vivid dreams, not too unpleasant. No need for Salbutamol up to that time. Felt reasonably well but a bit shaky. Thought maybe the mirtazapine treatment might be settling down (it's the 9th day). Walked less than kilometre in house and garden. Still not hungry by noon. To care home, slept 1.5 hrs. Urination frequency reduced. One puff of Salbutamol at 5pm. Feeling not too bad, Trying not to fear sleeplessness.

31st May/1st June
Relatively good night. Still very sleepy at 10 am. Hard to stay awake, Slow, unsteady walking. Shopped at supermarket with great effort. Felt very weak. Slept in E's room. Ordered taxi for visit to GP tomorrow. Needed reliever at 4 pm; don't think it worked. May need it at bedtime. Fear and depression hovering and need to be shaken off. Mirtazapine still not settled down. How long?

1st/2nd June
Woke at 2 pm with weird sense of time and space, then a long night of turmoil in which I tried to manage some sleep and counter breathing difficulty. Worried about Salbutamol inhaler efficiency, I may be over-dosing or under-dosing, how do I tell? Going to surgery for INR sample, will ask there about the inhaler. Feeling wretched mentally and physically. Saw GP; helpful about Salbutamol problems, can take

quite a few puffs with no harm and he prescribed a special device to ensure effectiveness. He said several people found paracetamol helpful for sleep; possibly a placebo effect. Advised keep going and see how it is in two weeks time when I see the other doctor - he's OK with my seeing her. Says it's unusual for the sleep-effect of mirtazapine not to last all night. Well, in my case, it seems to come back in the morning after receding between 2 am and 5 am, providing I'm not fighting for breath. See how it goes tonight - advises against getting up or doing anything stimulating. There's caffeine in chocolate, beware the stimulation.

2nd/3rd June
The worst thing was to wake at 1.30 am and not know how to get back to sleep (as in last November, with 'flu'), followed by the long night managing wakefulness. Almost as bad was the ambivalent reaction to dawn when sleep seemed to return but the light seemed too bright. Got up at 9.30 am. to get car to servicing dept. That was tough too. But mood and strength slightly improved when awake, now. The inhalers are really unreliable, which is a nuisance. Got to car-servicing by 10.45 am. Eileen did good walk with physiotherapist in care home tonight. I feel tired and rather scared of sleep disorders, otherwise fine, really.

3rd/4th June
The usual struggle to manage sleeplessness. How can this ever be sorted? A new development is that I feel obliged to stay awake in 7 am to 10 am period as a 'responsibility', which suggests that the wakefulness generally is connected with the needs of others, e.g. Eileen? The theme which ran through my mind was 'my life is for me' as if trying to convince myself of this (and not succeeding).

A long session with friend R and with Eileen in afternoon. No escape evident from the situation. I really just want sleep. The night was awful, hours dragged, no relief. Tried different bed, no improvement. Slight sign of sleep normality around 9 am. - too good to be true? Too late to know - tonight will tell?

4th/5th June. 14 days after starting mirtazapine. Probably no real improvement in mood and sleep for some days yet. I don't even know whether I feel better or worse than several days ago. Fatigue is clouding judgement. Feel a victim. Not convinced that 'my life is for me': still beating myself up, I guess. Will try to meditate, to rise above the jaws of the rat-trap. Had to leave care home at 4 pm. today, couldn't stay awake, felt ill. Got home, obviously. Less ill at 7 pm. but apprehensive.

Subsequently - 7th June: as I was feeling that I was in real crisis, I contacted various help-agencies. Finished up in out-patient dept. of hospital with an out-of-hours doctor, who advised me to double the dose of mirtazapine. I thought this was insane, considering what low dose was doing. But I had a second set of 14 pills from the supermarket pharmacy and the suspicion grew that they didn't have same toxic effect as the first 14 from a local pharmacy. In fact this seems untrue (it may just be change in my physiology, who knows?). Last night I took one pill and had no 'horrors'. I took the risk, then, of having a second pill. Still no horrors. The sleeplessness persists, but the mood is entirely different. It is a new situation. The difference between the pills will probably never be explained. I am tired of writing these notes, as well as of everything else happening to me, and will just get on with coping with the transition to mirtazapine dependency, which I am now told will take four to six weeks rather than the fortnight I was originally expecting. I have to keep reminding myself that my depressed state actually was serious and probably 'dangerous'.

The New Reality

The new reality is that I have to come to terms with the new reality. That is, facing what actually is rather than a state of being I would prefer but which eludes my grasp. I suppose it is now rather like the exploration of a previously unknown landscape, perhaps a scaled down version of seeking the source of the Nile or looking for an undiscovered civilisation or a remote planet. I must expect danger, bafflement, physical stress, and just possibly something interesting or beautiful. This prospect makes me realise how timorous I am, how my nature recoils from danger and desolation. I am not a brave, robust person. I am old and tired, as well, which is not helpful. Therefore, how should I do it? The safari consists of doing the safari? Is it a pointless search? How could I know, except by doing it? The solid fact that supports me is that, for all my fears, the situation is no worse than at any time in my previous eighty-four years. I am just more of a coward, that's all. So I must pull myself together and get on with it, must I not?

First I must start coming to terms with the chemical assault on my brain. This is the focus of everything because it is dominating my existence. Today, 10th. June, 2015, is the twentieth day of taking the drug. Although mildly annoyed that the original advice (that there was a two week settling down period) was misleading, and that I am still in the preliminary stage, I have to be where I am. It is a very difficult experience. How well am I managing it? More to the point, does the experience seem to be going somewhere interesting and useful? And, philosophically, does it make more sense than suicide, the only apparent alternative?

The Difficulty
It is hard to know just how significant is my dysfunctional sleeping in the general difficulty of living from here onwards. Although the debilitating effects of Mirtazapine are subsiding as I enter the fourth week of taking the drug, bad sleeping still assails me every night. I am living with this better than I was but do I now have to cope with terrible sleeping till I die? It is a tall order. I find it hard to think beyond it. Is there no way to remedy it, I ask? It would make such a difference. My GP practice will not prescribe sleeping-medication. Why not? All sorts or reasons. You do not question the custodians of the Hippocratic tradition. But I was allowed, even encouraged to try the hormone melatonin (after all it's not a prescription- drug): I tried it and it was ineffective (and also has a nightmare list of side-effects).

Now is the time, then, to try to tackle this sleep difficulty, which means trying to understand how it works in me. Maybe I should start with a surprise: for a few hours yesterday I felt cheerful, even skittish, i.e. frivolous. That is new; not experienced for months. This bloody mirtazapine does actually work. The price is high in terms of 'other effects', but to be light-hearted for a while is wonderful. It is said that this good effect becomes more pervasive while the downside diminishes with time. I will wait and see. Perhaps the difficulties will reduce, but there's no sign of normal sleep yet. And my mouth is like the bottom of a birdcage this morning (late June, 2015).

I am being helped. I am not as alone and feeble as I feel. Not quite; maybe not by a long chalk. Friends share their experiences and their stratagems with me. Psychiatry at its best is richer in resources than I had realised. And there is mindfulness, a resource I had almost forgotten. It shames me to admit it, but having been reminded of it, I intend to work with that inherent potential as much as possible. Therefore, specific mind-work is likely to dominate these pages for a while, and not mere generalised theory.

One thing, or the last thing, I expected was that my mind would be undermined. My mind is the only resource I have for assessing existence, both generally and mine in particular. I have always understood that it is not a trustworthy resource, but it has lately become clear that my mind can actually be a serious liability. Just one example may be sufficient: mirtazapine is psychedelic in effect and this sometimes involves a marked variation in reality, a variation which is not always readily identified and 'discarded'. I had not expected this and I am still trying to come to terms with it. Generally, the distortion of my commonly accepted reality takes the form of a didactic nightmare, in which I am set tasks or instructions that make no sense whatsoever. It is often hard to shake them off because they seem somehow firm and absolute. This raises big issues. Not least is the likelihood that my 'accepted' reality may be nonsense too. Judgements then become particularly fine and maybe the opposite of 'dandy'. In a way, I am comforted by this and similar distortions attributable to mirtazapine because I have always suspected the power of the mind to be relative and very non-absolute.

More disturbing, actually, are physical effects such as drying and taste-distortion in my mouth and swelling of my ankles and legs. They actually hamper me or worry me more than mere mental warping, given that the main objective is a fundamental change of mood to the positive, which has happened. The sleep problem, too, is persistent, making it necessary to find new and effective stratagems to cope with hours of empty pointlessness that I used to fill with unconsciousness. I rather like the way in which these difficulties have piled up and how the mixture of them has altered, if only in the sense that I see myself as a process rather than a person, a process largely if not wholly driven by the power of the brain lodged in my skull. I am astonished to have found it possible to move my 'self' so far off its pedestal.

So much for The Difficulty. I can't say that I feel any rancour towards it, but am happy to say they it all seems quite natural, in the bloody-minded but robust way in which nature operates.

The Outlook
Probably due to mirtazapine, and partly due to remembering mindfulness, I now have an outlook, of sorts, rather than a brick wall. With my partner in a home and myself alone at night and in the mornings, it is not an attractive outlook. I do feel bereft, lonely and isolated. But perhaps I could now focus on this and see how it could improve. It is a main element in the safari of the new reality.

My GP (one of them, that is) who has taken charge of my attempt to ditch despair and suicide, has recommended a book. It is called 'Being Mortal', written by a surgeon called Artul Gawande, and I am intrigued to see whether it makes sense of my outlook.

My immediate outlook is the uneasy relationship between my mind and the antidepressant. I suppose this is because it is such a good example of the limitations of medicine. And, indeed, that is a prime theme of the 'Being Mortal' book. It is now (July 8th) seven weeks since I started the mirtazapine experiment and, for all its horrors, this drug is certainly changing my 'mind' for the better and it's not just reduction of suicidal intent. In some ways I hardly recognise me at all. Apart from the physical effects, already listed, there is the 'disorientation' compared with my previous, 'normal', fixity of intent and comprehension. I wait impatiently for my old self to emerge from the smoke and wreckage, yet I have no idea whether that is ever going to happen.

Last night, for example, I thought I had put in place various ploys to outwit sleeplessness: timing, alternative activities, arrangements for controlling the light in the bedroom, that sort of thing. In the event, I thought, after taking the drug, that I had a colleague writing out his/her experience of what was happening to me, and I thought I would have my own detailed account of the night's work. In fact, though I did get up at 5 a.m., as planned, and spend an hour on the start of a new painting, and have the painting to prove it, neither of the other actions materialised. They had not even existed as plans in 'reality'. But I also did manage to sleep from about 6 a.m. to 9 a.m., as planned, which was a good result.

Another, more miserable, example; I went, as usual, to be with Eileen in her room from 2.30 p.m. to 7 p.m., and I looked forward to being with her and being in good spirits together. As soon as I arrived I was overcome by a distressing discomfort of mood accompanied by extreme need to sleep. It was hard on her and unpleasant for me, and I have no idea why it happened. I came home irritated with myself and regretful towards her. Well, at least I was aware of it.

Overall, I have reason to be happy. Physically, life is very tough, yet it's bearable; and mentally, notwithstanding the vagaries, I am certainly in a far better state than up to two months ago. A friend, who has been taking a similar medication since January is quite transformed (for the better) and that fact does give me some optimism about my own future.

The Philosophy

I return for this to the sketchy accounts that exist on the life of

Epicurus, the brilliant ancient Greek who dedicated his life to happiness and friendship. How did he do it? I mean, how did he achieve those objectives? How would I find the connection between an ancient Greek practice and a modern protester against standard practice. At least I have the whole book of Gawande's to work on. It is good yet I search in vain so far to find his method for achieving happiness in an old age context. It is no easier to deduce why Epicurus could be full of joy as he expired enveloped in the agony of kidney stones. Oddly enough, I can see how mirtazapine does it, but neither Epicurus nor Gawande seem to offer a psychedelic drug as the magic transformer.

There is a mystery here. Clearly, Epicurus was practising an advanced form of transcendence, perhaps aided by herbal medicines. Just as obviously, Gawande is both using and questioning the substances and techniques of 21st century medical practice. In their different ways, both Epicurus and Gawande want to focus on the whole person, not merely the medical aspects. But what exactly is this whole person, and how is it that there are such diverse views how best to serve the whole well-being of the whole person? Is it something we do well or, as Gawande asserts, is it something we do rather badly? I think this requires a new chapter.

Chapter Seventeen
How To Be Whole?

Is This A Whole Person?

As a footnote to the anti-depressant saga, here's the summary I gave my GP on the beginning of the eighth week:

8am 12th July - Typical daily situation.

Sleep: no sleep overnight until 5 am then about three hours. Experienced as very stressful and causes great anxiety. There's also light sensitivity now as well. I feel that it is impossible to continue at this level of deprivation and am obliged to sleep in afternoons to keep going.

Appetite: has become virtually non-existent, taste extremely distorted and mouth frequently dry. I am certainly not eating a sustaining diet. I take Horlicks at 2 am to try to promote sleep and add some calories. (I am awake then anyway). Food has become repulsive progressively.

Constipation: a recent development requiring aperients, e.g. Lactulose and occasional glycol suppositories.

Walking and exercise: am unable to do either. Very weak and struggle to cover a hundred metres. Have Achilles tendonitis which doesn't help.

Oedema: legs and ankles get very swollen soon after getting out of bed. I have to sit with legs propped up for hours at a time to have any positive effect. Legs and ankles normal after several hours in bed.

Mood: generally surprisingly good given the appalling side-effects, although I do feel desperation as a result of all the problems. I feel trapped in the medication and am very disappointed that my experience is worsening rather than improving in this eighth week of taking mirtazapine. I guess that withdrawal from the drug is unavoidable and I am very apprehensive of that.

Visiting wife in care home: I have managed to maintain a five-hour daily time with her, from 2.00 to 7.00 pm. Today, for the first time, I feel that I just cannot maintain that. To discontinue regular visiting would devastate her and add greatly to my psychological stress.

Overall: I feel completely weary and dispirited. I am desperate for a solution but cannot imagine one.

Question: until now I have been sustained by the belief that some kind of normality would re-establish after several weeks. There is little sign of this happening. Hence the despair.

Greater time-flexibility could be critical.

At any rate, it is a picture of me, as I am, at the time of writing. I will leave this as a milestone, or marker, of one of the most unpleasant episodes of my life, and it is one with an unknown conclusion at this time. Maybe I will return to it later, if I am still here.

This is undoubtedly not a whole person, if wholeness means healthy. But is it not whole in another sense? Is it not a picture of 'general purpose suffering', which more or less applies to all living things, sometime, sooner or later?

The question that seems most important to me is: how best to keep suffering to a minimum? I am by no means certain that this is a view shared by all members of my species. Quite otherwise, in fact. Now I have read Gawande's book I am far from sure that he is against suffering as much as I am. This is very disturbing. I would not feel safe in this man's medical hands nor do I trust his judgement. Why so?

Being Moral

He names his book 'Being Mortal', while pursuing various strands of morality. Mortality is clear enough, but morality is not. This is where his idea of wholeness diverges from mine, although I am not claiming superior knowledge because that is inherently suspect in matters of morality. At the risk of being simplistic, I feel that he is describing two main issues with a degree of inconsistency. First, he writes well of the existential trap into which unlimited medicine has led the society. He says, trenchantly and sympathetically, that the caring for elderly and sick people is an offshoot of clinical practice. Care homes have been created to take the weight off hospitals, where the search for ultimate clinical solutes has run out of sense and control. Half the book is focused on this rather muddled and unpleasant reality, his main point being that life-prolongation takes priority over autonomy of individuals who are old and/or sick. He provides some American examples of attempts to create a different solution, where happiness and enthusiasm are the objectives of care and nursing. So far, so good and so similar to Epicurus.

Then something strange happens to the book, almost as if a second Gawande takes over from the first. He deals in immense detail with a range of terminal cases. There is an almost loving attention to quite repulsive detail, a dwelling upon what almost seems to be the right of a patient to suffer as much as the system will allow. The philosophical plight of the doctor is the primary concern, it seems. Making the right diagnosis and offering the best treatment is right in broad principle, that is evident. Yet Gawande seems unable to recognise that the suffering usually involved for the sick person is beyond sense, purpose and humanity.

I should declare an interest. I am incensed by the refusal of our society's rulers to actively encourage and pursue the kindest and most agreeable death for anyone who desires it. I asked my GP why she had recommended the book to me. She said, 'It makes you think'. Indeed it does, but she and I think differently. As a doctor, she feels a commitment to keep people alive, primarily, and well or happy, secondarily. I understand the commitment, to the extent that a doctor committed to killing is itself an outrage - except, in my view, when the patient begs for relief from the agony he or she feels and the desolation of choice that is all-pervasive for such a person. To oppose this, as doctors do, is to deny the autonomy so highly praised and sought by Gawande in his book.

My GP, and Gawande, and presumably all medical people, are thereby denying the full wholeness of the people they purport to value and care for. I can be autonomous up to a point and not beyond it; my wholeness is rendered partial. Therefore I am not autonomous: therefore, I am not whole.

Always A Subject?
Is not human wholeness always in dispute, however, despite the attempts to assert or describe it? Aren't we, each and all of us, creatures in thrall? I have often referred to the Great Continuity, by which I mean the unity of life and experience, the fact, as I see it, that everything is connected, including all forms of life. If this is true, then I cannot be a separate wholeness, whatever my aspirations. The big danger is to feel free and whole and yet absolutely connected to only one section of existence. That bias is surely typical of the religions as well as most social theory and practice. The fear of dying and no longer existing is also part of the mindset. The medical profession is steeped in this kind of thinking. A doctor's job is seen, partially if not entirely, as keeping people alive - in a sense denying the Great Continuity. Animals and plants are regarded, generally, as disposable compared with the perpetuity of humankind. It is at best the most perversely warped kind of reasoning.

Therefore, my approach to wholeness should be how best to live without it, as it is a fallacy to suppose it actually exists. As if timed to perfection, I have now, suddenly, been identified by medical science as one of the legion of broken-hearted. I have the clinical condition known as 'heart-failure', it seems. Well, of course, what else could it be? All pretence at wholeness is nullified by this diagnosis, as if it were necessary to make the point.

Yet the point is something else, something more important than mere health, fitness or robust autonomy. Nature itself is broken-hearted. It struggles to exist. Death stalks the landscape. Nature is not healthy if by 'healthy' we mean hale and hearty, able to withstand all tests and tortures. The genotypes may be blueprints for survival, but the phenotypes struggle nevertheless. In other words the life of any individual organism is utterly provisional, that is without any form of absolute guarantee. The human organism, especially primed by centuries of occult and religious propaganda, does not understand, let alone subscribe, to this reality. Otherwise, we would not express surprise or despair when we sense the bleak truth - if bleak is how we prefer to view it. It is hardly any better for the collective groups: extinction is generally the rule not the exception. Humankind, not merely you and me, but all human creatures, will become non-existent sometime in the future.

So a minor personal problem such as my heart-failure is common coinage. How can we learn to come to terms with this unpalatable feature of existence? Surely it is a matter of relaxing the rigidity of the ego. The ego, which has its uses in certain kinds of tight corner, where pugnacity, assertion, or personal confidence may pay off, is otherwise frankly a bit of a nuisance. In it its subtlest manifestation it seems to make us believe that we have inalienable rights, and maybe even duties, in which merely staying alive carries inordinate importance. Life would be so much less onerous if we lacked these rather strange mental assumptions. I have used the term 'innocence' (as in my book 'The Tree Of Innocence') to draw attention to the fact that our ego feeds on things or events that don't actually matter at all.

Happiness, on the other hand, is something that matters a great deal. It is happiness that rules in the 'present moment of being' if only we will allow it to dwell therein. Very, very difficult that may be for most of us for most of the time, but it is certainly a high order need of the struggling psyche. Indeed, the irony is that whereas wholeness is a mirage we repeatedly try to impose on our lives, it is happiness that actually hangs about in the wings of the stage until we invite it to the centre. It seems that the question posed at the end of the previous chapter is the problem we can never solve, nor should we need to - because there is apparently no such thing as wholeness on this earth. Indeed, it is this inherent lack of wholeness that was identified by Gautama Buddha as 'suffering', the central theme of mainstream Buddhism. The story goes that he was the son of a wealthy nobleman who protected the boy from seeing the pain and ugliness of life until the young Buddha discovered it for himself and, one way or another, dedicated his life to the relief of suffering by, ultimately, 'mindfulness'. I am unsure of the systems practised in Buddhism, but, like Taoism, it is at least a realistic attempt to face life truthfully and thereby cope with it.

A Coping Strategy

I have, after some years of relative satisfaction with my way of living and coping, reached the stage of recognising that I am not, after all, very good at it. I suppose it could be the summary position on the Fifth Revelation. It is a revelation to discover that I am not a great practitioner of the art of living. I suppose that is also the heart of the depression that made me accept medication. It is also probably the root of my insomniac state. It is humiliating to have to accept failure after all these years. I am supposed to be serene, according to the Enneagram system, the perfect aim of perfectionism. But I am certainly not serene. What, apart from the obvious route of suicide, can I do about it? Am I being realistic, at last, in accepting that I have actually 'got it all wrong', or have I merely run into some nasty problems that I hadn't anticipated or thought more easily resolved than they have proved to be? All of these things seem quite true. Is this a beginning or an end, that is, am I facing a brick wall or am I being honest at last, with some room for manoeuvre?

As I do seem to have little alternative, I could assume that there are ways of making life more enjoyable despite the negative factors. It appears that the Buddha managed it, whatever the weaknesses of the system his successors have been unable to cure - as Buddhism, for all its undoubted grace, does not seem to serve our species all that well. Christianity, for all its dubious origins and foundations, seems to help people to some extent and is perhaps more comforting in its less inflammatory modes. What matters here, to me now, is what am I to do about my lack of strategic success?

Wiggle Room

Any action is likely to be limited and even mundane, because my problems are quite real and rather formidable. But I suspect the main problem may be the simple one of my expecting too much from life. Intellectually, I have analysed and understood the nature of the world, but I have failed to take the extra step of accepting the lack of control of my own personal existence. At best, I have some slight room for manoeuvre, but not much. If this is true, it must be the same for all of us. Do we behave, generally, like me and assume that we have, or should have, endless rights and opportunities? If that were so, does it not mean that I and all my kind are raving lunatics? Yes, I think it must and the state of our world bears that out. On the other hand, we are not fully responsible for who and what we are, a flawed species if ever there was one. I look deeper into the mirror and perceive my own absurdity and tragedy. I have certainly wiggled, and to a degree managed to outmanoeuvre my own limitations, but it's a pretty sorry tale really.

The Balance Sheet

As my physical integrity, my internal organs, heart, lungs, liver, etc, gradually falls apart, the fifth revelation becomes increasingly a weighing-up of my good and bad experiences to find what the overall picture is like. I am not suggesting that this is a particularly worthwhile endeavour, just irresistible. Let's get the negatives out of the way first. My arrogance, ambition, selfishness, and self-importance are fully recorded on these and other pages. I have not loved fully and well, nor have I drunk fully and copiously of the well of mystical and natural wonder that has constantly offered itself to me. I have been conscious always of a sort of important destiny, a magical place where my full glory would manifest, but have, of course, denied the existence of such a ridiculous mindset. I acknowledge that in several ways I may have appeared an attractive, even charismatic, person, yet weakness and self-indulgence has usually put paid to that as needs must in any Narcissist. I have been cruel, foolish, greedy, and insensitive.

I know all this but have somehow avoided doing much about it. Too busy searching for the next opportunity, I guess, to give full attention to the moving present. In later years I have made some attempt to live in the reality of the now, but I have not been very successful at that, and my extreme loathing of all religiosity has probably prevented me from living what might otherwise have been a spiritually aware existence.

So there I am, not much good, really. On the plus side, though, I have been a quite constant lover and companion of my wife for over sixty years, and generally have tended to cherish friends and tried to measure up to the massive role that friendship at its best involves. I was a reasonable scholar and a passable thinker. My behaviour to my family was just about adequate, though marred by the fact that they usually exasperated me. I made enough money, and honestly, to live comfortably, though it took half my life to get to that point. When I retired, lost and exhausted, in my mid-fifties, I searched for and found a new way of living which corrected some of the failures of the past.

Writing and painting have been increasingly important and emotionally rewarding activities though, I'm glad to say, have not been commercially successful. In these, my last years/months/days/ minutes (whichever they prove to be) of my life, a wonderful friend is going to get my paintings 'out into the world' where she says they belong. My books are already out there, more or less meritorious and more or less ignored. I have also been capable, at last, of some generosity and then deeper importance of selfless loving has gradually encroached. I am grateful, oddly enough, to have remained an inveterate sceptic, especially as that has saved me from the worst of the self-indulgences.

The End

...Maybe not quite here yet, but not far off. I end this book with an experience that leaves me shaken and shriven. A bad sleeper nowadays, I was awake an hour ago (five a.m.) struggling with an extraordinary muddle of memory and anxiety. At last, I realised I had to get up and finish this book with an account of what was happening.

Thirty years ago I was in charge of a business that included fuel distribution and the 1984/5 Miners' strike was tearing Britain apart psychologically and financially. I was anti-strike in an off-hand way, but glad to be able to 'help' by keeping some of the CEGB production going. I good friend at the time, a composer, ironically dedicated a fine piece of music to me, music that was the opposite of any strike-breaking belief-system.

This friend, call him, Sven, visited my wife and I last night at the Nursing Home. He is obviously in fine fettle, and he was disturbed to find us so wretched. Poignantly, I had just been told by my GP that my heart valves are in a parlous state. And I had only just given this news to my wife. Sven was sympathetic but wisely focused on the project of getting my paintings out of the closet. It was a lovely meeting despite or because of everything.

Back to this morning's vision. I am on the sunbathed lawn of our headquarters and we are entertaining press and shareholders. I am one of the senior trio running the whole company. Energy is my game. I am tired but triumphant that the miners have provided us with bonanza profits. Then I discover that one of our non-executive directors, probably running on excess Chablis and confused about which side he's on, is declaiming quite loudly that the CEGB has been robbed by us. I pin him down and tell him that every litre of oil was ordered, invoiced, delivered, happily accepted by the CEGB so what the hell does he think he is doing?

Nothing happened of course. I was disappointed that he was forgiven by the chairman (who had, of course, appointed him anyway) and my life moved on to further 'energy-related' distress. But at five o'clock this morning this empty vignette wouldn't go away and let me get some desperately needed sleep. I am uncertain of the meaning of this. I will probably never know. But it feels as though I am at last brought to book, somehow, and that the medical synopsis proves how wretched I have always been. I can explain it away by shock or anxiety or even sheer senile rambling, but this doesn't work - as explanations usually never do. The fact is, I suppose, that I now, at last, feel really 'done-for', and that no more bluffing it out is going to convince anyone, least of all myself.

If, as I suspect, my life has been totally, though secretively, dedicated to some variety of absolute success, then it is now far past the time of wondering whether it's going to happen. What has happened has already happened, and even if my paintings were to achieve recognition I would not be appeased. As it is, anything is likely to make my distressful failure even more unbearable.

I think that really is the fifth revelation in its pristine perfection. Goodbye.

We probably won't meet again.